SHEP
My Autobiography

SHEP
My Autobiography

David Shepherd

with David Foot

ORION

Pictures supplied by kind permission of David Shepherd,
Express & Echo (Exeter), Western Morning News (Plymouth),
Bill Smith of Sports Photography, T R Beckett, Bristol Evening Post,
www.sporting-heroes.net, *The Guardian*, PA Photo Library, David Munden,
Philip Booker, Isobel and Ron Hodgson, Baths Photographic,
Sandra Yeo, North Devon Cricket Club and Mike King.

First published in Great Britain in 2001 by
Orion
An imprint of Orion Books Ltd
Orion House, 5 Upper St Martin's Lane, London WC2H 9EA

A CIP catalogue record for this book
is available from the British Library.

ISBN: 0 75284 592 6

Set by Selwood Systems
Midsomer Norton

Printed in Great Britain by
Butler and Tanner Ltd
Frome and London

To my partner, Jenny,
without whose constant encouragement and support
this book would not have been started, let alone completed.

Acknowledgements

I would like to thank everyone who has helped me in producing this book. They are too numerous to mention but I would especially thank David Foot who helped me write the book and Richie Benaud for writing such an interesting foreword.

I must also thank all those umpiring colleagues who have helped me during my umpiring career.

It is an honour to be involved in cricket at the highest level and most of it has been great fun!

Contents

Foreword

The best umpires I have known, in fifty years of playing and observing cricket, are those who are scarcely noticed. They go about their job in a calm, unflurried manner, and they give their decisions having also given thought to the relevant part of the Laws of the game. David Shepherd is one of half a dozen umpires in the top bracket of the modern-day game, and in the time I played, Sid Buller of England and Colin Egar of Australia were the best two I knew.

Like players, umpires come from all kinds of backgrounds, Buller was an ex-cricketer, Egar owned his own business and, as you will see in this charming autobiography, 'Shep' was a player, didn't mind having a beer at the end of the day and had an appetite to match a couple of the best trenchermen I've come across on the cricket grounds of many countries.

These pages tell of a delightful background and I guess he has had something of an advantage in living in Instow and being near the Taw and Torridge rivers. The thing that strikes me most about this book is that there are so many Australians who developed a love of cricket, and all that goes with it, by living in the country in this way. It is a compliment to the people of Devon that the wonderful environment in that part of the world, quite a distance from the big cities, lends itself to having a calm mind and the ability to make considered decisions.

It is certainly an advantage these days, if you are an umpire, to be able to do things in a calm fashion. There may be some players who endeavour to make life easier for an umpire, but you do need to search hard for them. It's the way of the game in the modern era though, hopefully, the introduction of the Preamble and the Spirit of Cricket to the Laws, will make a difference. Showing dissent, rushing at an umpire to pressure him, ignoring an umpire before he answers an appeal and then looking incredulous when he says 'not out', have all become regular occurrences in recent years. They may now disappear, depending on how firm the umpires themselves will be.

Unfortunately, the introduction of the ICC idea that will have an umpire never again able to stand in a Test match in his own country will also bring changes. The idea seems to be that we are to have independent umpires in every Test match and that will mean, to use the obvious example, that English spectators will never again see David Shepherd or any other English umpire, on a Test cricket field in England. I can see the idea, but the result is clouded. Mind you, there is a precedent to this and it happened way back in 1992–92 when the World Cup Final was played between Pakistan and England and Shep wasn't permitted to stand in the game because England were taking part. He had one of the most outstanding competitions I have ever seen from an umpire and, although all the players knew, and said, he was the best umpire, he wasn't allowed to stand.

This book is the story of a burly cricketer, built for comfort not for speed, and one who has been slowed down a little in recent times by the advent of diabetes. He will handle that with the same aplomb as he did the Wayne Phillips decision at Edgbaston in 1985, the Warne-Hudson one-sided fracas at the Wanderers in Johannesburg and the fact that Jenny bought an ice cream for the dog rather than him.

Characters are good for cricket, and Shep is one of the great characters we have seen in the game in England and on the international stage of umpiring, and, when he puts away his red barrels, the game will be the poorer.

Richie Benaud
July 2001

Testing Time

30 May

It's my fifty-sixth Test tomorrow at Old Trafford. England vs Pakistan.

The sun is shining in Devon and I'm up before 6 a.m. to do my paper round for my brother Bill. Then it's a brisk walk with Skip, the dog. I'm quiet and a bit preoccupied as the big match approaches. Yes, I'm a worrier. Nothing changes.

You never quite know what is going to happen with Pakistan, of course. They have so much talent – pace, spin, wristy shots, but they're also the most volatile of all cricketing nations. Jabbering away excitedly in a language I can't understand.

As I pack my bag I have absolutely no idea, of course, what a traumatic Test (in the personal sense) is facing me. Especially the last horrendous day. It's going to turn into the lowest point in my cricketing career, leaving me utterly depressed and perilously close to giving up Test and international umpiring on the spot. But not so fast, Shep. There will be time, a little later, for you to reflect and try to detach yourself from the sport that has been your life – and work out whether, at the age of sixty, you need the stresses, the brutal TV close-ups and the critical headlines that go with the job.

Match referee Brian Hastings has already rung me. He's worried about the recent race troubles in nearby Oldham and the need for reliable security at Old Trafford. Just after nine o'clock, I climb into my

Peugeot. I say my goodbyes to Jenny, turn on to Radio Devon and, when out of range, switch to Terry Wogan. He amuses me – and I need relaxing. But, despite Terry's best efforts, it's difficult to shut the Test out of my mind. Old Trafford was where I did my first Test against the Aussies and where I stood with Roy Palmer for that notoriously 'awkward' and bad-tempered one with Pakistan in 1987. It was Roy's first appearance as a Test umpire and he had to warn Aqib Javed for intimidatory bowling at our tailender, Devon Malcolm. As I say, there's always plenty going on with Pakistan.

On the car journey north, I think back to when I was in the same Gloucestershire side as the graceful Zaheer Abbas. He used to hint at the politics and differences that always seemed to be present in Pakistani dressing-rooms. Indeed, in the run up to this Test, there is the news that Javed Miandad has been fired from his position as team coach for the second time. And now Shoaib Akhtar, once viewed as the fastest around, has been left out of the Test team. Scare stories about his health abound. There are clearly plenty of fragile temperaments and highly competitive natures amongst their team. I've read for years about the so-called factions, followed by the placating statements that there's nothing wrong apart from an occasional squabble or two 'in the family'. A Pakistani Test is seldom without some kind of incident. What can I expect to find this time? There's a lot going on in my mind as I near Manchester.

I reach the ground by early afternoon. I look around for the referee but can't see him, so I wander out to take a look at the pitch and have a word with head groundsman, Peter Marron. It looks a very good track, with a nice even covering of grass. I'm surprised at how firm it is. 'Should be a good flat one,' says Peter. We also talk about what the weather is likely to do.

Darren Gough is launching his book at the ground, so there are plenty of press and other media people milling about. I steer clear and bring my kit in. I'm told that the other officials have gone back to their hotel, the Copthorne, so I motor there myself, passing the famous football ground and Sir Matt's statue. At the hotel reception I ask where the others are staying. 'Mr Hastings is in Room 112 and Mr Nicholls is in 111.' Wow, that was a near one, I muse, deep-rooted superstitions never far away. I'm put in 207, not that far from 222. I settle myself in and make contact with the referee who invites me down to his room. With all the usual pre-match routines to go through, I'm less worried about the race troubles. Later on I get in touch with the third and fourth umpires, Ray Julian and Mark Benson, and we have a drink together.

After a sandwich in my room, I'm in bed between 8.30 and 9 p.m., having arranged an early call for the next morning. Paper delivery boys like to get a decent night's sleep. As I drop off I'm still thinking about the match. . .

31 May

Over fruit juice, tea and toast in my room I take a look at the TV weather forecast. It's not good. Distracted, I cast an unseeing eye over the runners and riders in the *Telegraph*. I prefer the jumps to the flat, in any case. I've arranged to take Brian and Eddie Nicholls to the ground and we get there in plenty of time. As we stroll out to the pitch, we speculate on whether England will play a spinner. I feel certain Pakistan will include Saqlain. Prophetic words, if you know what I mean!

The weather turns to showers and everyone is asking us what is going to happen. One of the enquiries comes from Ian Botham's daughter, Sarah, a lovely girl who's doing some work for Sky. They want me to do an interview, 'Just a couple of minutes,' says Paul Allott. These can be a bit of a distraction but I suppose we also have PR responsibilities.

The match starts at 11.30 a.m. I ask Ed which end he'd like and he says the Warwick Road one. I've only stood with him once before, in an Oval Test against Sri Lanka. He's a policeman at home in Guyana. Pakistan win the toss and the fourth umpire takes the new balls to the

3

fielding captain, Alec Stewart, for him to choose which one he'd like. Goughie is bowling at my end.

I'm equipped with my ECB walkie-talkie, so that I can remain in contact with the third umpire, in theory at least. More of that in a moment. The walkie-talkie's clipped to my shirt and is a bit cumbersome but I can see the advantages. What else do I take with me? My six red counters, a pen knife (to clean studs), a pair of scissors, a stud key (in case a player loses a stud), a ball ring (to measure if the ball goes out of shape), a pen, some paper and a notebook, and a rag to dry the ball, if necessary, although nowadays players are inclined to take their own rag on to the field.

The first session goes quickly enough and before long it's time for lunch. The referee and the other umpires go into the dining room. I prefer a quiet lunch and stay in my room with a couple of ham rolls and a yoghurt. At tea-time I just have a sandwich. Desmond, the attendant, makes sure there's a drink waiting for me at the close of play.

It's early to bed again, so I don't watch the highlights on TV. I'm more interested in how the county scores are going, in any case. It's important to keep life in perspective.

1 June

The second day and there's some very good cricket out there, but there are also some matters I don't approve of. It isn't all one-way. I've already reported Andy Caddick to the referee for his attitude on the first day. His manner was getting up his opponents' noses. As for Pakistan, how I wish I could understand some of the things they're saying. I did take modern languages at school, but not Urdu.

Let's get back to the cricket. Inzaman-ul-Haq's 114 was a gem. And now there's Michael Vaughan and Graham Thorpe. When anyone mentions Thorpy, I think back to a match at Guildford, soon after he'd broken into the Surrey team. A wicket fell and it seemed like an eternity before the next batsman came in. It was Graham; someone I'd never met previously. 'What kept you waiting so long, young man?' I asked. The reply surprised me. 'Couldn't find my bat.' That was a new one. Disorganised – or was it the nerves of a newcomer?

Back in my hotel room at the end of the second day I go over the events and decisions of the match so far. Did I get it wrong with Younis Khan? The TV replays apparently suggested I did. Oh dear! I put in a call to Jenny, back in Instow, as I do every evening. 'Well, how did it go?' she wants to know, detecting the concern in my voice. 'I can do without this, Jenny.' Her initial silence carries its own eloquence. 'Think of all the decisions you get right,' she has often said. We don't talk just about cricket. How's the village looking? What about Bill at the post office? Have you taken Skip along the dunes for a run?

4 June

Where do I begin my tale of woe? How do I analyse my compounded torment? How close am I to walking away from big-time cricket?

Those who watched on television the uncompromising, magnified errors of the two match umpires probably forgot, like some of the commentators, that we'd had a pretty decent match up to this final day. All the players seemed to agree about the latter. Today, the match was boiling up for a result, despite periods when England concluded it was a matter of staying there and Trescothick was padding-away consciously negative over-the-wicket bowling.

So what about the alleged ball-tampering by Waqar Younis? An undeniable fact so, according to TV, I'm told. The camera lens zoomed in mercilessly to show him rearranging the seam. I saw nothing of that. As usual I examined the ball at intervals throughout the match – and had no reason to be suspicious. When the allegations were made publicly, Waqar promptly denied them. So did Yawar Saeed, his manager.

I'd like to block out the memory of that final day forever. I was as attentive and conscientious, at least at the 'business' end, as I've ever been. So how did I slip up so badly and so publicly? They say all umpires, like wicket-keepers who miss catches or strikers who fluff open goals, can have bad days. To quote dear old mum (as I do more than once in these pages) . . . 'there would be days like this . . .'

But I'm not going to make any excuses. That's never been my style. I failed to spot three no-balls when Saqlain took three wickets. It doesn't bear thinking about. They were basic mistakes on my part, and I'm concerned about it . . . very concerned. Earlier in the day, I allowed Trescothick to survive a glove/pad catch. He'd already reached his hundred, so it wasn't a case of sub-conscious sentimentality from a fellow West Countryman!

Why, for goodness' sake, didn't someone pass on a gentle warning over the walkie-talkie? People said to me again and again that that was surely something the third umpire should have done. I hadn't a clue about the no-balls until twenty minutes or so from the end. My walkie-talkie had packed up and if my third umpire was trying to tell me something I needed to know, I wasn't getting a word of it. In the end, Benny, the fourth umpire, came out with a replacement radio. His only murmur to me was, 'Watch the front foot.'

So Pakistan won a fine game of cricket by 108 runs, on one of the best Test pitches I can recall.

I came off the field with no real inkling of what was in store for me. I asked Ray Julian, 'Everything all right?'

'I think you got all the decisions right. But three wickets fell to no-balls.' I was horrified. I went cold.

I picked up my medal at the official presentation and hurried back to the umpires' room, showered, packed . . . and was away. No hanging around for shared anecdotes. There were reporters lurking. 'It was a difficult match out there,' I told them. Nothing more. Despite that, one or two fanciful lines about my future intentions found their tortuous way into the tabloids the next day. Within an hour of the end of the match, I was on the road.

It's too easy to say that we shouldn't let things get to us, but I can't help it. It's a long car journey back to Instow and I was thinking about those bloody no-balls for most of the way. Anxiously, I turned on the car radio and heard nothing about my mistakes. It's those newspapers tomorrow, I told myself.

I stopped for cup of tea at Taunton Dene service station and arrived home at midnight. Jenny was waiting up for me.

'So how did it go?'

She probably knew. 'Not an easy one, Jenny. How's Skip?'

5 June

My mind is virtually made up. At my age I can do without this hassle and bad temper. I can't think of a match I have enjoyed less. I'm feeling more depressed than I can ever remember. I didn't sleep well and I'm up at 5.45 a.m. delivering some of Bill's papers (and taking a peep at some of the match comments). They're not as bad as I'd feared in most cases – but bad enough. Especially those reproduced images of Saqlain's no-balls, taken from the TV screens.

Back at home I talk things over incessantly with Jenny. She points out that any decision I make about my future as an international umpire must be for the right reasons and not made in the heat of the moment. I tell myself it's time to ease off. After all, I've a few more years on the county circuit. No, I don't want to make a complete break. Oh dear, my spirits *are* low.

6 June

I phone Lord's and speak to Tim Lamb, the ECB's chief executive. I speak to him frankly about how I'm feeling, and tell him that I'm thinking seriously of walking away from my senior umpiring duties. He seems shocked and does his best, with a sympathetic manner that I appreciate, to dissuade me. Later in the day the ECB put out a statement of support for me. This should be good for the ego but it isn't. I remain in a state of confusion.

By now, the letters are beginning to arrive at my North Devon home, some from people I don't even know. Friends ring to add their support for me. Ex-players are also in touch. One of my early letters is from Eric Hill, the former Somerset opener. Another is from Peter Roebuck who assures me that I'm held 'in high esteem around the cricket world'. He adds that Sachin Tedulkar recently named me as his favourite umpire; timely praise, indeed. Umpires, including Dickie Bird, ring me with good wishes. But I'm still on a low. My confidence has been shattered.

7 June

Maybe it'll help when I'm back in the middle. My first game after the Test is between Northants and Australia. It's heart-warming to discover how many Aussies come up to me and, with reassuring words, give me a lift. They must know what I've been going through.

And what happens? Near the end of the match, I wrongly give out Darren Cousins, caught at the wicket. In an instant, self doubts resurface. That's it, I tell myself.

9 June

Saturday and for me, as I see it, this is official decision day. I ring Tim Lamb for the second time. I know exactly what I'm going to say. As tactfully as possible, I'm on the point of telling him that I feel it's time to quit. Tim is on his mobile, just about to enter Sophia Gardens, Cardiff for the Australia vs Pakistan match. He says he'll settle in and then ring me back. I'm hardly off the line before I get another call.

It's Bev Price, a long-time friend from Wales. I first met him when we were training to be teachers together at St Luke's College in Exeter. Bev doesn't go in for humbug or smarmy phrases. I tell him what I intend to do – and he goes for me. He lectures me for nearly an hour and gives me a dreadful rollicking. Of course you have to keep going, he says. When Tim Lamb phones the next time, I tell him I'm ready to complete my contract. I put down the phone and turn to Jenny, 'So the Price is Right!'

Since those few days of inner turmoil, I've been heartened by several things I've read. Mike Atherton, for instance, came out and said that the umpires hadn't cost England the Test and he felt they'd actually had a good match (thanks, Mike, but the evidence suggests I have to pass on that one). And I read in the *Racing Post* a column by Paul Haigh that was far more about cricket than horseracing. I think what he says has some significance:

'If cricket (or football) really wants to win back public confidence, it has got to follow racing's example and never again allow a TV audience to have more information about what is actually going on than the officials who are supposed to be in charge.'

That brings me to the vexed subject of technology, which has revolutionised the game of cricket at the higher level and will be discussed by me at some length in this book. For the moment, I'll simply say that it can be good for the game if used properly. But pity the poor old umpire who lacks the visual and scientific aids available to others. Anything that helps the game – and that includes the proposed 'bleepers' for no-balls – should be considered. My reservations will become evident later.

In the weeks that followed, my experiences at Old Trafford occupied my thoughts on many a car journey or quiet night back in the hotel or guest house. I can't possibly begin to catalogue all the distractions that took place during the match. It wasn't merely the sledging or the less savoury exchanges that we have come reluctantly to accept. At one point, when Alec Stewart was batting and Waqar Younis was bowling, I called the pair together. I reminded them of their responsibilities and told them they had to sort out their players. The England captain also claimed that a racial remark had been directed at his team, a case of prejudice, particularly misplaced, if true, in the context of what had just taken place in the streets of Oldham. I'd heard nothing but made it clear that I would crack down on it at once if any derogatory racial slur were repeated.

There was also the deliberate scuffing of the pitch, although this is hardly a new trend and happens on the county circuit at times. No excuses, however. England had to bat last and were going to suffer. When I saw two Pakistani batsmen surreptitiously at work on the track, I had a prompt word with them. They apologised profusely and, with touching innocence, assured me it had not been deliberate. Similarly, between overs, as the Pakistani fielders crossed over, some made a point of doing so 'on a length'.

Nor are diplomatic injuries particularly new. But the absence in the field on the last day of Inzy and Saeed Anwar, arguably not the most nimble fielders on the Pakistani side and their replacement by more agile players, aroused some comment. I take a charitable view. Inzy came up to me and said his head, which he had injured the day before, was causing him trouble. Atherton heard him and said, 'He seemed all right to me when he was whacking the ball about.' My reply was, 'I'm an umpire, not a doctor, Athers.' In fact, I spoke to the match referee, not knowing if it was a genuine injury. It was confirmed that Inzy saw the doctor when he left the field.

Most of my cricket, whether as a rotund player or a talkative umpire, has been accompanied by smiles and good humour and I don't want to give the impression that the second Test, my nadir, was devoid of either.

Back at the hotel one evening I was talking to some of the media boys when Jonathan Agnew suddenly turned to me and said: 'You know what happened today, don't you Shep? You missed 333.' He meant that I'd failed to dance my little jig for the magic figure. I laughed but it troubled me – it was a very rare miss on my part. 'I was concentrating so much out there, Jonathan.'

What's that you say? No time for Devonshire superstitions? That evening there was a minor earthquake twenty miles off Hartland Point in North Devon. Jenny felt the tremor. I have no comment to make.

Rivers Run Deep

So where did it all start? I couldn't do better than with Taw and Torridge. What a pairing they make – strong and physical, tempestuous and yet wonderfully constant. Yes, I have to put them ahead of even Courtney and Curtly.

Taw and Torridge aren't cricketers, of course. They are noble and timeless Devon rivers which between them make up the estuary that sparkles and frets only a few boundary lengths away from my home at Instow. All my life I've strolled the sand dunes with my dogs, gazing out across to Appledore or perhaps through the wintry haze to Lundy. The sound of these two rivers' names has its own exciting ring and they could never be separated in my thoughts and imagination, in the same way that Trueman and Statham always belong together.

I lie awake at night and smell the salt coming in off the sea. Devon is permanently in my nostrils. My umpiring takes me around the world, to beautiful grounds and exotic locations. Back in England during the summer months it would often be more convenient for me if I lived in a less remote corner of the country. But my roots are important to me, as these pages will reveal, and whenever I'm having my bags packed for a distant tour, I make sure that my emotional priority is not overlooked.

The return ticket to North Devon . . .

I accept that this makes me look mawkishly sentimental. Some will probably see me as an old stick-in-the-(estuary)-mud. The fact is that local culture is ingrained deep in the way I speak, look and think. No-one is going to change me now. Once or twice during the lunch interval of an overseas international when I've been umpiring, I've found myself asking a plainly puzzled waiter: 'I don't suppose you've got any 'Ockings, have you?' It isn't an affectation. Hocking's ice-creams are a renowned delicacy from Appledore. I've licked and loved them since childhood. Of course, they aren't going to be rustled up from the fridge at Melbourne Cricket Ground or St John's, Antigua. It's crazy to ask, but I can't help myself. My unusual request is followed by a self-conscious attempt at an explanation and a weak smile that leave the waiter even more confused.

While I began my story with the Taw and Torridge – and the invigorating scent of the sea – in truth, the wonderful whiff of linseed oil is the most influential of all. And that brings me to the Sandhills, Instow, one of the loveliest and most romantic cricket grounds in the country and the home since 1837 of the North Devon Cricket Club. Nothing could be more central to my life and ambitions. It fired my enthusiasm for the game. It was where my father umpired and my brother skippered, where I threw my old bike against the fence to watch my first Minor Counties matches and saw villagers I idolised stroke fours more elegantly, in my imagination, than Hammond's. It was where I sprawled on the grass to marvel at the accents and the colourful variety of blazers worn by midweek tourists on their annual visits. I helped to roll the pitch and chased away the rabbits. I practised my shots, learned as I watched, and went on to play at a ground which was so picturesque that photographers and artists travelled miles to capture its charm.

The boundary is no distance from the water's edge and it is some-times suggested that fielders at third-man can discreetly combine their duties with a spot of spontaneous fishing between the fall of wickets. As for the rabbits, they have continued to multiply on the adjacent sand-dunes at a spectacularly faster rate than I ever amassed runs during my schoolboy days of incautious aggression. When the rabbits encroached on the lovingly tended outfield, they rarely seemed inhibited by the brandishing of a twelve-bore by a succession of groundsmen.

But above all, it is the pavilion, a beautiful rustic symbol of sporting architecture, that everyone seems to admire most of all. The roof is thatched, just like that of the quaint little whitewashed scorebox. It dates back to the eighteenth century, and the interior, full of historic club treasures and mementoes, is equally handsome.

Sandhills was for a time home to two clubs. North Devon held the lease, it was their ground and they regularly entertained dozens of famous touring sides. Instow CC was composed of members with less free time. They had work to do during the week, so they played on Saturdays. Brother Bill and I watched Instow whenever we could, arriving on our bikes and eagerly practising on the edge of the boundary. Our constant hope was that one of the players wouldn't turn up and that we'd get a game.

Father was a regular umpire for Instow. All right, I'd better come clean before my mates waggishly have their little joke: Dad had lost an eye in the First World War some years before. So, yes, I suppose I can honestly confess that I come from a line of one-eyed umpires.

Looking after the ground and preparing the pitches for the numerous fixtures was Les Bircumshaw. While studying at Oxford University, he liked to spend his vacations in the village, playing for both North Devon and Instow. He was an accomplished cricketer, a fine batsman and good leg-break and googly bowler. Bill and I would help him with the ground and in return he'd practise with us in the nets. Imagine what a lesson that was for us. We learned the importance of watching the ball all the way while he skilfully and cunningly turned it both ways and offered timely encouragement.

North Devon and Instow amalgamated in 1955. It made sense as by now the defiant social divisions were disappearing. Growing up in the area, young lads like the Shepherds were still conscious that they were expected to know their place. Hadn't one commodore of the Yacht Club previously been blackballed for the unpardonable sin of being in trade? North Devon had a reputation for being elitist. We only had to look at the membership and study some of the minutes of past meetings: plenty of ex-military types and country gentry; plenty of double-barrelled names. Youngsters, however enthusiastic, were on occasion told to keep their distance from the pavilion and one day a club official got into an almighty lather because a spectator was seen in Bermuda shorts. But cricket has always seemed to me to be a valuable destroyer of archaic barriers and since those days North Devon CC, once a haven of clean-cut sporting endeavour and privilege, has become as democratic as society itself. Once a succession of captains' voices indicated the best of public-school pedigree; now I relish local voices of contrasting modernity at the Instow ground: 'You bide over there at mid-wicket, boy.'

It's the cricket – the competitive skills as well as the humour – that means more to me than mere social standing. I was lucky enough to see great club touring sides at the Instow ground: the Oxford and Cambridge college teams came, as did the Free Foresters, the Gloucestershire Gypsies, the Somerset Stragglers, the South Oxford Amateurs, the Yorkshire Amateurs and Yorkshire Puddings, Dorset Rangers, Eton Ramblers, the Shrewsbury Saracens, the Derbyshire Friars, the Hampshire Hoggs and the Devon Dumplings. And many others, almost all of them laden with genuine talent. I chuckled at the clubs' names and the flamboyant caps that many of the players wore. I lay on the grass, applauding the fours, retrieving the ball from the sixes, and not missing a delivery. My head was already buzzing with un-realistic thoughts that I might one day make a living from this enchanting game.

My father Herbert was Welsh. He'd come from Penarth and was a natural sportsman, playing both rugby and cricket for the town side. It's a lasting regret of mine that I never saw Dad play. I'm equally dis-appointed that he died in 1962 and didn't live to see me play county cricket or to umpire. He had played rugby at full-back and centre and I understand he even had a trial for Wales. He was particularly proud of the fact that he had been in the Penarth team which defeated the Barbarians in 1913. Later he joined the Merchant Navy and rose to become a chief engineer. During the twenties and thirties he travelled the world, but he never talked of his experiences. I suppose it's a weakness of children that they don't ask enough questions – and end up regretting it. Because of the worldwide slump, many ships had to be laid-up. My father's finished up on the banks of the Torridge, which was a free harbour. Ever resourceful, Dad stepped ashore and never really left again. He settled quickly in the village and before long had married the local postmistress. His wife was to die in childbirth in 1933 and, sustaining the post office tradition, Dad went on the marry Dolly Smallridge, who was already working there and doing a paper round on her cycle. Her father, Bobby, was a familiar figure as he ferried the daily mail to and from Appledore. Our parents needed to keep the post office going throughout the year so had to take separate short holidays. Bill and I would go with Mother to Sidmouth, where we seemed to spend all our time watching the cricket on that impressive ground on the Front.

Mum was solid, well-fleshed Instow stock and was the youngest of seven children. She became the postmistress and was still working there when she died aged eighty-one in 1990. She had an easy manner and the kind of welcoming personality that helped to make the post office one of the focal points of village life. The locals didn't merely call to pick up their pension or a book of stamps. They exchanged good-natured gossip about every local issue you could imagine. Mother knew everyone, their parents and grandparents. She also had the necessary air of authority for the job and Bill and I were in awe of her: the efficiency with which she ran the shop, the time she had for the customers.

For those who run our rural post offices, Christmastime is hectic and I can't have helped matters, having been born on 27 December. She'd been beavering away, sorting the letters and weighing the parcels up to virtually the last minute. We apparently only just made it to the hospital. As usual, Mother's timing – whatever the scares on the way to the labour ward – was immaculate. She had so many solid Devonian qualities and remains one of the major influences on my life. I even quote her, indirectly, in one of my recurrent and doubtless boring sayings: if I'm having a fraught time and everything seems to be going wrong, I'm apt to mumble, 'Mum said there would be days like this – and she was a very wise woman.'

When it came to cricket, however, Mother was inclined to be a bit naïve. She viewed it with engaging innocence and I remember the occasion when she was watching a Test match on TV and saw me give out Graham Gooch leg-before. The next time she saw me there was a long, deliberate stare from her. 'And what did Graham say when you gave him out?' She'd never met Goochie, of course. But somehow she didn't approve of my action. I chuckled quietly at the sympathetic way she referred to him as *Graham*.

Brian Johnston was a good friend of mine and it happened to be Mother's birthday on the first day of one of the Tests. 'Do me a favour, Johnners. Slip in a birthday mention for Mum.' And he did. Back in Instow apparently the whole of the village heard it and there was much excitement in the post office. When I saw Brian later in the day, he said, 'I spoke to Mum this morning, Shep.' It was his way of telling me he'd remembered to broadcast her birthday greeting. He did better than that – he also sent her a birthday card the following year.

My brother Bill is seventeen months older than me. He's continued in the family business and looks after the post office in Instow. He was an outstanding cricketer, the kind of prospect who, with a little luck, would have established himself as a county player. I didn't have his talent. So I continue to feel some guilt that while I had fifteen seasons with Gloucestershire and then jetted around the globe as a Test match umpire, he ultimately stayed at home. Bill did have three years at Lord's, where the coaches, among them Harry Sharp and Len Muncer, enthused about his natural skills as a slow left-arm bowler and discerning left-hand bat. On the day an invitation arrived from Lord's to renew his contract, there was another official letter in the post, summoning him for National Service. Talk about cruel timing.

He had shown enough quality to captain the MCC Young Professionals, batting with enough composure to score a hundred in the middle at Lord's. Once he played against me at that famous ground, where I was representing English Schools. As a slow bowler, he nagged away with the subtle variations of an older player, and everyone assumed he would end up as a county cricketer. He takes, at this distance, a more cautious and unnecessarily modest view: 'I don't think I'd ever have stuck the county game. Wasn't quite good enough. I don't lose any sleep over it. Dad died and, well, needs must, I put the cricket thoughts out of my head. There was a busy post office to help Mother run.'

We'd shared so many cricket daydreams. The two of us, with an old bat and battered ball, had spent hours practising on the beach when the tide was out, as well as on a corner of the Instow ground. On Sunday mornings we would cycle up to Mutton Hill for our improvised matches. As its name suggests, Mutton Hill was only really a field for sheep, but Ken and Maurice Pedlar, who lived near by and were the sons of Archie the postman, would conscientiously roll the pitch. There'd be ten or eleven of us; Bill and I were the two youngest. Everyone except the batsman would field. This was all part of our cricketing education. It was a Sunday morning ritual more willingly practised by some of us than matins at the parish church. I'm not sure what the vicar or the non-conformist ministers made of our alternative form of worship. We may not have turned out in whites but the game was always taken seriously by the Shepherd boys. We had our own bats and pads, and we tried to play the kinds of shot that we saw and envied at the Instow ground. Our innings at Mutton Hill didn't find their way into any official scorebook, but we still treasured some of them.

One of the other enthusiasts was John Huxtable, an ex-gas fitter whom I still see most days when I'm in Instow. Another was Ivor

Stevens, who became known as 'Ivor the Engine' because he worked in the booking office at Barnstaple Junction. Gerald Lee and Ray Cook were every bit as keen. Yes, I could make out a case for placing dear old Mutton Hill alongside a few Test arenas in my affections. That's keeping life in perspective; Devonians, from Sir Francis Drake onwards, were pretty good at that.

I was impatient even then to hit balls out of sight. Bill, meanwhile, was already bamboozling the older boys. He was a terrific all-round sportsman, going on to play rugby, and soccer for Bideford Town. Everything in his life and leisure needed to be fitted in around the opening hours at the post office, however. It must, at times, have been very frustrating for him. At least he had one full season for Devon in 1966, after coming out of the army. In one summer for North Devon, whom he captained, he took 138 wickets from weekend matches alone. Alf Robinson, a Yorkie who bowled swinging medium pace, took 157 wickets in the same year. Clearly a good season for the bowlers. 'Robbie', an ex-copper, was something of a character, apart from being such a capable club seamer. In his Devon days he worked as a commercial traveller and often had difficulty getting time off to play. He was known to turn out under an assumed name, so that his employers wouldn't discover his sporting whereabouts by way of the local press. He regularly arrived late for matches, relying on his dubious stock-phrase: 'Oh, I thought we'd be batting first.' A big man, he incongruously drove a Mini; I used to say he wore it rather than drove it.

There are so many, in addition to Robbie, that I should mention. Bill ('Wasp') Walter, as good an upholsterer as he was a cricketer, was one. He used to play for a fine local side, Alwington, before joining North Devon CC. A seam bowler and middle-order batsman, he helped the club, under my brother's leadership, to win the County Knockout Cup. Wasp went on to play for Devon and I always thought he might have progressed much further in the game. He was a natural sportsman, whether at darts, skittles or golf. On a personal level, he was a good family friend who had my brother over for Christmas Day when Jenny and I were away. Others like John Phillips, David Lea and Bryan Palmer come to mind among the hard core of club workers.

They Called Me 'Titch'

My small local primary school in Instow provided good, conventional teaching, and no fancy theories. Our headmaster, Reggie Way, made it clear to all the boys how much he loved his sport. He happily watched us kicking a ball or trying to hit a six at every break-time, and openly encouraged us. He probably thought we needed it as North Devon was, after all, somewhat isolated: the nearest county cricket ground was Taunton; the nearest league soccer at modest Exeter and Plymouth.

Mr Way came up to me one day when I was nine. To my surprise he asked, 'What would you like to do when you leave school, sonny? How about a professional footballer?'

My reply was immediate, even if I was a trifle intimidated by the question. 'No, sir.'

'What about a professional cricketer, then?'

I still vividly recall the fleeting exchange. That second question needed some consideration, even from a nine-year-old. 'Oh yes, sir.'

Mr Way, a stocky, paternal figure, lived in Barnstaple and came to Instow every day on the bus. He had an old-fashioned sense of discipline and kept a cane for wayward behaviour. I hope it doesn't sound smug if I report I was never one of his victims, though several of my young chums received what they painfully described to me as 'a fair old wallop'. He was, as he needed to be in a small village school, a versatile teacher, taking us for everything, including arithmetic, which in those far-off days was my favourite subject. There were about sixty pupils and the headmaster was assisted by Miss Cutland and Mrs Parsons. The Second World War hadn't long been over; there were still hollow cheeks and demob suits to be seen. Nor had rationing disappeared altogether. At home, influenced by the strictures of the war, I was expected to clear my plate every mealtime. At school, in the playground, the stumps and the goalposts were in rotation chalked on the side of the surviving air-raid shelter. The shelter was quite a talking point and the children used to chat with some retrospective excitement, if vaguely, of the German aircraft which had dropped a bomb not far from Instow after a raid on Bristol.

In his distinctive manner Mr Way gave us a rounded early education. It's possible he favoured me slightly because he liked to talk rugby with Dad. I inherited that passion for sport and there was plenty of mathematical practice for me each day as I totted up the various county innings, to make sure the papers had done their sums properly. School was never a drag for me. The penny bus fare was money well spent.

Village boys in those drab post-war days had varied ambitions. There were those who wanted to be bus or train drivers – or, even more glamorously, RAF pilots. But I think Mr Way planted the seed that day for me. Yes . . . a cricketer! Not that I had the remotest idea of what a professional cricketer's life was like or how to go about becoming one. I hadn't even seen a proper county match, though I'd listened, like the rest of our family, to John Arlott's Basingstoke burr, rather different from some of the posh accents I'd regularly eavesdropped on when those touring amateur sides were paying their annual call on the Instow ground.

From primary school I went to Barnstaple Grammar School. My nickname also changed: back in Instow my classmates had called me 'Titch', a reflection on my size and lack of strength in those days. All right, it's hard to believe but I really was the smallest of our particular gang of boys. I liked to think I compensated for what I lacked in inches with extra skill. At the grammar school I was more often known as 'Bunny' because of the gap in my front teeth.

I don't suppose I did so badly, considering that my mind was constantly on cricket. I was in the A stream and got eight O levels. My academic studies went rather off track after that. In the sixth form I took French, German and geography. I don't know what possessed me – it was one of the worst decisions I ever made. I should have stuck with the sciences. But, then, I liked the geography master, Basil Hargreaves, who was a cricket man at heart. Basil and another master, Dai Williams, used to spend hours of their own time after school and at weekends supervising practice sessions and matches. In only my second year at the school, I had been selected for the 1st XI. That was when I found myself, as a twelve-year-old, playing against boys who were much older. It was another chance for me to make up for what I lacked in size with skill and determination.

We used to play two fixtures every week. On the Saturday we competed against another school and on Thursday evenings we entertained a local club side. One snag was that I lived seven miles from the school, so it was always difficult to play even a home game. The Thursday matches started at 6 p.m. and finished at nine o'clock. It was impossible for me to get home after school and be back in time to start the match so I'd stay at school. The ritual was to leave home in the morning at eight-thirty. When it got to four o'clock I would mark the boundary lines and then have my sandwiches. After the match I would catch the last bus home, arriving at 10.30 p.m. This was a long day for every Thursday of the summer term. But how I enjoyed it. I'm not too certain how I managed to squeeze in my homework, especially as I had so many other interests, in addition to cricket.

The post office atmosphere generated an interest in stamp-collecting, something I continue to pursue. Among the stamps I treasure is one, issued in Grenada, of Curtly Ambrose and myself. This pales, however, in comparison, with the First Day Cover of Sir Don Bradman. When I was in Adelaide for a match, I met someone who was off to see the great man. Sir Don, one of my timeless heroes, with kindness and courtesy signed my cover for me.

Sailing held little appeal for me, maybe because I didn't naturally warm to one or two of the more seemingly self-important people who belonged to the Yacht Club. You can possibly detect the glimpse of an inferiority complex here. I loved the water, all the same.

I spent hours swimming in the estuary. Like many of my pals, I used to jump off the jetty and got into trouble with the ferryman, Norman Johns, for splashing his passengers. And there was me thinking I was naturally graceful and sylph-like as I dived in! Then there were the enjoyable attempts at fishing. A group of us lads bought lines and hooks and, at low tide, we'd stake out both ends of the lines and attach anything up to a hundred hooks. We would use lug worms, dug up on the beach, as bait. Our preparations completed, we'd go home and wait for the tide to come in and cover our lines. Six hours later we would return and see what sort of a catch we had landed. If it was a good one, we might sell some to the fishmonger, before baiting up again. You couldn't really live just off the water's edge and not be in some sense a fisherman. The prospect of a little extra pocket money was another attraction, of course.

It was impossible to live in Instow without hearing, and often going cold at, stories of the fierce local tides. Whenever I stood on the Front watching the ferry crossing to and from Appledore, I thought of the tragedy on that regular run at the beginning of the twentieth century. Three Appledore fishermen and two passengers were drowned in the waves which had been whipped up by a hurricane. I also heard many tales of small boats breaking loose from their moorings and saw at first hand the sea walls taking dreadful poundings.

North Devon was also hunting country. Like my pals, I sometimes followed on foot but didn't like to see the huntsmen digging out a fox, exhausted, after it had gone to ground.

Life moved at the kind of gentle pace that suited me. Time to stand and stare, as Nailsworth's supertramp poet, W.H. Davies, said. Boys of my age at Instow stared for hours at the boatmen as they rowed across in all weathers to our traditional rivals in most things, Appledore; at the misty outline of Lundy Island (I've still to go there); at the ceaselessly mating rabbits on the dunes; at the railway station and the one-track line.

Like so many others, the station was a Beeching victim. We'd been proud of it. At one time the trains had puffed in, during the summer months, and the compartments were bulging with tourists. I can remember them coming, the kids with their buckets and spades, right into the fifties, but by then cars were taking over. Train traffic, for us, was sadly on the wane.

I remember, too, the toffs stepping on to the platform with their cricket bags. They'd come from all over the country, picking up a branch connection for Instow, to play a tour match here. The blazers were the giveaway. Looking back, I'm not certain North Devon CC's opponents were all in the prime of youth, but I would gaze at the cricket bags, ignore those civilised, flushed complexions, and imagine the players were at least county standard. Boys with shining eyes are wonderfully uncritical.

In small villages like ours, the railways had their own glamour. The train driver would poke his head out of the cab and we accepted he was a man of importance. We knew our local porters and signalmen, who traded jokes with us as we walked to school. For our part, we were never too sure about the safety of the level-crossing, or the slightly suspect flashing-light system that followed.

Remnants of the station can still be seen: I'm thinking of the lovely little signal-box which has survived as a Grade II listed building. It deserves that accolade.

Once in school I was always grateful for the time and effort that Dai, Basil and other teachers put in to make sure we were able to play regular sport. It doesn't appear that such dedication is very evident today: as far as I can see, few comparable matches are played between state schools any more. This has certainly had some effect at national level. Sermon over, for the time being.

I was in the school's 1st XI for six years, ending up as captain, as well as being head boy. I liked to keep wicket and in those days also fancied my off-spinners. In my last summer I topped 1,000 runs with an average of more than 50. It was a record for Barnstaple Grammar School and they presented me with an inscribed ball, which is proudly displayed at my home. It looks as though it took quite a battering so perhaps it's the one I hit to all corners of the ground as I went past my thousand!

Like a good Devon lad I worked at my rugby, too. I began as a full-back and then 'progressed' to scrum-half. Where else should someone so neat and nimble play? Now, although I say so myself, I must have been reasonably good. I was selected for Devon Schools Under-19s and usually turned in a decent performance for my school. Apart from getting the ball out to my fly-half with an accurate pass before being charged over by the opposing flankers, I took the kicks. My left foot served me well and I was entrusted with all the penalties and conversions for both Barnstaple and South Molton, the club I'll be telling you more about in a moment. In one game the club side scored ten tries and I landed all ten conversions; it seemed like a case for the Monopolies Commission.

There was no school game one Saturday. Chris 'Taffy' Thomas, a mate of mine who played for South Molton twenty miles down the road, came knocking at my door: 'Feel like turning out for us? We're a man short.' No need to ask twice. I suspect that South Molton were often a man short in those distant days, but it appealed to me and from then on, whenever the school was without a fixture, I'd do my level best at the base of the South Molton scrum – a slightly lopsided pack of burly farmers and locals, some recruited at the last minute.

South Molton RFC played in an all-black strip so were rather grandly known as the All Blacks around the country lanes of Devon. We changed in a local pub, the Unicorn, and had a unicorn as an emblem emblazoned on our shirts. Playing in an open field bereft of facilities, our team was said 'to kick everything above the ground'. This was a bit harsh in my view, but there was no denying that this was Coarse Rugby on the grand scale: energetic, enjoyable, none too skilful. Although we did have one very good player, John Shapcott, who was equally accomplished at cricket and golf, as far as I remember. He was twice as talented as most of us. If South Molton were in trouble, confused in their tactics and not sure what to do, the cry would go out: 'Give the ball to John.' It was probably our only hope – and he served us manfully and at times single-handedly.

As a club we were hit-or-miss. Our players didn't train, or anything like that: they shoved as only farmers can, and they liked a drink. My own early alcoholic apprenticeship, however, whether at rugby or cricket, was suitably modest and discreet. Although he liked the occasional glass of beer, Dad hardly ever went into a pub and would certainly not have approved of such premature tendencies on my part. So I didn't tell him about my first halves of shandy.

Team selection was a weekly hazard, at least to the overworked secretary. One week, a big Welsh bloke suddenly turned up to change with us in the pub before the game. No-one had ever seen him before. 'Where did you find him?' Denys Budd was asked discreetly.

'Marks and Spencer's! Saw him in there this morning and thought he was a useful size.'

Bryn Wood played in the second row for the next two seasons.

I was responsible for some offbeat administration myself. We were due to play Exeter B the following week and the secretary handed me a card, addressed to the opposing club official. He asked me to post it when I reached home. 'It's like this,' he told me. 'Exeter also play in black, so as the visitors I'm asking them to come in a change of colours.'

The next weekend, on my way to the ground I put my hand into my pocket – and there was the postcard. So we had thirty players all in black. The only difference was that Exeter, slightly more sophisticated than us, had numbers on their backs. I was very apologetic and told the referee, Wally Gibbs, someone I knew, that it was all my fault. 'Don't worry, Shep. We can still have a game.' And we did, after a fashion. The trouble was that our boys needed to check the back of a player's shirt before they tackled him.

In time, South Molton developed into a flourishing club with even a ladies' team. Bob Holmes's influence was behind the progress. He had the knack of catching the school-leavers and encouraging junior sides. Matters were more hazardous, though never less than convivial, when I was playing. What did it really matter if we could only muster seven forwards? We were an earnest, amiable and unfit team. And we certainly boasted an odd, interesting assortment of professions – car mechanics, a chemist, an accountant and a hotelier were all in the team. Plenty of farmers, too, as I've mentioned: there were the Prideaux twins, Dave and Frank, the Kingdom brothers, Maurice and Gerald, and Maurice's son Peter, as well as Mike and Ray Currie (the latter went on to marry Edwina). John Rowe, John Tucker, Roger Nichols, Denis Cronk . . . the names come back in a joyful rush.

I liked my rugby, and discovered I had a strong competitive streak to complement what others amiably claimed was a face of deceptive innocence. But I knew inwardly by now that cricket was my game. It wasn't simply the 1,000 runs I'd just scored for my school. I wanted to go on improving, playing at a higher standard – and yet still daring to hit impishly over the top as if it was a village match at Westleigh or Fremington.

My scoring consistency was earning approval, and not just in the north of the county. I was chosen to play for Devon Colts and at the end of the 1959 season, my last at Barnstaple Grammar School, I learned that I had been selected to play for English Schools at Under-19 level. That was when, for the only time, I had the privilege of opposing my brother's team of MCC Young Professionals at Lord's. We were soundly beaten and I made few runs but that didn't really matter. The scenario, at the home of cricket, will remain with me forever. It was a breathtaking experience, especially as this was my first sight of the world's most famous cricket ground. I just stood there on the edge of the boundary and gazed in boyish wonderment all around me. Was this really Lord's – and was I about to play here? I'd come up on the train from Instow, waved off by the family. In my hand was a small cricket bag; in my head was a glorious amalgam of dreams. The occasion was almost too much for me. I was exceptionally nervous, I remember, though the fact that Bill was around – even if on the other side – gradually helped me to calm down.

Harry Sharp, later to be the Middlesex scorer, was in charge of the Young Professionals. Years later, by which time I was an umpire, I took Bill to Cardiff to watch a John Player League match when Glamorgan were playing Middlesex, and I introduced him to Harry. He admitted then that for years when he'd seen the name 'Shepherd' in the Gloucestershire team, he'd assumed it was Bill. There's a picture of Harry, in a touring team group, hanging on the wall of the Instow pavilion and I had it copied and sent to him. He was a valued tutor to Bill and I'm sure numerous other aspiring cricketers in his Lord's days.

I made my Minor Counties debut for Devon at about the same time as my Lord's appearance. It was against the Somerset 2nd XI at Taunton. Two of the stalwarts in the Devon side were Deryck Fairclough and Dereck Cole, one a lecturer at Exeter University and the other at the Royal Naval College at Dartmouth. They were both fine players, and they both had a considerable influence on the course of my sporting life. They turned up at Instow one day to see my father. 'Now tell us, Mr Shepherd, what's this boy of yours going to do?'

'Well, you know he's mad about cricket. He's been for a few trials. He's even thinking about it as a possible career.'

They were talking in the back room and I could hear every word. The visitors were quite emphatic. 'Whatever you do, don't let him go into cricket without something behind him.'

I could sense the way the conversation was going. Whatever their good intentions, they were dissuading Dad from letting me do anything hasty. It couldn't have been more disheartening to me. I appeared to be waving goodbye to all my private hopes.

Back in the Easter holidays I'd gone to Kent for a trial. I stayed with

Les Ames, who encouraged me and told me to come back later to play in some 2nd XI matches. There had been an invitation, too, from Lancashire. But Somerset were closest at hand and I sounded out a few Devon officials when I played against them in the Minor Counties game. They suggested I come for a trial match but I'd broken a thumb in a school fixture and the invitation wasn't extended.

It was time for a serious talk with my father, who knew well enough how I was feeling. He also understood the advice passed on by Fairclough and Cole. The result was that I was sent to St Luke's, Exeter, to qualify as a teacher. So, for the time being, it would have to be college and club matches – and Minor Counties when available.

Clubs like Devon had restricted budgets and cost-cutting was on the agenda. If they were playing at Torquay, young Shepherd's travel arrangements needed to be monitored carefully. I lived miles away, up in the north of the county, and the last train back there didn't wait for cricketers. The cost of an overnight stay in a hotel was out of the question so, when possible, I was allowed to leave the field early – and discreetly – to catch the train. Substitutes were ingeniously rustled up. Graham Wiltshire was just one who came to my aid in that endearing, slightly unofficial way. I was later to know him well as a conscientious Gloucestershire coach, someone whose enthusiasm was conveyed to hundreds of schoolboys. He was a gangling, warm-hearted police-man's son from Chipping Sodbury who gave more than forty years' service to Gloucestershire. As a player his county appearances were limited because he had to take his place in the seamer queue behind George Lambert, Colin Scott and David Smith. Maybe he deserved a little more scope; after all, he did take a hat-trick against Yorkshire with his deceptive out-swingers. And, oh dear, in his teenage days back at Sodbury he dared to dismiss both Charlie Barnett and Tom Graveney in a benefit match. Charlie no doubt gave him a look of withering disapproval.

Graham's most valued skill was in instructing young and potentially talented cricketers. He did it with a rural, unconventional charm, travelling miles to talk to improvised classes of schoolboys in out-of-the-way villages. His method bubbled with humour. Grahame Parker, who became Gloucestershire's manager and historian after giving up teaching, used to say that 'Wilts' had Pied Piper appeal. He was also someone who loved Devon and, in particular, Cornwall. He talked about fishing off Penzance harbour with almost as much enthusiasm as he displayed when discussing cricket. And that's saying something, for he was enormously enthusiastic about cricket. He was always willing to step in and play at the last minute and countless times for Gloucestershire he was a jovial and uncomplaining twelfth man.

That brings me back to the occasion when he came to Devon's assistance, though hardly by design. He was coaching at a school in Sussex when Ted Dickenson, Torquay's captain and a mainstay of the club, rang him up: 'How do you feel about playing a game or two for us?' Such a request was seldom wasted when directed at Graham, so he decided to travel to the ground to meet Ted. He ambled out of Torquay station and into the nearby cricket ground, where Devon were playing Oxfordshire in the Minor Counties competition. Dereck Cole, the Devon skipper, looked over the players' balcony and was clearly surprised to see him: 'Have you got your kit?' You don't expect that kind of question late in the afternoon after a lengthy railway journey but luckily Wilts had brought his with him. 'Good, do me a favour. One of our boys has to leave at teatime. Be grateful if you'd take over.'

Graham didn't even know me or realise I had to chase away to catch the last train back to Bideford. But he assumed Oxfordshire would win – they always did against Devon – and that there would be a few pleasant, untaxing hours in the evening sunshine. He should have known better. Against all the predictions the match swung Devon's way. We had a left-arm spinner, Jack Kelly, who took the wickets that mattered. As the game became increasingly tense (I'd already left but heard graphic reports of the finish later), all the fielders crowded the bat. My substitute found himself at short-leg. We beat Oxfordshire for the first time and Graham was heard to say: 'All that for a cup of tea and a cake!'

Not long afterwards, when Wilts was ensconced in his coaching duties at the County Ground in Bristol, he was told that some lad from North Devon was turning up for a trial with Gloucestershire. Would he go to Temple Meads station to pick up the newcomer? I'd better let him complete the story.

'I didn't even know the name of this trialist but we were to look out for each other. And then I spotted him. Roly-poly. Grinning. All I could say was "My God, aren't you the bloke who buggered off at Torquay that day and left me fielding at short-leg?" '

My relationship with him remained warm. He used to say I had a touch of the Colin Milburns about me, a judgement I conclude that had something to do with my comfortable build rather than ability. He had plenty of stories to tell against me, claiming that I once brought the fencing down at mid-wicket in a vain attempt to stop a four at New Road in a 2nd XI match with Worcestershire. He was, too, one of the few who appreciated my vocal accomplishments, citing my rendition of the 'Blackbird' song with our ex-chairman Frank Twiselton while precariously perched on a table in our hotel, on the night we won the Gillette Cup. Above all, we both kept laughing as we played or when he supervised my practice.

Hasty exits or not, I enjoyed my cricket for Devon. The other day I came across a copy of the county's centenary yearbook for 1962. Deryck Fairclough, who had first skippered Devon in 1952 and was still in charge, had this to say about me: 'David Shepherd continues to show brilliance and is acquiring, through experience, a judicious mixture of caution and clouting.' A nice bit of alliteration, Deryck – and very flattering – for at that time the most I dared hope for was Minor Counties cricket.

Nevertheless the competitive element and the standard, one removed from North Devon and rather a lot removed from Mutton Hill, was introducing added disciplines.

Friendships were forming all the time, as we quaffed our post-match pints and swapped stories. I was still very much the listener as an eighteen-year-old, thrilled to eavesdrop on the accounts of individual feats and to chuckle at human follies and eccentricities. Doug Yeabsley was a good friend. We'd played together, when I was fourteen, for Devon Colts. He was born in Exeter and went on to take nearly 750 wickets over thirty-one years for Devon with his accurate and often awkward in-swingers. In any assessment of the county's cricketing history there would have to be a prominent place for Doug. Somerset enviously noted his regular tally of wickets and invited him to play a few Sunday games for them. He must have been tempted, at least fleetingly, for as a challenging bowler he was made for limited-overs cricket. But as a chemistry master at Haberdashers' he had his career sorted out.

It was Doug who noticed how nervous I could be before an innings, pulling on a succession of cigarettes. This was a habit which continued well into my years with Gloucestershire. Many players, some with years of experience, were affected in the same way. That wonderful, wristy batsman George Emmett seemed to consume whole packets as he waited his turn. The nicotine-stained fingers gave him away years after he'd given up playing and was by then frightening the life out of dreaming or indolent young pros as he brusquely rapped his orders. He was one coach who stood no nonsense.

Whenever I see Doug Yeabsley now, the ancedotes fly. They include inevitably our stay at Caversham Bridge while we were playing Berkshire. We were booked into the local hotel and had every reason to be pleased with our progress in the match. We decided it called for a spot of nocturnal enterprise and, without permission, it has to be said, planned to take out a Reading rowing boat. According to Doug, I took it upon myself to organise the crew for the unofficial jaunt along the Thames. It was quite a daring operation by our innocent standards. Suddenly, as they say in all the best cop shows on television, all hell broke loose. The guilt-ridden crew was thrown into complete confusion as we were illuminated by police searchlights. Our little prank was over almost before it had begun. As we discovered later, the law had turned up and seen with some amusement what was going on. They delayed switching on the lights till the last second. I suppose we're grateful that they took such a lenient view and at least one of the officers arrived at the ground the next day to see us play.

Doug clearly had a liking for the Thames, as I have a distinct image of him on another occasion diving into the river and swimming to the opposite bank. Whether he was still in his white flannels I can't recall.

Doug used to recall my tendency to get caught at mid-off and then reflect, back in the pavilion, 'Sorry about that, lads – I thought I could clear him.' But he had to admit that 'Shep could hit the ball in the air a long way.' He was particularly enthusiastic about one innings of mine on a poor pitch at Liskeard, where he recalls – more vividly than I do – how I kept whacking the ball over a shed and out of the ground. Cornwall, our perennial rivals, were beaten and I got a hundred. In spite of my occasional impetuosity (on and off the pitch!) Doug knew I was a loyal team man, aware of the needs of the side and ready to take the difficult end if the ball was doing something or if one bowler was well on top.

Friendship needs to be returned, of course, however subtly. Some years later, Doug was playing for Devon against Nottinghamshire at Exmouth in the NatWest Trophy. His intention was never to bowl a wide and it was one of his outstanding virtues that he made the batsman play almost every ball. In this match he was perilously close to a wide and I was by now the umpire. 'That was very tight, Doug. Don't put me on the spot.' He knew that I didn't want to spoil his record, and I think I can be excused that momentary concession to sentimentality. We looked at each other, and our expressions said it all. What would cricket be without a soul?

There was frequently an amusing sting in our exchanges. I remember when Doug was playing for, and probably captaining, Minor Counties against Gloucestershire. Mike Procter, shirt-tails flying, was hurtling them down. It was faster and more intimidating than anything the opponents had faced before. Doug, probably with no desire to prolong his stay at the crease, instinctively pushed his bat out, and to his astonishment the ball scorched away through the covers for four. Applause on the boundary, and a sheepish shrug of disbelief from Yeabsley, someone not especially renowned for his batsmanship. I was fielding at mid-off and as Procky, expression set, walked determinedly back to his distant mark, I stage-whispered to my chum: 'He'll have you for that. Get ready to duck.' It was an obvious prediction and carried some affectionate relish on my part. Facing Procter, one of the fastest in the world, without a helmet wasn't an attractive proposition. He didn't take kindly, I imagine, to a tail-ender creaming him away to the boundary with what looked like perfunctory ease. He rapidly ended that uncharacteristic gesture of bowling levity and wickedly dug one in. Doug was out, and glad to get his pads off.

Cricket for Devon, and the invitations to play club matches, often alongside Bill, was all very well. But, as my father insisted, my studies at St Luke's had to be the immediate priority. As I was being repeatedly assured, I needed something behind me – something less romantic and unrealistic than cricket: 'Get your head down, son. You could turn into a decent teacher.' I was far from convinced.

St Luke's came as quite a shock to me. The place appeared to be overrun with Welsh students, virtually all of them mad on rugby. The college understandably had a terrific XV, loaded with talent. Martin Underwood couldn't even get in the college's 1st team and soon he'd be playing on the wing for his country! I didn't sniff recognition as a scrum-half and had to be satisfied with the 4th XV.

Bev Price and Graham Reynolds, who both came from Gwent, were in the next room to me. At cricket they were opening bats in the college's 1st XI, so we had plenty in common. I went in at No. 5. Sport was the perfect therapy for the more onerous studies. Bev remembers what I was like in those days:

Shep was boyish in appearance, younger than most of the others who had completed their National Service. One evening we all went down

35

the road to a cinema in Exeter, to see *Psycho*. Shep was very worried that because of his youthful looks he wouldn't be able to get in. He just about managed it. He was jovial, popular and, well, overweight. We used to call him 'The Bear', probably because he was inclined to be cuddly. I suppose you could say his appearance was a bit unlikely for the PE course he had chosen.

When it came to cricket he didn't have to run too much because he hit the ball so hard. In one six-a-side match between the hostels at the college, he hit a huge, straight six over one barrack-like hostel and into the swimming-pool beyond.

Graham went on to play soccer many times for Newport County at centre-forward and is now a scout for Tottenham. He remembers me being called, by contrast, 'The Cat', based on my efforts as the goalkeeper in soccer friendlies, I assume, and as a tongue-in-cheek reference to some-one much more deserving of the nickname, Chelsea's Peter Bonetti.

'He had a good brain for both rugby and football. At soccer, you'd hear great shouts of 'My ball' from him when he came out for crosses. Defenders were inclined to have a bit of a moan when he got in their way, but he was confident and had good hands.

Geography was his second subject and he couldn't have picked a worse one. It involved a lot of hard work. Standards were high and 'Dosie' Rest was a demanding geography lecturer. In the case of PE, there was much changing of clothes.

A word about Shep's card-playing. He was the worst I ever played with or against. He smoked all the time. We'd play 'river boat', which is similar to three-card brag. At first he'd stand around and watch us. Then he decided to join in. You always knew when he had a good hand because he'd go red in the face and puff nervously on the latest fag, so he hardly ever won. Others would throw in their cards because they always knew when he had a good hand. He could never quite understand how we knew.

When he went home to Instow for a weekend, he would return with a hamper of goodies, prepared by his mother. We'd have a real Billy Bunter feast. He was invariably generous to his chums.'

I suppose I should do a spot of self-analysis and admit that I probably wasn't the brightest student at St Luke's. Dutifully I attended the lectures and envied Graham and Bev, who were doing history which seemed to me decidedly easier than geography, my second subject. I'm sure they didn't have so much work to get through. The cricket came easier to me. One Whit Monday we played a twenty-over fixture against ex-students on the college ground. It was one we badly wanted to win as there was pride at stake. I hardly paused for breath and hammered my way to a hundred off ten overs. It became quite a talking point. The local *Express* and *Echo* got quite lyrical over it and suggested, with maybe a bit of journalistic licence, that I'd smashed two windows in the process, at least I assumed that's what they meant. I'd hate to think that it *wasn't* a printing error and I'd really smashed two widows!

This is a good moment to reflect. Here I was at college in Exeter, training (largely against my instincts but on my parents' sound advice) to be a teacher. Soon I'd be on my way to a secondary modern school, to discover what sort of fist I'd make of supervising the vaulting in the gym or, more worryingly, of standing in front of a classroom of boys and girls to teach them geography. Was that to be the direction of my career? Was I destined to be holding marked exercise books rather than my trusted cricket bat? Had I, to return to my maritime roots, missed the boat?

For the record, I was a teacher for three years. I started as a supply teacher at Bideford and then Ilfracombe. There followed a full-time appointment. I took games, which I enjoyed. In the classroom I did my best, but feel it was a weakness of mine that I invariably wanted to be one of the boys and share their sense of fun and even mischief. In my resolve to introduce a measure of discipline I occasionally let fly a piece of chalk. By today's standards I imagine that would be considered politically incorrect but back then the class would grin and not hold it against me. The other day I bumped into one of my former pupils and he marvelled that I always seemed able to anticipate trouble and so nip it in the bud. Jenny says it's a useful quality of mine.

Dawn Deliveries

Whatever the future held for me, my heart was never going to drift far from Instow. My duties as an international umpire take me to Australia and the Caribbean, where I find myself booked into five-star hotels. But life is often a little unreal, too glamorous and sophisticated for my Devon taste ... too far, emotionally, from the estuary village that has been my home and my haven for more than sixty years.

So what, I have to ask myself, is Instow's deep, timeless appeal, an appeal that is as strong as ever? The thought of it fills my head with joy and relaxation whenever I step down from the plane and point the car for home. It means that I'm ready still to get up before 6 a.m. and carry on the tradition of delivering newspapers from Bill's post office and shop, through the winter months or whenever I don't have a match. As a family, in the years I was growing up, we never had a car. All of us, including Mother, did our turn at delivering papers on our bikes. We puffed up the hills, often when it was still dark and found time to have a chat, as we knew all of our customers personally. We also found time to listen to the birds: dawn is a wonderful part of the day.

Gloucestershire's Arthur Milton, England's last 'double' soccer and cricket international and someone full of wisdom, has started delivering papers again in Bristol. He's in his early seventies and remains enchanted by the signs of nature coming alive at first light. For the same reason, he chose previously to be a postman. Arthur was so popular on his rounds that householders where he delivered the letters organised a wine-and-cheese party to mark his retirement.

Milt is an urban lark and I'm one from the country, but we share the same regard for early mornings.

Instow is many things to me, retaining imperishable memories that glow with innocence and good humour. This cocooned community, halfway between Bideford and Barnstaple, is defiantly holding on to old customs and standards, even though it has moved with the times in some ways. When I was a boy, I'd see the milk-churns and the fish-and-chip van on Friday nights, and cycle past thatched cottages. Bideford and Barnstaple were too far away so we made our own entertainment. Mother would call us in to listen to *Dick Barton, Special Agent* on the wireless. Bill and I joined the youth club and attended the village shows, so maybe within my shy exterior there lurks a comic actor. I later found myself recruited for the cast of several Women's Institute pantomimes at the village hall. I liked attending the rehearsals and riotously practising the slapstick routines. In one production I was cast as the Sleeping Beauty in a musical. Now that was really taking a chance on me, as I'm tone-deaf. I had all sorts of trouble learning the words, or more so the tune, of 'One Day My Prince Will Come'. My producer was in despair, concluding that I'd never get it right. But the sight of me, decorously gender-bending on stage, brought its own solution for any lack of vocal confidence on my part: the audience went wild, their continuous laughter blocking out my tuneless efforts. I'm not going to say that the show should have transferred to London's West End, but it was a big local success.

Villager Vera Richards, who played my nanny in that panto, still recalls our exchanges whenever we pass in the street. Apparently I established my claims for an Equity card in that Christmas show and to this day I get asked whether I'll be available for the latest panto-mime. The temptation is there and perhaps I should enlist an agent to look after my interests. More seriously, I seldom know far in advance whether I shall be needed for a spot of umpiring on the other side of the world, so it looks as though my Sleeping Beauty costume must be put away for some time yet.

Before I'm accused of immodesty, I should make it plain that my theatrical experiences were strictly limited and that the parts to which I was entrusted demanded no exceptional acting skills. The fact that I was a bit of an Instow celebrity carrying a few extra pounds at the midriff no doubt added to the enjoyment of the spectacle. As far as memorable comic acting is concerned, our most famous exponent must have been that bald master-craftsman of West End farce Robertson Hare, who came frequently to the village; not, alas, to perform but to play cricket for North Devon CC. I was too young to see him, or Jack Hulbert and Cicely Courtneidge, a famous husband-and-wife act from radio and London's stage, two other regular holiday visitors.

An equally famous caller I missed, again because I was too young, was Sir Francis Chichester. He had relatives in the village and one popular story, recounted in Alison Grant's excellent history of Instow, is that his success as a solo round-the-world sailor in his ketch, *Gypsy Moth IV*, could be traced to unlikely tuition from the daughters of the local house where he was staying.

Someone I *do* know is the long-distance runner and international coach Bruce Tulloh. His mother lives in Instow, where he spent his early years. From time to time I see him, during his visits home, running barefoot along the beach. We usually have a few sporting thoughts and memories to exchange. Bruce has often turned up in Instow with well-known athletes and has taken part in local marathons and fun-runs.

Ours was a tight little community. As cars became more widespread, the Molland brothers, Joe and Monty, were around to repair them in the garage started by their father, Frank. There were the butchers, Reg Slee and Bill Smallcorn. There was the local bobby, Charlie Bolt, who dispensed justice with a clip about the ear and who ran his own police cricket team. So many names from those days come back to me. While we're talking about characters, I mustn't ignore Arthur Look, a farmer from the Glastonbury area who came to live with his wife in a chalet near the Instow ground. The place was a shambles when he arrived, but Arthur set about clearing the brambles and sprucing up the surrounds. With a countryman's enthusiasm, he planted vegetables and flowers. One day the vicar walked past and stopped for a chat.

'Arthur, you and the good Lord have made a fine job of improving the appearance.'

'Thank you, Vicar. But you should have seen it when the good Lord was doing it on his own.'

Arthur never lacked a sense of humour. At the cricket ground the ladies' loo is at the back of the pavilion. Full of mischief, he put a dead rabbit in the bowl, its beady eyes looking out. Poor Margaret Tyers had the fright of her life.

Another local character was John Harper, who was the chef at the Marine Hotel, and did the scoring for us in the numerous darts and skittles matches that were played there. When we bought a round of drinks, it was always 'Stick one on for Chef.' As far as I recall, he stockpiled his free drinks for future matches. It was a classic case of drinking on credit. As for the skittles, Instow was a veritable hotbed. There were eight leagues and more than a hundred teams in the Bideford and District League. Instow itself had four teams. The division winners used to play each other to determine the 'Champion of Champions'. I played for Instow Town and we triumphed, in beery delight, both in 1982–3 and 88–9.

Someone whom everyone in the village knew was the railway signalman, Jack Frost. He was described in the official history of the village as 'a one-man neighbourhood watch'. I can certainly vouch for that. From his lofty position in the signal-box he was among those who raised the alarm when the post office was raided.

It's time for me to come reluctantly to my family's experience of crime. You just don't expect it at Instow, where for generations the villagers, like so many in rural areas, would never even think of locking the front door at night. There was so much mutual trust. The first robbery at the post office came in the mid-sixties when I was in Bristol, taking my early tentative steps as a county cricketer. I was phoned to be told of the family's ordeal and it left everyone, including myself, in a dreadful state. Three thugs had entered the post office when no-one else was around and asked to see a road-map. Before Bill knew what was happening, one of the raiders threatened him with a knife. A second man went round the counter, said he had a gun and instructed my mother to hand over the money. Bill nodded and she gave the intruders a cash-box which contained, in total, £480. The three then made off.

My brother phoned the police immediately. Road-blocks were set up; luckily there aren't too many roads out of North Devon, and there were even fewer in the sixties. At one point the raiders were flagged down but didn't stop, which led to a chase. Sensing they were trapped, they abandoned their car and made off across some fields. Two of them were quickly caught, and the other was overpowered after a struggle. He had hurled a rock at the police officer and hit him. Later a sheath knife was found in his pocket. When the case reached Bristol Assizes, the policeman was commended for his bravery. One of the raiders, who came from Liverpool, was sent to prison for five years and it emerged that he had twelve previous convictions. His confederates, younger men, were sent to a detention centre and Borstal.

It was a ghastly business and for weeks was the talk of formerly crime-free, easy-going Instow. The police had done a great job and the cash was recovered, but the raid and the threats on her life had shaken up Mother terribly. Dad hadn't been dead long at that point. Was nowhere safe? The psychological scars would stay with Mum, and with Bill. I was away playing cricket and enjoying myself, and can't help feeling guilty that I wasn't there to help. At home, in the post office on the Front, where I'd grown up, a knife had been menacingly placed across my brother's throat.

There's an odd postscript to that raid. Some years later, a woman called at the post office. She said she worked with prisoners and told Bill that one of those thugs would like to come and visit us. The social worker may have been full of compassion and the prisoner full of remorse, but my brother didn't want to know – and who could blame him?

Before I turn to more pleasant matters, I should mention a recent break-in. Again I was away, this time in Australia. I was enjoying the millennium celebrations, umpiring matches and spending the last day of the century with old friends, Mike and Myra Pratt. I'd asked not to travel on 31 December for fear of the millennium bug – superstitious old me. As ever, when miles from home, my thoughts weren't far from the North Devon coastline and my family. Were they all well? Was the dog safe? How was Bill coping at the busiest time of the year?

We arrived back in England on 3 January and I called at the post office to see Bill. The news was shattering. Intruders had got in over-night, but my brother had disturbed them and they'd fled. 'They'll be back,' the police said. So they were, a week later. The fact that the raiders again left in a hurry, empty-handed, was only a partial com-pensation. It isn't difficult to imagine the amount of stress and anxiety it caused Bill.

Post offices in rural areas are always at risk. Even going back to the days when Dad was the postmaster, there was the occasion when he and a local policeman were tipped off that a raid had been planned for that evening. They lay in wait, Dad gripping a shotgun, and he later assured me that he'd have used it. Fortunately the burglary didn't take place.

I'm a serious bloke at heart, whatever the apple cheeks and ready smile imply. Those break-ins shattered me. What kind of society do we live in when a village postmaster, providing an essential service for the local community, has to live in fear?

Three months before I returned from Australia I'd been in Dubai, umpiring a tournament in Sharjah. We had a day off and were being shown the sights. An hour or so into the trip I realised that I had left my wallet in the foyer of the hotel. 'Don't worry,' said my driver, 'it will still be there. I'll go and get it for you.' Sure enough, he returned with the wallet, which was untouched. This is a different society where the punishment for theft is far greater than it is in this country. Who's got it right?

Strangler and Axeman

Enough of that. Now where was I before I got distracted?

While at St Luke's I was scarcely a one-club man. As I've mentioned, I turned out for the college, for North Devon and in Minor Counties matches. Basically I helped out anyone who was short. That might mean a twenty-over beer match or occasionally making up the numbers for a village fixture, where the pitch was a 'natural' and you hoped the ball would miss the mole-hills on its way to the boundary. 'Have bat, will travel' was my motto.

Village games were always fun. As, of course, were some of the local characters. We gave them fearsome names. There was that ageless and capable cricketer, Derek 'The Strangler' Blanchard. There was Ian 'The Axeman' MacIver (who worked for the Forestry Commission), Colin 'Werewolf' Payne. And I could go on – 'Doodle' Cutland, 'Uggy' Tythcott … I heard of some serious drinkers in one club who were known as 'The Cyanide Seven'.

The visits to Tavistock were always fun, not least because of the links there with my long-time pal and later Gloucestershire team-mate, Jack Davey. The North Devon players liked to stop for a few drinks before the game, usually at the Dartmoor Inn and most of us remember one time we lost the toss and had to field. The trouble was that the first wicket took a dreadfully long time to fall. When the batsman left the field, so did the whole of the North Devon team, including Bill and myself. We just about made it to the toilets.

Talking of Tavistock reminds me of one of their players, Stuart Munday. He came to watch a Test match at Edgbaston years later when I was umpiring. Stuart asked where we were staying and I gave him the name of the hotel. He boldly walked up to the reception desk and said: 'I'm a friend of Mr Shepherd. Could I have the same cheap rate?' He probably got it. But the thing about this hotel, the Norfolk, in Birmingham, was that it was a temperance one. I ask you, no drink for cricketers after a long day in the field? Stuart didn't make that mistake again.

My connection with the Norfolk went back a long way. Bert Avery, the scorer and 'travel manager' when I played for Gloucester, once booked the whole team in. Only once we had arrived did we discover its alcoholic limitations. Mike Procter, who had a healthy thirst, exploded. Bert, not averse to a drink himself, rapidly adjusted the booking.

I remember when the newly formed Fremington village side, a few miles from Instow, decided to launch themselves early in 1964 with a game against a North Devon XI captained by local schoolmaster Nick Madgwick. Maybe Fremington slightly underestimated the strength of the opposition. We batted first and in no time scored 267 for five declared. I went in at No. 3 and rattled up 91. Bill, at No. 4, made 102. Fremington, who were playing at the local army ground, should perhaps have been slightly less ambitious: they were all out for 28 and I hope their initial fixture didn't demoralise them too much. Bill came on with his slows for a couple of overs at the end and took two wickets to polish off the innings. 'We should never have invited these damn Shepherds along,' our good-natured hosts said. We adjourned to the Fox and Hounds pub. I'm sure Fremington had every reason to blame the track, at least in part, for their failures. The ball would fly around a bit and a succession of wary batsmen would pop catches to the close fielders. Self-preservation was a required art. 'Doodle' Cutland quickly cottoned on to this and positioned himself as Fremington's regular silly-mid-off. Opponents found themselves helplessly fencing simple catches to him.

Doodle was a canny fielder, but also a brave one: he stood only a yard or two from the bat. In one match he was struck by a ferocious drive in the most delicate area of the anatomy. It looked bad. Everyone went quiet, except for a few whispers of the black humour that is part of the game. No-one quite knew what to do as village cricketers aren't usually too proficient at first-aid. Fremington were playing Witheridge that day and suddenly several of the opposition emerged, carrying a five-bar gate which had been lying on a dung heap near a cowshed. They placed poor old Doodle on the gate and carted him off to the boundary with soothing words. He no doubt suffered a sore bottom now, too, from the improvised stretcher.

Mike Snell, one of my many pals from the local cricket side, is a great source of Fremington stories. He'd come out of the Merchant Navy and, after a lapse of more than seven years, played for the village team in that disastrous first match with North Devon. He still sentimentally retains the relevant page from the scorebook. It reveals that he scored 2 not out as his team collapsed around him. That wasn't the only occasion my brother Bill helped them out. Mike reminds me: 'We were playing against an army side in the late sixties. Bill had just gone along to watch. He was in his cap and working clothes but we were short and persuaded him, without any kit, to play. The army had some very good players and were well turned out. When our mystery man walked to the crease in late middle order, we saw the military blokes looking at each other as if to say: "Whoever have we got here? Does he know which end of the bat to hold?" He certainly did. Bill took a quick look at the bowling and then started smashing it all over the ground. It was tremendous stuff. One ball got lost in the hedge and a fielder emerged with a duck's egg. What could you ask is more rural than that? And yes, thanks to Bill, we won.'

In those days the army in the area had a fiery and talented opening bowler by the name of Tony Hoyland. One day he went into the local barber's and told Keith 'Rastus' Ruse that he'd just been playing for the army at Lord's; no boasting, he really had. Rastus was an opportunist member of Fremington CC, and reckoned they could do with someone of this undoubted calibre. In no time Hoyland had taken 72 wickets for the village side at an average of just over 2. Oppositions feared him; he was simply too good for most of them.

The tracks varied a great deal around the parishes of Devon. You learned the hard way to protect your throat. For me, it was part of the learning process, although I must say that the majority of pitches on which we played were excellent, tended lovingly by groundsmen and their bands of helpers. Laughter was rarely far away. There was a match at Filleigh, a tree-lined ground on Lord Fortescue's estate, between Barnstaple and South Molton. Just one minor snag, as I recall: after the tea interval a herd of Friesians, on their way in for milking, would meander behind the bowler's arm, where a sightscreen might have been placed on a more well-to-do ground. This could be a bit of a distraction for the batsman. During one game, the cows were in even less of a hurry and Bill eventually stepped away from his wickets. The bowler didn't know what was happening.

There are so many memories to cherish: not just the runs and the results, but the priceless stories, the drinking that went on longer than the best innings, and the pranks. I'm told, for instance, that after a match at Sidmouth we were known to come home unaccountably with a deckchair or two. Not guilty, m'Lord.

Maybe I should admit that I was once dismissed twice in a day – by the same bowler. John Edwards, a retired headmaster, had come to Instow first with South Oxford Amateurs and this was where he returned to live. As a prominent member of the North Devon club, he was responsible for running many of the midweek matches. He was playing against us, however, firing in his medium-pace seamers, when he had me twice, before lunch and after tea. John also reckons I must have been one of the last batsmen out to an under-arm delivery in a proper match. It happened in the early sixties during the holidays. I was guesting, alongside him, for South Oxford Amateurs against the Somerset Stragglers at the King's College ground, Taunton. Eccentric or unpredictable bowling was not unknown in some of these games and when I was confronted by such levity, I thumped the ball straight to mid-on for a straightforward catch. That made me blush. 'I could have hit the bloomin' ball anywhere,' I told John. He graciously reminds me of that terrible shot only once a year.

Then there were the ladies: the ones who played cricket for North Devon, I mean. In a light-hearted match against them the men – with not a sexist thought in their heads – played in Wellington boots and batted left-handed if usually right, and vice versa. Unfortunately, one of the ladies, fielding recklessly close in on the leg side, was hit in the face. She lost some front teeth and was driven off to hospital. The men fidgeted a bit with embarrassment, then noticed that the teeth had come out in a clean break and were lying near to where the intrepid short-leg had stationed herself. 'Let's have them,' the hospital requested. And, do you know, those clever medics inserted them back in the fielder's gums. The wonders of medicine!

Schoolteaching or not, my passion for county cricket resurfaced whenever I was on my own and left to reflect on my options for a career. I had five years with Devon, playing in the holidays; I scored three centuries. There'd also been tons for the college and North Devon.

Bristolian John Budd, a useful club cricketer and rugby player in his own right, was then living in Barnstaple and was expected, according to George Emmett, Gloucestershire's little martinet of a coach, to be keeping an eye on potential talent. Emmett's letter to John was curt: 'What about this fellow Shepherd? Why haven't you told me about him?' There was a prompt response to Emmett: 'Yes, he's good. He'll do anything asked of him: go after the runs if that's what you need; bowl off-breaks; keep wicket.' John talked to me and suggested I should have a shot at county cricket. By then, of course, the decision had already been made for me to get down to some studies in Exeter.

John was disappointed. He'd played cricket against me when I was still at the grammar school. And at rugby – he played at prop or in the second row, a big bloke with a mind of his own – we opposed each other when I was turning out for South Molton. So he knew all about me, and he argued that I was capable of doing a decent job for Gloucestershire.

I suppose it was really my cricket for Devon that clinched it. Reg Sinfield, the former Gloucestershire all-rounder and incidentally the first professional in the county to achieve the double of 1,000 runs and 100 wickets, also had a big hand in my career transition. He saw me, on a good day, crack a hundred for Devon against Oxford in the Minor Counties. Andrew Hichens was bowling and, by our standards, he was a bit sharp, but I took a liking to him and whacked him over the sight-screen. 'Not bad, young David,' Reg said to me. 'Do you know, they were coming off for bad light until you hit that six?' Reg, who coached the boys at Clifton and Colston's, in Bristol, after retiring as a player, put in a word for me with the county. Things were suddenly happening. Dad, such a good friend and guide, had died and I realised that from now on I had to make my own decisions.

As I mentioned earlier, I went to Kent for a trial and was told to come back for a few 2nd XI fixtures. At the start of the 1964 season I was invited to play in several 'Club and Ground' games for Gloucestershire. At Malmesbury in Wiltshire I scored a pretty forceful 60-odd. Back in Bristol, and my first appearance at the county ground, we played a Mashonaland XI from what was then Rhodesia. I improved on my Malmesbury innings and reached a century. Not bad, but the county were apparently worried about my shape. I'm afraid the size of my waistline is going to be a recurrent theme in this book! The murmurs from those committee members who'd seen my ton were to the effect of: 'Well, yes, he knows how to hit the ball, but can he field?' They decided to find out.

It happened that Gloucestershire were playing a championship match against Middlesex at Lord's and I was sent to join them. *Not* to make my county debut, I should rapidly point out. I arrived at the team hotel to meet the others in the evening. Ken Graveney was the captain, and none too fit, at the time. Others there were John Mortimore, Arthur Milton, David Allen, Tony Brown, Barrie Meyer, Sam Cook, David Smith, Ron Nicholls, Bobby Etheridge, Martin Young and Harold Jarman; all, as far as I was concerned, famous names, real pro cricketers. The scorer and 'paymaster' was Fred Dudderidge. They struck me as a very happy team and equally sociable in the bar. I was going to enjoy myself.

The next day I went to Lord's and had a net with the rest of the team. After this session most of the players returned to the dressing room. Morty, Barrie Meyer and Ethers were left on the Nursery Ground. I won't easily forget what happened in the next half-hour. Morty, who was temporarily in charge of the side as vice-captain, had Bobby and myself tearing (or more accurately puffing) in all directions around the ground. Our job was to catch, field and hurl the ball back to Barrie. There was no let-up.

A few years later Morty reminded me of that day. He said I'd returned to the dressing room, collapsed in a chair and asked: 'Is every day like this?' He went on to explain that he'd been told by the captain to discover what I was like in the field.

'What did you tell him?' I asked.

'I said that if you could get to the ball, you would catch it.'

That unflagging half-hour had knocked the breath out of me. I returned to play for Devon and represented the Minor Counties against Australia at Bedford. Our side included Norman McVicar, who went on the play for Warwickshire, and two Durham lads who could well have become established county players in my opinion: Russell Inglis, an accomplished batsman, and a super fast bowler, Stuart Young. Minor Counties were soundly beaten but I managed 30-odd runs.

At the end of the season I was invited to play for Gloucestershire 2nd XI in their final match of the summer, against Hampshire at Southampton. I compiled an aggressive hundred and, after what I can only assume were a few hesitant opinions at committee level, I was offered a contract for the following season.

That match at Southampton coincided with the end-of-season party. One or two were leaving and the atmosphere was decidedly relaxed. The evening was quite an eye-opener. County cricket seemed pretty good, at least when the last game was out of the way and there were no more tensions and anxieties for those suffering from loss of form or worrying about a new contract.

I was a special registration so the club were obliged to offer me a three-year contract. It was going to be a new-look team: Ken Graveney, Sam Cook and Martin Young had retired; Tom Graveney had gone just before and was now qualifying by residence to play for Worcestershire; Old Etonian Tom Pugh, the cause of Tom's displeasure, had come and gone. There were several new faces for Gloucestershire – and I was one of them. I'd made it. Faithfully, if not quite with unabated enthusiasm, I had done what my father had wanted and prepared myself for another career, but my heart had always told me it had to be cricket. Now that adventure, which for so long I had feared was no more than a fat Devon boy's dream, was beginning for real.

Century Debut

I joined Gloucestershire for the start of the 1965 season. The annual salary was £500. Ah well, at least beer was still cheap in those days. But expenses – digs and food – had to come out of that princely sum. I was twenty-four and my head was buzzing with the realisation that I'd made it; or at least that I was on the way.

The county was not in the best of spirits. During the previous summer they had gone till the middle of July before winning a championship match, and they lost to Yorkshire by an innings in the final fixture. It must have been bad enough coping with Geoffrey Boycott (177), but then, according to my new team-mates who had played, the weather conspired against us. All out for 47 in the first innings. Oh dear! There was much talk in the pre-season sessions about a new resolve.

I wasn't the only newcomer. Sid Russell, the Brentford footballer, had arrived from Middlesex, where he'd struggled to establish himself in the side. We shared digs at 77 Effingham Road, not far from the county ground in Bristol. Don and Pat Davies looked after us and it was a homely environment, just what I needed. The substantial fried breakfast was equally to my liking, certainly more so than the yoga Don used to teach. He persuaded me to attend a few of his classes, but it wasn't really for me, all a little too energetic.

The opening fixture was against Oxford University. I hoped to be included but thought I'd probably have to wait my turn. After all, it was understandable that experienced pros like to get a few runs under their belts – and The Parks must have appeared as good a place as any: benevolent bowling, a nice, reassuring start to the season. However, to my delight, the new skipper, John Mortimore, included me. I travelled up to Oxford with Tony Brown and Arthur Milton; they sat me in the back and told me I was the rear gunner. My job, they said, was to keep an eye out for the speed cops. We cracked along at a brisk rate, as far as I remember, but my mind was really on other things. We stopped for a round of golf en route but as I had no clubs I just walked the course in awe of my new companions, listening rather than talking. They chatted mostly about their contemporaries and mischievously dropped into the conversation the names of a few of the more ferocious fast bowlers I might be coming up against for the first time. 'Just try to play your natural game, Shep.' It was the only advice I was given. Did they realise what my natural game was? In the Bristol nets I hadn't tried to put every ball I received into the distant back gardens around St Andrews, attempting to demonstrate that my powerful shoulders were made for hitting the ball hard and straight.

On the morning of the match I had no intention of changing the habit of a lifetime so opted for a hearty breakfast.

'You like your food, Shep.'

'I'm a growing boy,' was my instant retort. It still is.

Just as well we fielded first. By the time we'd reached the ground, that lovely parkland with students already strolling around the boundary, their textbooks under their arms, I was getting nervous. When it was our turn to bat, I was rapidly qualifying for a mention in the *Guinness Book of Records* for frantic chain-smoking. I don't remember too many details of my innings, even though it provided one of the margin notes of county history. I even needed to check the record books to see where Morty put me in the order.

Oxford had a reasonable side on paper. They included Richard Gilliat, the New Zealander Michael Groves, once seen as a possible captain of Somerset, the county he represented seven times that summer, and another short-term Somerset player, John Martin. They opened with Peter Gibbs, who went on to do the same for Derbyshire when not writing plays. But we beat them by an innings and 106 runs. The impression I carried back to Bristol with me was that Devon would have given them a decent game and personally I couldn't have asked for a more encouraging debut. Gloucestershire made 394, of which my beefy contribution was 108. There were two sixes and fourteen fours, and *Wisden* generously recorded that 'he dominated the cricket to such an extent that he made 108 out of 139 runs scored while he was at the wicket'. It pleased me almost as much that my flat-mate, Sid Russell, was also among the runs. He and his fellow-opener, Ron Nicholls, scored half-centuries. So did David Brown, who was with me as I moved into the nineties. He came down the track to me at one point and said, 'Do you realise that if you get a ton on your first game, you're in the *Wisden* records for ever more.' Well, I got there and then swung across the line, to be bowled by Giles Ridley, the Rhodesian who was playing in the first of his four Varsity matches. I suppose I still had reason to feel pretty satisfied with myself, but Morty immediately brought me down to earth with a bollocking: 'Well done. But once you get a hundred, your job must be to go after another – and not give your wicket away.'

The telegrams of congratulation arrived all the same. One was from county headquarters back in Nevil Road, Bristol, another from North Devon CC and from an old Instow chum, George Rumsam, a car mechanic, whose two great loves were following the hounds on foot and a drop of whisky. John Budd, whose recommendation and progress reports had had some bearing on my cricketing career, was another to send a telegram. Mind you, I'm not wholly sure about his judgement. At the same time as he sent the telegram he placed a bet of twenty-five pounds with a Barnstaple bookie that I'd play for England within five years. I ask you! That really was going over the top, John.

There were also congratulations from my colleagues in the team. 'Nice shot selection,' said Milts. Valued praise from one of the game's technicians. I dutifully bought my round of drinks. But in my more introspective moments, on the journey back to the West Country, I started to ask myself a few questions. Was I creating added problems for myself by cracking a century on my debut? Was there going to be too much to live up to? Was Oxford's bowling a proper test? Would championship cricket be very different? At home I didn't live so far from the Somerset border. I recalled the stories I'd heard about Harold Gimblett's wonderful hundred in his opening match for Somerset at Frome. He won all the headlines and everyone started making premature predictions. He hated it, admitting – to himself, at least – that he could never sustain it.

The next fixture was away to Yorkshire, at Harrogate. Time to face F.S. Trueman. Christ! This was it. I puffed myself silly as I waited to see if I was in the team and consumed a few more packets on the car journey north. They had decided that the apple-cheeked newcomer would have to stay in after his crash-bang debut. I talked it over with Sid Russell before we set off. In his dry, canny way Sid said, 'Don't worry, Shep. Fred can only bowl one at a time at you.' This was meant to be reassuring.

Harrogate in early May wasn't all it's cracked up to be: the weather was cold and showery. We won the toss and batted. I was again at No. 4, between Arthur and Tony Brown. When we were off for rain, Ron Nicholls turned to me in the dressing room. 'I'll tell you one thing for sure – Fred will be in before long.' It was apparently well known that Trueman liked to visit the opponents' dressing room. In he came – and he stayed. The stories tumbled out in that throaty, familiar voice which later, of course, I was to become so used to as I listened on the radio. On that wet day in Harrogate his tales about his fellow-players were familiar enough to my more experienced team-mates but they were thrillingly new to me and I chuckled away. He had a captive one-man audience from Devon.

When he'd gone, there was the inevitable bit of mickey-taking at my expense. 'The Yorkies will know all about you, Shep. They do their homework. They'll be aware that you've just hammered a hundred. They aren't going to let you get away with that.' Milton, a quiet, perceptive man was turning into a kind of instant mentor to me. I broached the subject of walking out to bat. 'Say good morning to them,' he said. That sounded nice and civilised to me. 'And don't be upset if you get nothing back.'

Then it was my turn. I stubbed out my fag and there, leaning against the boundary fence as I walked out hesitantly, was Trueman: 'Good morning, Shep.'

He'd got in first. 'Good morning, Mr Trueman.' That was respect from a newcomer for a famous fast bowler.

It wasn't the end of our conversation. Fred was clearly conscious that this was my first championship match. 'I hope, David, that this game of cricket gives you as much pleasure as it's given me.' What a warm-hearted welcome. I've never forgotten those boundary words.

Five minutes later I was caught in the gully by Ray Illingworth off Tony Nicholson. I hadn't scored. So I'd nose-dived from a century to a duck in my two opening innings of first-class cricket. Maybe it was the leveller I needed. It can happen in cricket like no other game.

Now it was our turn to lose by an innings. Yorkshire made only 191 but we were out for 74 and 65. Trueman took nine wickets and I was left to conclude that lurking beneath that cordial 'Good morning' were the hard eyes of the executioner. I always enjoyed my matches with the Yorkies – and never for a moment took them lightly. Crafty, too. In the second innings I was at the non-striker's end when I distinctly heard Brian Close tell a fielder to go down to third-man and make sure he saved a two. In other words Closey wanted me, a nervous new boy, in the firing line. It was in that second innings that I received my first bouncer – and yes, it was from Fiery Fred. There were no helmets in those days and I don't suppose it occurred to anyone that there should be some kind of head protection. Self-preservation was part of the game: you ducked or rapidly tilted your head out of trouble, offering the bowler a brave grin or perhaps an eloquent glare. As a novice cricketer, I probably pursed my lips and accepted the hint of danger as a necessary part of my sporting education. Trueman had delivered one straight, good-length ball which, in the best traditions of the batting manual, I played back to him. That was when he said, 'Right then, Shep.' Nothing else. Those few casual words meant nothing at the time to this naïve batsman, but Arthur Milton had also heard them. 'He's telling you that he is now going to let go a bouncer. Better be on your guard, old son.' Milt was dead right as usual. I was prepared and made sure I kept out of the way as the ball reared up. A bouncer from Trueman ... it was an early experience of which I could be proud, a psychological badge to be worn.

Cricket, as I quickly found out, carried a constant element of fear. In my case, I think I could honestly say that I was never truly frightened by a bowler's aggression. The quickies came to know those who were, and they ruthlessly exploited it while for the most part staying within the laws of the game. But if I wasn't frightened, I was on occasion *concerned*. Many of us were, when the track was full of pace and the bowler was quicker than we'd anticipated. Remember that we played on uncovered pitches and of necessity we learned the hard way how to deal with the vagaries of damp surfaces. An early conclusion I drew was to respect how good, and not merely how fast, the bowler was. Derek Underwood on a wet pitch was virtually unplayable.

That first season was a revelation, a university course in a fleeting summer of new locations, new sensations, new-found mates and a healthy amount of dressing-room cynicism thrown in. As I'd feared, it was never going to be so easy again as at The Parks in front of the strolling scholars. Sid picked up early half-centuries against New Zealand and Glamorgan as he put his Middlesex frustrations behind him and headed for 1,000 runs. By comparison, I struggled.

We beat Derbyshire but it certainly wasn't down to me, more in the end to Tony Windows, Matt's father, and Barrie Meyer. By the time Gloucestershire got to Cardiff I was dropped in the order to No. 8, but it didn't make too much difference. We went to Old Trafford, a personal treat for me just to go there (I was so unworldly, I assure you, that I hadn't seen a single county match until I played in one). Brian Statham bowled me – he finished with eight wickets in our first innings – but not before I'd scored 51. In Bristol, playing against Hampshire, Derek Shackleton dismissed me for 8. Was I being found out at the higher level? I accepted realistically that I would soon be playing for the county's 2nd XI.

Confidence was starting to sag a little, though kindly advice was being offered, and at this time I hung on grimly to any crumb of encouragement. One, from Tony Brown, I recall, gave me a temporary lift. We were playing Hampshire again, this time at Portsmouth, it was a lively wicket and we had to face Shack, Butch White and Bob Cottam, a formidable trio in those conditions. Perhaps I can immodestly allow Tony, thirty-six years later, to recall: 'Shep got the full treatment from Butch White in particular. He was battered and bruised – and here, after all, was someone who'd come virtually straight from club cricket. The old boy really got hit. I decided that here was a thoroughly good and brave team man.'

One surprise for me was to discover how few people watched the game. I was convinced that first-class cricket must be dying on its feet. Nothing made sense economically. Having grown up in a post office and shop, I was conscious of the importance of balancing the books. I looked around the county ground at Bristol and other venues and was demoralised by the lack of support. So much seemed to depend now on the limited-overs matches and the registration of talented overseas players. Which brings me on to Mike Procter and Barry Richards.

They had come to Bristol on the recommendation of David Allen. Our county secretary at that time, Richard McCrudden, had written to the off-spinner, then with Mike Smith's 1964–5 Test team in South Africa: 'Are there any exceptional young players out there who might like to join us?' David went straight to Jackie McGlew and asked if he could suggest anyone. David himself had already experienced at first hand the precocious assurance, the arrogance as he saw it, of the teenage Richards, who had come in five minutes before lunch to face him: 'He charged five yards down the pitch, missed and was stumped. The timing may have been bad but I admired so much the sheer confidence of the young man.' McGlew had no reservations about Richards. 'And there's another lad called Procter. No one has heard of him yet. They will.' David recommended both players and they turned up for some 'Club and Ground' and 2nd XI matches for Gloucestershire in 1965. I found myself playing alongside them, marvelling at their natural ability. They were primarily rated as batsmen, until the fair-haired Mike Procter started knocking over castles, too. Very shortly he'd be taking the new ball for South Africa. We can only regret the Test limitations that followed.

David Allen used to say that during my early seasons with Gloucestershire I was apt to try too hard to please. He cited a match at Northampton on a very flat wicket. David was deputising as captain and he impressed on me the need to *impose* myself. He said I misunderstood the advice, went impetuously for an attacking shot and was out for a duck. More words from the stand-in skipper: 'Get your head down first.' It must have worked as I developed a sense of responsibility – and David considered my second-innings contributions at No. 3 of 40 not out helped us to win by one wicket. Not that I feel too much praise should come my way. Mike Procter took eleven wickets in the match, while in our first innings Mortimore had raced to a century in 113 minutes and was in a big stand with David himself.

Talking of our Test spinner reminds me of one mild difference of opinion we had soon after I joined the county. He'd been asked by an officer of the club whether he considered Gloucestershire were wise to sign me. He shook his head and implied I was unlikely to be any better than one or two, including David Carpenter and Dennis A'Court, who had not had their contracts renewed. His reservations were leaked and they got back to me. David was upset that a matter of confidential opinion had been made public in that clumsy way. 'Shep tackled me about it. We had a quiet chat, he understood my sense of loyalty over players not being kept on, and we shook hands. We remained good friends. That incident proved to me that Shep was a big man. And I'm not talking about his girth.' I'd forgotten the incident but I can fully understand a conflict of views when it comes to contract time.

Back in the 2nd XI after my undistinguished run, I realised it was time to sort myself out technically. Graham Wiltshire, among others, could see that I was too far over with my left foot. As a result I was out too often LBW. Years later, in my umpiring days, I would see a batsman with the same tendency and, subconsciously at least, I'd wonder whether he was going to be out the same way I used to be.

In my greenhorn days, when Hampshire were playing at Bristol, I was having a net. Suddenly I noticed Derek Shackleton, that fine, inch-perfect seam bowler, standing behind the net. He wasn't saying anything but I'm sure he detected more than a few flaws in my batting technique. After the session I nudged Sid Russell and asked, 'Did you see old Shack hovering? What was he doing that for?'

'He was probably rubbing his hands in glee and saying to himself that here are four wickets for him over the season.'

It was a fact, as I came to discover, that older pros from the opposing counties liked to take a surreptitious look at newcomers they'd soon be facing out in the middle.

A few years later Derek's son, Julian, was on the Gloucestershire staff, and we were both playing in a match against Warwickshire. Bob Willis was spearheading their attack and he was pacy, all right. Julian was the next man in and I said, 'Just watch him – the first ball he'll give you will be a yorker so don't lift the bat too high.' My colleague walked to the crease, pondering my words. He didn't lift the bat at all. To my private amusement and maybe the frustration of Willis, young Shack left the bat in his blockhole and the ball didn't get past. Not maybe quite the style recommended by the manuals in dealing with yorkers but effective nevertheless. He wasn't at the wicket too long but he was still pleased with the manner in which he'd thwarted the England fast bowler. 'You're dead right, Shep,' he said on his return to the pavilion.

Back in the sixties, though out of the championship side, I had the reassurance of a three-year contract and the knowledge that my headmaster at Ilfracombe was prepared to have me back during the winter months. But I was worried. When Sid Russell was away with the team, life could become strangely lonely, so I looked for other distractions. At the start and end of a season, when the footballers like Harold Jarman and Bobby Etheridge were back at Eastville or Ashton Gate, there were evening matches to watch. Our good-natured physio and trainer, Les Bardsley, the bandy-legged wizard at Bristol City, would look after us for tickets. Arthur Milton would say, 'Come on down the club' meaning Eastville, not so much to see Rovers as to play a few frames of snooker or go to a dogs meeting. Arthur, a highly intelligent man inclining to mathematics – one could only marvel at the way he could judge the timing of the winning runs – was an undisputed expert when it came to the local greyhounds. He attended time trials and generously marked the cards of the players, including opponents who went with him to the races.

I could write a book about Milts alone. He was a marvellous athlete who was as fast chasing singles as he was sprinting down the wing at Highbury and we had no better fielder. But he hated the limelight; that's why he, like myself, continues to deliver papers before dawn breaks.

Uncertain Future

Three years of county cricket – and it was a world away, in standard and attitude, from North Devon CC or the Minor Counties. Did it mean it was now time for me to cut my losses, in the emotional sense, and return to full-time teaching?

My future as a Gloucestershire player was increasingly a matter of speculation among the spectators and in the local press. Big headlines in Bristol's evening paper made no bones about it: the reporter knew my name was high on the agenda when it came to contracts and it wasn't at all certain that I would be kept on.

Milts, my mentor, tapped me on the shoulder. He'd seen the headline and could imagine how I was feeling.

'I haven't exactly set the world on fire, Arthur.'

'Now listen. I'm going to follow Morty as captain next season. And I want you to come back and play for me.'

That swayed me – and for twelve more years I played for Gloucestershire. I never again had anything more than an annual contract. Every August I was looking over my shoulder, pulling on an extra cigarette, wondering whether I had played as well as I should have done. In my personal profit-and-loss account, there was much I loved such as the conviviality and camaraderie. But I could have done without the rigorous training and battle to control a fleshy midriff. It's popularly believed that fat men always have a smile on their face, that the Friar Tucks and Falstaffs are eternally jovial and carefree. Alas, it isn't quite true.

Let me have a word first about the social side of cricket. It's one of the game's attractions, of course, whether we're joking, singing and boozing under a thatched roof alongside the water at Instow or in the Lord's Tavern. As a true Devon boy, I suppose it has to be admitted that I like a drink. My long-time Tavistock mate and county colleague Jack Davey, with whom I later shared a benefit, arrived at Bristol the year after me, and moved into those trusted Effingham Road digs. We shared many a pint – and a few adventures. In fairness, I'd better give him the floor for a moment.

Shep could be merry. No doubt about that. He'd lead a sing-song at the Robin Hood, for a long time the cricketers' pub. Tom Hennessey, the landlord, was on the county committee, and was a friend to all the players. He was rather like a father to Shep, having him into the back room for supper and to watch television.

On the night of an infamous match at Old Trafford, when Gloucestershire played in semi-darkness and lost, Shep was in a pretty bad state. It was a matter of drowning sorrows. I shared a room in the hotel with him and I suffered from my pal's excesses through the night.

A couple of years later, after he'd won the man of the match award against Surrey, we ended up at the Robin Hood. We were still there at midnight. Well, I don't want to tell too many stories out of school, but it took two of us to get him into a car and back to his digs. We went through his pockets and found the door key, with great difficulty, because he was dead weight, we got him inside, where he toppled over, setting off some chiming apparatus and waking the whole house.

Mr Davies, of yoga or was it karate skills, came charging down the stairs. It now took the three of us somehow to get Shep upstairs and into bed. He didn't wake up but to our surprise we found he'd lost his shoes. Next morning, HTV, the local TV company, arrived to do an interview with the Gloucestershire match-winner. It wasn't a very good interview. Shep wore dark glasses and it was agreed that the cameras would remain above knee level. The shoes were never found.

Yes, he liked a celebratory pint. We all did – and Shep was always good humoured and a popular member of the side. There was the evening when we decided for a change to go to the Pineapple pub near the centre of Bristol. We travelled in Shep's faithful and slightly clapped-out Morris 1000, in which he liked to drive at a steady 30 m.p.h. When we got out, we used to feel we needed to wipe our feet, there were so many fag ends on the floor.

We stayed, to put it discreetly, for a skinful at the Pineapple. We didn't remember too much about getting home, but next morning Shep was in a bit of a flap: his car had gone. He checked all the local streets where he normally parked. Sheepishly he phoned the police to report a stolen car. The following day he received a call at the ground. The dear old Morris had been found ... in a car park near the Pineapple. Don't ask me how we got home or how we forgot the car.

I'd like to say that you shouldn't believe everything that 'Jolly' Jack Davey tells you. But I have an uneasy feeling there's more than an element of truth about those late-night episodes.

Oh dear, they are now queueing up with their rather boozy and, I'd like to think, embroidered stories. And I thought Andy Brassington, who'd arrived as a seventeen-year-old, fit and ever cheerful, was a friend of mine!

I'd been a young goalkeeper at Port Vale and now I hoped my trial in Bristol would lead to a career as a county wicket-keeper. I turned up, influenced by the comparative strict disciplines of professional football. I was athletic and eager, instructed to look after my body and be careful what I ate.

Meeting Shep was a complete eye-opener. On my first lunchtime after some training I was dragged down to the Robin Hood. Shep wasted no time: he ordered ham, eggs and chips, and got stuck into a pint. Is this how they prepare themselves for a season's cricket? I asked myself.

But it was great fun. He took me under his wing and over that first week of mine in Bristol, the Robin Hood was my second home. The players used to drink till closing-time. Then the ritual was for them to make a show of leaving, before returning, ten minutes later, down an alleyway. We'd this time go through the kitchen of the pub and wait in a back room until the last of the locals had gone. It was then back into the bar.

It must have been about two o'clock in the early hours, on one occasion, when there was a knock on the door. Tom, the landlord, opened it. It was two police officers. The law – shit! As a seventeen-year-old, away from home, I was panicking like mad. But to my surprise the bobbies took off their capes, hung them behind the door and joined us for a drink. I had the distinct impression that they'd done this before.

That's quite enough, Andy, thank you. The trouble with those young cricketers was that they had such fertile imaginations. They continue to tell these tales about me. The fact is I don't remember half of them and am not at all sure they happened.

I always thought rugby was the most convivial of games, once the last bloodied scrummage had ended and we were back in the bar as bosom friends, singing our saucy songs. But the communal warmth in cricket is something I cherish just as much. I mentioned my lonely days in Bristol, when the runs weren't coming and I was out of the side. That was when I most needed the company of fellow-sportsmen. Procky and Barry Richards stayed at my Effingham Road digs for a time, as so many others did, and someone could be guaranteed to suggest that we should all slip down to the Robin Hood for a strong pint or two.

I relished all of that but not, by any means, the physical demands that came with the training. Perhaps nature didn't deal me the best of hands: I lacked the graceful physique of a sprightly colt. But there were, honestly, several less mobile players than me. I was grateful to hear Tony Brown, on his appointment as captain and discussing the merits of his team, say: 'Shep is light on his feet, especially when running between the wickets. In some of our exercises he comes second or third in speed between the wickets. Some may hint he's a bit like an old steam engine, but he's genuinely quick – and good on the turn.' I'd like my detractors in the team to ponder those words ...

Grudging praise? Possibly. On the other hand, how many of my contemporaries can claim to have run-out Gary Sobers? Now that surely is a conversation-stopper. We were playing Nottinghamshire in the County Championship at Newark, and because of an appalling mix-up, two of their batsmen – one the great Sir Garfield – found themselves stuck at the same end. I was at mid-wicket, typically lithe and alert, and instinctively I knew what to do, lobbing the ball to wicket-keeper Meyer with faultless precision. It was fielding at its finest, unfazed by the international reputation of the opponent. (My version has probably been augmented and refined a little in the retelling.) The only other contact I had with Sobers was one day when I was twelfth man and he asked me to put on a bet for him. His weakness for horse racing was well known, of course. I can't remember if he won; I don't think any commission came my way in any case.

With such natural ability as I showed in dismissing Sobers, you'd think they might have let me off training! But not a bit of it, and like everyone else I was obliged to attend the pre-season stint one year at the Royal Marines centre at Lympstone. Whoever dreamed up that sadistic idea? Devon is somewhere to enjoy ambling walks and relaxing holidays, not perspiring runs over rough terrain and other military-style exercises, fiendishly invented to jar joints and break bones. I simply wasn't built for it. I stumbled around, joining in the black humour and wishing I was back on my bike delivering letters and papers. Back in Bristol we did far too much road work for my liking. We would have to drive out, over the Clifton Suspension Bridge, to Redwood Lodge, a country club. That would be our base for three- or four-mile runs around the village lanes. Half the team were footballers and disgustingly fit. I'd lag behind the others and soon get detached from the main body. And I suppose I had better tell what happened one day (well, they think it was only one day!) several of the senior pros, including Browny, were becoming a bit suspicious. When they got as far as Long Ashton Golf Club they moved behind a hedge out of sight. What they saw caused much hilarity but probably little sur- prise: as a milk float rounded the bend, the rest of the team could see me, not puffing along the road, but sitting up front with the driver. They'd finally discovered why I dropped so far behind!

Sometimes I used to think we had a better football team than a cricket one. In addition to Milts, Ron Nicholls played in goal for both Bristol Rovers and City. My chum Barrie Meyer, later to stand along- side me in the middle, was a striker who played for the two Bristol clubs and one or two others as well. David 'Smudge' Smith was a winger at Ashton Gate; he was a fine bowler off that short, deceptive run, and good enough to play in five Tests. He made the complete break from Gloucestershire when his career ended, helping his wife in their fabrics shop in Fishponds, near where he was born. Bobby Etheridge was an engaging chap, full of self-confidence; if he'd possessed a little more speed, he could have played soccer for England. His team-mate John Atyeo said he never played alongside a more intelligent passer of the ball. Technically he was a highly skilful wicket- keeper, but he had to put Bristol City first. Barrie Meyer took his place and never let it go. Ethers, now sadly no longer with us, was confined mostly to 2nd XI cricket, where he talked non-stop and showed great gifts of intuition with some of his stumpings.

And there were yet more footballers at the county ground. Harold Jarman scored more goals than any other winger in the history of Bristol Rovers. The top clubs were always coming to watch him but

Rovers then had a policy to buy or sell rarely. Harold had his own fan club at Eastville and it was vocally boosted on those days when the Gloucestershire team stood loyally on the terraces. David Allen and Tony Brown both played high-class amateur football. I thought it just as well not to publicise that I'd once been known as The Cat in my intermittent goalkeeping outings while at St Luke's.

As you can imagine, with that assortment of soccer stars and Les Bardsley in charge, there was plenty of football in our training schedules at the county ground. Touch rugby, too. My grounding in my all-black strip at South Molton came in useful. Not the fastest, perhaps, and inclined to run out of puff, but I invariably enjoyed the 'thinking' aspects of sport. I like to believe I had a little of Etheridge's intuition and powers of anticipation. They compensate for a good deal.

At the end of my first three years with the county, I would lie on my bed, light my last fag of the day, and reflect. That first match had got me off to a dramatic start and, as I've said, put me in the record books. Apart from that it did me a disservice. I'm not a hoarder, a collector of news-paper cuttings and personal records. Frankly there weren't too many to drool over. In my second year I had a couple of decent knocks at Bristol against Derbyshire, encouraged by Morty, I remember, from the other end. Then, at the Wagon Works ground in Gloucester, Tony Windows and I helped to squeeze us home by two wickets against Glamorgan. The ground, with a history of valiant deeds – not least from the lanky Tom Goddard, who had a carpet shop a few streets away – wasn't by any means everyone's favourite, but it suited me well that summer. We followed the Glamorgan match with one against Worcestershire. Tom Graveney, whose parting from Gloucestershire had been so painful and probably needless, was now playing against us. He retired injured after making 7. I was more fortunate. Enjoying myself and finding form that had been far too elusive, I cracked three sixes and a dozen fours in a briskish 118 in the second innings. That was the time David Allen came in at No. 8 and scored an undefeated 82, as if telling us his batting should be taken more seriously. We declared, it rained and the match was drawn.

When we travelled to Cheltenham for Ron Nicholls's benefit game against Sussex, I wanted to do well. I had a high regard for him, knew he had an attractive range of shots and couldn't understand why he was apt to get bogged down. It's the inconsequential things we remember about our team-mates – like the time we were arriving at a hotel to book in. Ron came charging out, horror in his voice: 'We can't drink here,' he told the rest of us. 'Do you realise that beer is three bob a pint in the bar.' Three bob in old money; fifteen pence in new!

Ron came from Cheltenham and hoped for a full match and big crowds. He did all right financially but Gloucestershire flopped and lost by ten wickets. I managed 4 runs in total. Ron's 35 in the first innings was the highest by a Gloucestershire player in the match. Our spinners, Morty and 'DA' took most of the Sussex first-innings wickets between them. We argued with optimism that the two of them might do it again on the last day. What we hadn't imagined was that Buss and Snow would run through us.

Over those first three years as a paid cricketer I failed too many times. There were useful thirties and forties, but not enough. Too often my wicket was lost to a careless stroke – or when my front leg was in the wrong place.

'It's up to us, now,' Sid Russell said to me solemnly as we went into our third year. Again my championship appearances were limited. I was never an automatic selection and I accepted I was vulnerable. So many county cricketers know the feeling; don't let anyone ever tell you first-class cricket is a game of eternal smiles and carefree exchanges – every dressing room is laden with insecurity. There are always players – good, honest journeymen in many cases or talented young players never quite good enough – who worry themselves sick when August arrives.

In 1967, that crucial summer for me, I'd had virtually no championship cricket when we went to Romford in June. 'Get out there and score some runs, Shep,' the other players urged me in kindly encouragement. I did my best and followed a duck in the first innings with a hundred in the second. Nick and I tried to prove, with our mid-order partnership, that it wasn't a lost cause; but it was and we were defeated by nine wickets.

Later that month, when Yorkshire came to Bristol, we once more lost by nine wickets. Freddie rolled me over, but not before I'd rattled up 123. Closey had been in his most playful, or should I say astute, mood by declaring 129 runs behind. After that, Morty was probably too generous with his declaration in the second innings. Yorkshire had no real trouble and there were a few inevitable groans around the vast Nevil Road ground. I suspect that the single-minded Geoffrey Boycott may also have had a quiet moan: he was 98 not out at the end. I can imagine him saying to Phil Sharpe at the other end: 'Could have let me have a bit more of the strike to that I could get to three figures, Phil.'

We may have lost, but the ton was important to me. I was glad that Sid, my flatmate, was among the runs, too. So was Mike Bissex, an ambidextrous all-rounder (like Matt Windows years later) who was born in Somerset.

The variety of the county grounds is for me part of the fascination of the sport. Worcester's New Road, with its cathedral and horse-chestnuts, is perhaps my favourite. It's the intimacy I savour, so Taunton, surrounded by its church towers and distant view of the Quantocks when the morning haze has lifted, also has a high place in my regard. Cheltenham, too, of course; I liked playing there, unless I was engaged on an unavailing chase down the slope towards the hospital building. There is always a nice mix of accents at the College ground. I can still detect peppery military voices recapturing the Regency town's aura of long ago; still the more gentle conversation of the academics and clerics; and, for balance and new-found social equality, warm rustic Cotswold banter. Once, when I was fielding there at the bottom of the slope and with the sun in my eyes, I lost the ball completely and it went for four. The nearest tent was, I fancy, being used by the local RAFA; there were certainly plenty of handlebar moustaches around. As the ball crossed the boundary, a voice from that direction, and behind an expanse of facial hair, bellowed good-naturedly: 'Bad luck, old chap. Just like the Huns, coming at you straight out of the sun.' That same afternoon, a beefy drive went straight past me and into the entrance of the RAFA tent. I couldn't pull up and pounded in after it. With exquisite old-style RAF timing, a pint mug of beer was magically produced in an instant for me. I gulped it down with gratitude and reasonable haste as I affected to search for the ball. My glass empty, I wiped the foam from my mouth on the back of my hand and rejoined my unknowing team-mates on the field. There are obvious advantages in being stationed in the vicinity of the hospitality marquees during a Festival match.

It's pointless to say we have specific grounds where we do our best work. I had already in my relatively brief career reached a century at Gloucester. Now I was back against Derbyshire: two ducks and private misery. Thanks, Messrs Rhodes and Morgan. The umpires had been far from pleased with the state of the pitch before the game started but I mustn't make excuses. John Mortimore took ten wickets in the match and we won. There's nothing more dispiriting to a batsman than to find himself with a pair, as I did against Derbyshire. The following month, when we played Pakistan at Cheltenham, I did it again. At that lovely ground the spectators know their cricket. I sensed that they were looking at each other and shaking their heads, a much more eloquent response than mere words, when I was dismissed a second time.

For me it had been quite special to find myself playing against a top touring side. Not quite a Test appearance, but in my imagination the next best thing. I took a moment or two to gaze at the Pakistan players as they took the field. There were, to me, quite famous names in that team – Intikhab Alam and Hanif Mohammed among them. I still recall how neat they all looked – and I'll never forget how well their spinners bowled.

In the past, you could always rely on the ball to turn at Cheltenham. That was why Charlie Parker, that wonderful mixture of temperamental mischief and magically twitching fingers, and Tom Goddard so much enjoyed playing at the College ground. In the 1967 fixture with Pakistan, we lost a low-scoring match by 50 runs. Nineteen of the tourists' wickets were taken by John Mortimore and Mike Bissex, and seamers didn't get a look-in: poor old Jack Davey was given only nine overs in the match. But that was usual for him at Cheltenham; he was generally left out for the Festival. 'It's my holiday time off!' he would say.

Pakistan were delighted, of course. Intikhab gobbled up seven wickets in the first innings and four more in the second. He was such a wizard with his leg-breaks and googlies, and he accounted for me in no time at all, tempting me far too early to whack unwisely a simple catch to someone in the deep. I didn't really have a clue how to read the spinner and I perished in identical fashion in the second innings, then a victim of Pervez Sajjad's slow left-arm cunning. I remember that he was a graduate of psychology and he certainly out-thought me.

So those were international cricketers, I said to myself. I marvelled at the way they, especially Inti, could turn the ball at will. I'd seen nothing like it – not that I saw much at close quarters in that particular fixture.

Committee members were apparently divided in their support for me. They congratulated me on the big scores when they came, or when a defiant innings, seen by some as out of character, had helped to turn a game. But there were, too, the less sensitive assessments: 'Trouble with Shep is plain for all to see. He isn't fit. He's carrying too much weight.' It was pointless for me to say, 'Well, so does Colin Milburn.' I didn't put myself in the same class as him. He played nine times for his country; he was technically ahead of me.

Among those who defended me at committee level was John Budd, who after all knew my Devon CV inside out and had advocated in the first place that Gloucestershire should take a chance with me. As I came to the end of my contract John was worried for me: 'I knew that the county needed to offload a player for the following season and Shep was clearly vulnerable. At one meeting, I told them that if they wanted a six off the last ball, he's your man. And if they needed someone to block out, he'd do that, too. I emphasised his qualities. But they were worried about his weight, so I gave them a guarantee that I'd have a word with him and do what I could.' A burly sportsman who has doubtless had a few weight problems himself, John came to Instow with the intention of having a serious talk with me. His version is that my first reaction on meeting him was: 'Let's go into the Marine and have a few pints so that we can discuss it.'

Before I leave John Budd, an incident during the Folkestone Festival comes back to me. After the close of play I was walking with him across the field to a tent where we'd been invited for a drink. I was wearing my Gloucestershire blazer and was feeling pretty knackered. We'd been out in the field most of the day and no-one had been too keen to face the Kent attack for a few overs in the evening, but I had agreed to open. Now I was really a bit too tired for a lot of conversation in the club tent. As I walked towards it with John, I said he should go in my place. We swapped blazers, though he claims he had difficulty doing up my buttons. In the tent supporters and committee members of Kent noted John's comfortable build – he did look a bit like me and was wearing my official player's blazer – and they converged on him, asking him what he thought of the Kent bowlers and about his career in county cricket. I kept my distance, chuckling to myself. John did his stuff, putting on a Devon accent and carrying on with the charade. And he likes to tell of the evening he stood in for me.

Gerry Collis is a one-time Kent architect who came to Bristol and ran with affable charm another of the city's popular cricketers' pubs, The Duck, in the suburb of Westbury-on-Trym, and ended up as president of the county in 2001. His enthusiasm for Gloucestershire is considerable. He travelled to many of our away matches and it wasn't unusual for the whole team to look in for a late drink on the return to Bristol. Arthur Milton did a few serving shifts there, on condition that he was left free for dog meetings, and Gerry also employed Jack Davey behind the bar during the winter months of his benefit year.

As the licensee, Gerry couldn't always get away to see the cricket. There was a limited-overs game at Nevil Road, where the visitors were Middlesex. It was being televised and Gerry, stuck in the bar, was watching as he served the pints. Someone apparently hit the ball in the direction of deep third-man and I set off for it, my little legs 'hammering away', as he saw it. Again you have to accept someone else's version of what happened next. This is the Collis one: 'The ball crossed the ropes and a pounding Shepherd managed to pull up just short of the fence. Tony Lewis, who was doing the commentary, said, "And the fence gave a sigh of relief!"' Fair enough. I'm on the fat side and I've always enjoyed a joke at my expense. Nothing at all wrong with a bit of Falstaffian humour, I've lived with it all my life. Les Ball, who helped with some of the bars at the county ground, one day walked through the dining room where the players were seated for lunch. He took a long, quizzical look at my helping and said, 'Blimey, Shep, you're doing well for yourself. You'd need a bricklayer to get any more spuds on your plate.'

But I did get fed up with the county's insistence that I should take more care over my diet. They said they were acting on the sound, professional advice of Richard Bernard, a former Gloucestershire player who as a GP was then keeping a watchful eye on the team and medical matters. I was ordered to cut back and, while I tried to comply, I felt that when I lost weight I also lost some of my strength and zest. Fortunately others saw things the same way and the campaign to make me diet was discreetly shelved.

And yes, it is true that I once gave David Allen a bad time during training. Not that it was my fault. One of the exercises that Les Bardsley had introduced involved strenuous and competitive piggyback races over short distances. It just happened that DA had to carry me and we collapsed in a heap. He didn't have much luck with me during training. Once in the nets I hit a hard return and he claimed it nearly had his hand off. He missed the first two games of the season.

Losing weight was never easy. I put it on every winter, no doubt causing looks of consternation whenever I reported at the county ground for the start of a new season. Some of the advice occasionally carried a ruthless streak. Like many who are destined to be fat, my size could depress me, but dieting made me worse, at least psychologically. I'm convinced that losing weight didn't help my form and that's why, in the end, the club left me alone. They knew I liked a generous helping on my plate; they knew I liked a pint of beer.

The trouble was that the extra pounds I was carrying had their effect on hot days. I was too easily out of breath, though I did my best to disguise it. 'Bit red in the face, Shep.' My half-convincing reply would be, 'That's my normal colour.'

I remember what happened when I joined a close-season tour to Sierra Leone by Mendip Acorns, then a highly resourceful club side from the West Country, organised by Norman Teer. Their travels took them to many distant parts of the globe. Norman, renowned for his comically slow deliveries that seemed to get lost in the clouds so high and optimistically were they thrown up, liked to include one or two county players in his tour party. Tony Windows was on the tour and so was Richard Cooper, a prolific scorer in club cricket around Wiltshire and briefly a one-day asset for Somerset. Richard looked and played rather like Colin Milburn. Perhaps he was invited because he shared a comfortable build with myself.

There are various reasons for me not to forget the tour. On the second day there, some internal political problems confined us to barracks. We had absolutely nothing to do and were pretty bored. I was taught backgammon but all we wanted to do was play the matches that Norman had arranged for us. Unfortunately, there were too many guns out in the streets.

Gerry Collis, who had left the Duck in safe hands back in Bristol, was with us and we discovered it was his birthday. It was safe to go out by this time and we all went to an upmarket beach restaurant just outside Freetown. Solicitor Herbie Alpass, whose father had been a good friend of Wally Hammond and who had himself played a few matches for Gloucestershire in the twenties, got up from the table to make what appeared to be a spontaneous speech in praise of Gerry, the pub landlord who devotedly followed us everywhere. 'We can't let the moment pass without making a little presentation to him,' said Herbie. He walked out of the room and returned with two attractive local girls. It may have been that they were searching for a bit of nocturnal business. Gerry admitted he was frightened to death. Looking back on it, the incident was one of the highlights of our truncated tour. And it was all so innocent and tongue-in-cheek. Come to think of it, I hope the girls were reimbursed for time spent on a fruitless mission.

During this, my one and only visit to Sierra Leone, I experienced if not quite a lost weekend then certainly a lost evening. Gerry can explain it: 'We'd all gone back to my room for what we jokingly called a happy-hour. Shep for some reason was drinking dry Martinis. Suddenly we spotted him completely unconscious on one of the beds. We had a doctor, Brian Coles, in the party and he stayed with Shep while the rest of us went down for dinner. And we all became most concerned some time later when we were still missing our star cricketer and the doc.' Don't blame the Martinis. It was the heat and humidity of the place – and, I suppose, that I wasn't as fit as I should have been.

That was a scare for me, in the same way as was my stumbling and assisted exit from the field at Bristol, during a Gillette Cup game with Worcestershire. It was a hot day. We batted first and as Worcestershire had batsmen like Glenn Turner, Basil D'Oliveira, Imran Khan and Phil Neale, we argued that we needed a lot of runs on the board. So that meant a lot of running. Zaheer was in his most wristy form, hunting for singles, twos and threes. We once even ran a five. Worcestershire's fielding became a little ragged at one stage and there were overthrows to be taken. By now I was flushed and breathing heavily. At last Zed was run-out for a century and in came Tony Brown for the final overs, saying, 'We must take everything that's going.'

One of the umpires, John Langridge, had seen me panting and asked with concern, 'You all right, son?' I nodded, I'm sure without conviction. I just about saw my way through the sixty overs – and then they had to help me off the field. I don't know how I made it to the pavilion. Les Bardsley saw my distress and took over, placed a chair in the shower and gently eased me into it. Then he turned the water on, warm at first, then cooler and cooler. It was an acute case of de-hydration and I was in a dreadful state. Team-mates kept poking their heads round the door to see how I was. There was an air of anxiety and rumours were buzzing around the ground. Reporters came to make enquiries. Les, practical and deadpan, said, 'He'll live!'

And while all this was going on another drama was being enacted. Worcestershire were being asked about our using a sub in the field. There wasn't the remotest chance of my taking any further part in the match. Norman Gifford was their captain. 'Come off it,' he said. He reckoned that Gloucestershire were pulling a fast one. I wasn't con-sidered by any means the quickest thing on two legs – and here they were planning to bring on a young, specialist fielder in my place. Or that, as Giff saw it, was the gist of it. He was told, 'The poor old sod is half dying in there. Come and have a look for yourself.' Giff was clearly shocked when he saw me. My eyes were closed and I was barely conscious. Water was dripping from me. 'Looks as though you've just landed Moby Dick.' He conceded, no doubt reluctantly, that we had every justification for a sub.

Mike Procter and Brian Brain took three wickets each and we won by 18 runs. I only heard about it later. Gloucestershire were worried about me and they decided I was in no state to go back to my digs. Instead I stayed for several days in a rambling old Victorian house in Redland, Bristol, tenderly looked after by Jenny, in particular, and by five other young women, mostly teachers, who shared the house. They all made a fuss of me and I couldn't have asked for better care.

Those Superstitions

Maybe I should get my superstitions out of the way. I can't delay any longer. 'David Shepherd? Let's see,' say many who have little interest in the game of cricket but who idly tune in when there's, say, a Test match on TV. 'Isn't he that fat chap who dances around on one leg?'

Some see it as amusing eccentricities that bring colour and a welcome distraction to the match. Others, I suspect, think that I'm just a show-off conscious of the camera. To the latter, I plead not guilty – even though, if I'm honest, I do play on it just a fraction. My hops and jumps, all done with a straight face and genuinely based on my superstitious nature, have become a light-hearted talking point. I can live with that. If there's just a suggestion of theatricality about my personalised actions, perhaps you had better put it down to my latent talents in the am-dram world of Instow's pantomime season.

Let me try to explain. Devonians are, of course, a superstitious lot. The undulating contours of Dartmoor, for instance, are rich in folklore, and the dozens of parishes around where I grew up all have their favourite blood-curdling tales. As a kid I used to hear the legends and myths from elderly villagers, some of whom had never gone farther from their homes than a bus ride to Bideford or Barnstaple. It would have been hard not to be touched by this aura of mystery and the unknown. On one side of me was Bodmin Moor, reeking wonderfully of Cornish legend, and Tintagel, which many, if not necessarily the historians, see as Arthurian Camelot. To the other side are Exmoor and *Lorna Doone* country. To the south is Dartmoor, silent, eerie and captivating. I defy anyone to grow up in this strange, mystical, exciting and beautiful corner of the country and remain unaffected by the superstitions that are an integral part of our history down here.

Nothing would have persuaded me, as I've already recounted, to play chicken with the millennium bug and to fly back from Australia, as was intended, on 31 December 1999. I don't much enjoy air travel in any case and the threatened bug was another hazard I reckoned I could well do without.

My whims go back to club cricket days. As long ago as I can remember, the score of 111 had its special significance. It was a bogey number. In the same way, the Aussies' comparable number was 87. For me, however, 111 was the one to be feared. Cricketers look on it as 'Nelson' – one eye, one arm, one ambition, if you like. Back playing for North Devon, I kept an eye rigidly on the scoreboard. Privately I confronted the illogical, deep-rooted dangers that lurked by lifting a leg off the ground. It became an automatic gesture, just like some people throw salt over their shoulder. It was my own little statement of resilience and to offset any bad luck. I didn't tell anyone. In my heart I reckoned it served me well. I saw no reason to discontinue it when I got to Gloucestershire. On a few village grounds, with their improvised scoreboards and suspect calculations, occasionally I'd been in a kind of torment as I tried to estimate how close either of the teams, or even I, was to the dreaded Nelson. No excuse when it came to championship matches: the scores were prominently displayed. My apprehension, though, was all the greater. Should I do my best to cut out my jumps? 'Why should you?' countered Collis the Drink. So I continued to do my hops and skips but I was inclined to be self-conscious about it and went through the ritual with as little animation as possible. Not too many noticed. Those who did scratched their heads. Was it a bee in my pants, or a nervous twitch I'd developed?

My eccentric behaviour, as it was eventually perceived, only really became public property after I'd become an umpire. It happened in my second Test, England against Australia at Edgbaston in 1985. Someone – was it a mischief-maker from the West Country – had written to Brian Johnston at *Test Match Special*. This was made for him: here was a visual jape that offered rich scope for Johnstonian whimsy. Cream cakes and Shepherd gymnastics, dual diversions for this warm-hearted broadcaster who in spirit had never quite left the third form.

I had no idea of the letter to him, of course. Suddenly, as the score reached 111 and I did my little skip and jump, a relatively subdued version by my normal standards, there was a shout from all around the ground. What the devil was going on? It honestly didn't occur to me that I was the cause. Nor did I know that Johnners had referred to my superstitious traits in his commentary, preparing the spectators for the supposedly bizarre demonstration by an umpire in an austere Ashes series. But many who go to watch a Test match take a transistor with them, to listen to *TMS* at the same time. On this occasion they were all party to the jocular Johnston research. The total stayed on 111 and next ball I jumped again. More whoops of jollity. I was puzzled and looked in all directions for an explanation. Could it be a streaker? Gradually it dawned on me. I kept my obligatory athleticism in my umpiring repertoire after that. Maybe it was expected of me. It certainly was by the singularly good-natured Brian Johnston.

I've been asked countless times to explain my sequence of jumps. One conversation in my playing days went like this.

'What's 111, David?'

'Well, it's Nelson.'

'And 222?'

'Oh, that's Double Nelson or, if you like, Lady Hamilton.'

'That's all very well, but what's 333?'

'If you're playing for Gloucestershire, it's a bloody good score!'

As far as I can remember there were only three occasions when I failed, during my playing career, to survive the dread 111. The county had gone on a tour to Malawi and one of our fixtures was against the Limbe Tobacco Company. It was a pleasant game and I did rather well, but the scoreboard gave limited details, and certainly no individual scores. On my return to the pavilion I discovered to my horror – and I mean that – that I'd been dismissed for 111. My reaction was one of great unease. It hadn't been my fault or carelessness in not knowing my total, yet I was convinced that if I'd done my calculations in my head and had been more conscious of any hovering bad luck over the dark bogey number, I'd have progressed. Call it silly, if you wish.

In May 1970 (see what an impression these things make) I was so keen to get beyond 111 that I took a liberty with Tom Cartwright, something no-one should ever have done. I always knew why Mike Brearley used to call him a master-craftsman. There were consolations in that I'd just hit a three-hour century, but I daresay a few of the spectators on that chilly day noticed how disconsolate I looked on my preoccupied walk back to the Bristol pavilion. Didn't I lift my padded legs high enough, I was asking myself?

Once I was driving our amiable scorer Bert Avery to Canterbury from the previous match. I used to call him Bert the Book, to distinguish him from Bert the Boot, our dressing-room attendant at that time. Bert the Book was a good friend of all the players: he looked after our hotels, did his level best to make sure they weren't teetotal, sank a pint with some style and enjoyed our sing-songs. In the honourable tradition of our most valued scorers and travel managers, he was also the perfect confidant. Not that there was anything particularly confidential about that trip to Canterbury. I pulled into the hotel car park and Bert got out.

'Hang on, Bert. Get back in.'

He didn't know what was happening. Without explanation I drove out of the car park, went round the block and returned to the hotel.

'What's that all about, Shep?'

'I chanced to look at my dashboard. We'd done exactly one hundred and eleven miles. Couldn't have that, could we?'

Bert and other members of the county team regularly attempted to put me into Room 111 or 222 in hotels all around the country. They never succeeded.

Those of us cursed by superstitious thoughts realise they aren't all simply a matter of mickey-taking and mirth. There are the blacker aspects. If a Friday falls on the 13th it continues to frighten the life out of me. It has a personal significance: the last time I saw my father before he died was on Friday 13th. Whenever it comes around, I make sure that I am touching wood: I fix a matchstick with an elastic band to my wrist without fail.

Misfortune is never too far away, though what happened once in a county match at Lord's I was umpiring on a Friday 13th was, at least in retrospect, lightened by the dry Glastonbury humour of Graham Burgess, who was standing with me. At the close of play, he sat down in the corner of our room and read a paper as he relaxed. 'You go and have your shower,' he told me.

As I took off my umpire's coat, I said what I always say to my fellow-umpire. 'Just in case I get knocked down by a bus, here's the ball in this pocket.' Budgie takes over the story. 'Shep went off to have his shower. Before long there was an almighty commotion. I rushed in and there he was, starkers and feet uppermost. He'd slipped and fallen heavily. I have to say it wasn't a pretty sight. As I hurried over to ease him as gently as I could to his feet, I couldn't help myself saying, amid my stifled grin: "Where did you say you'd left the ball, Shep? Which pocket?"'

I was grateful for Budgie's concern, if not his joky manner. Surely he hadn't forgotten what day it was. We got on well as two West Countrymen with comfortable builds. Mind you, I did consider it slightly ironic when once, after the close of play at Uxbridge, he decided to take a kindly hand in my calorie intake. He told me to cut out breakfast completely the next day, to have the lightest of lunches and to make do with a modest evening meal. He claims that I admitted I was feeling a good deal better, and lighter, the next day. I did go through the motions for a few days, but it was altogether too drastic for me.

A final word about my superstitions and idiosyncrasies. I'm not likely

That's me on the far right, not looking overly impressed with having to be at Sunday school.

I wasn't the only sportsman in the family. Here's my brother Bill with an impressive haul from a school sports day.

One of my earliest cricket line-ups at Barnstaple G.S. I'm standing on the far left.

If it wasn't cricket it was rugby. Here I am at South Molton R.F.C. sometime in the early sixties on this occasion. That's me, second from the right on the back row. Bill is second from the left at the front.

And if it wasn't cricket or rugby, it would be football. I am second from the left at the back. Bill is second from the right on the front row. We've turned out for the Bideford G.P.O. team. Some would say that my build was better suited to rugby . . .

The St Luke's College cricket team. How I wish the smiles were so ready in cricket today.

A proud moment. This is me being presented with the Devon cap at my home village of Instow.

At the crease for Devon vs. the Royal Navy at Plymouth in the early sixties. Just the one slip. Lovely.

1965. And I could bowl a bit too. Well, I did get two wickets in my first class career . . .

As my career began to fall into place, Bill's life, despite his great talent for sport, was moving in a different direction. Here he is outside the post office, which he runs to this day. I deliver the papers for him . . .

That same post office received a famous visitor when Fred Trueman arrived for drinks the night before a match at Instow. Could that be nervous laughter from yours truly?

Another very proud moment was when I received my Gloucestershire cap in 1969. Note a twenty-three-year-old Mike Procter, third from left. And the, ahem, generous build of the freshly-capped first class cricketer.

Still, it meant I could get some weight behind the ball!

1973. I always enjoyed playing my shots.

And winning! Sadiq Mohammad and I hold up captain Tony Brown after winning the 1973 Gillette Cup final against Sussex at Lord's.

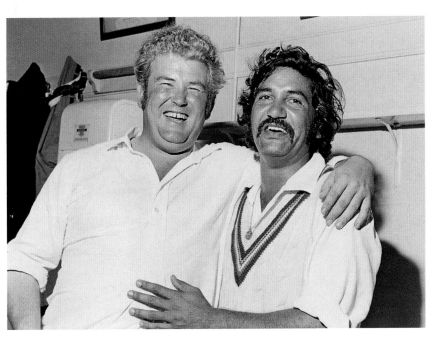

Celebrating afterwards with Sadiq in the dressing room.

And later with Mike Procter and Tony Brown.

The team on the open-top coach tour of Bristol. Procter holds the Gillette Cup high. He contributed a marvellous 94 in the match.

1976. A fine figure of a man! It's difficult to imagine a player of my build playing the first class game today.

Winners of the Benson & Hedges Cup 1977. We beat Kent by 64 runs. Andy Stovold (71) and Zaheer Abbas (70) provided the foundation for our winning score. Note the profusion of moustaches!

By 1978, the following year, we were mostly clean-shaven again. Here we are at Cheltenham.

ever to change, it's no affectation. I'll continue to keep an eagle eye on my car mileage reading; I'll never go out on Friday 13th without a matchstick next to my skin; at home, as I go up and down stairs, I've no intention of ending my habit of coming off the last step with my left foot. That's a Devon boy for you: taking no chances. Mind you, I've an idea that I get on Jenny's nerves at times.

I was mentioning my light-hearted associations with 'Copperplate' Avery. We shared so many journeys and laughs. What about the day when the Gloucestershire pair, David Graveney and Andy Stovold, were awarded their county caps? In traditional fashion that meant drinks for the rest of us. We were playing in London and staying at what was then the Westmorland Hotel, near Lord's.

'What are you guys going to have?'

We were never so impolite as to turn down such an offer. Bert said he'd have a gin and tonic. It seemed a special occasion so I asked for a Bacardi and Coke. We waited with growing thirst to celebrate the double achievement within the team. The drinks arrived in the grandeur of the cocktail bar. For Bert: gin and Coke. For me: Bacardi and tonic.

I was with Bert and most of the players, again in London, back in the hotel after the close of play. We were starving but didn't particularly fancy what was on the menu in the dining room. With a magnanimous gesture – and perhaps thoughts of a quick call or two at pubs on the way – we volunteered to bring back generous helpings of fish and chips. That was more like it, the players agreed. En route to the shops, I saw some lads walking towards us. I was feeling nice and relaxed after scoring a few runs, and spontaneously decided to parade my linguistic skills, those that survived from my sixth-form days.

'*Ou est les fish and chips, s'il vous plaît?*'

I'm not sure I looked especially Gallic but, in my phoney show of worldly verbal confidence, I tried hard to give the impression that I came from across the Channel. The retort was pretty shattering. They saw through me. 'We are from France, *monsieur*.'

A Cap Hard-Earned

It's time for me to get back to the practicalities of batting. I had to be persuaded by Milts, the new skipper, that there was still a place for me at the county ground. The first three years had been less than productive and those murmurs of criticism from the committee room had probably been justified. Were my defiant good-luck superstitions letting me down?

My fourth year, 1968, offered precious little improvement. I could hardly score a run in May and early June, was dropped and felt I was letting down my captain. Brought back against Cambridge at Bristol I eagerly accepted some batting practice, even if it was against bowling that didn't seriously challenge us. I scored a hundred and so did David Green as we put on 183 for the second wicket. We won by an innings. Greeny was the best batsman by a mile that summer. Later that same month, at Hove, I watched in admiration as he stroked his way to a double century. In that match I realised what a fine, maybe ultimately unfulfilled, batsman he was. Here was a player who once scored 2,000 runs in a season without a hundred. He took on attacks and built his innings with good-looking, at times daring, shots. I was surprised to discover how nervous he could be before going out to bat. That's why he had to open; he couldn't bear waiting around. It reminds me of that wonderful cavalier Roy Marshall, who similarly with Hampshire simply needed to get his pads on and open the innings. He found it insufferable waiting his turn.

For reasons that one can imagine were not too far removed from the brewery trade, Greeny was a great friend of Mike Procter, and for that reason he could afford to take the occasional risk at the South African's expense. Greeny used to field bat–pad at times for Procter, and that was what he was doing, without helmet or protection, of course, on one occasion against Sussex. Ken Suttle was the batsman. Procky was steaming in off a forty-yard run when Greeny hissed to the batsman to step away with the pretence, I suppose, that he had something in his eye. He did it three times in an over, each time after the fast bowler had come halfway down his fiery approach. It's safe to say that Procky was fuming by this time. Greeny was tactfully looking in the other direction, chuckling to himself. All would have been forgiven later in the bar.

Once we were playing Warwickshire at Coventry and had the Sunday off. Procter and Green doubtless had a civilised pint or two at lunchtime and in the afternoon the two of them organised their own 'single-wicket' rugby match on the hotel lawn. Both were good rugby players, both were burly and muscular, and it was a thoroughly bone-crunching affair. They charged at each other in ruthless competitiveness while the rest of us, watching from a safe distance, winced. I'm not sure who won. I was just grateful that there were no serious casualties. Gloucestershire certainly couldn't afford to lose either of them.

I often wished I had David Green's style to go with my forceful approach. In that fourth season of mine nothing too much went right. After my hundred against Cambridge I waited till the end of July and into August before I scored another. This time, against Middlesex, I had Procter in command at the other end and scored a career-best 153. The two of us whacked forty-six boundaries between us. All for nothing as Mike Brearley's side settled for a disappointing draw.

That season Gloucestershire finished one from the bottom.

David Smith chose Cheltenham for his benefit match against Worcestershire, whose own supporters are in effect neighbours and help to boost the gate. Professionals like to do well for their mates on these occasions but again I failed, dismissed twice by Basil D'Oliveira.

We lost but Smudge, who used to complement his professional sport with stints as a driving instructor, deservedly had a pretty good match in financial terms. Would I ever have a benefit, I began to wonder? It means so much to journeymen cricketers.

I have every reason to recall the 1969 season. Indeed, I experienced the full range of emotions. The high point was to win my cap. Some might say it had been rather a long time coming. My satisfaction was in feeling I had *earned* it. Not everything had gone so cheerfully as I had my share of injuries that summer. I also shared in the overwhelming disappointment when, after being on the top of the table in mid-June and touted as favourites for the County Championship, we fell away to finish in second place to Glamorgan.

We went to New Road, Worcester, in early July. By then we knew that every point counted. It did my confidence no good at all when I was run-out for 4 in the first innings. Brian Brain took four wickets in that first innings. In those days he had limited opportunities with the new ball because of the presence of Len Coldwell, with his big shoulders and in-swingers, and Jack Flavell, both of them talented enough to bowl for their country. I rated Brian highly as a county bowler and he turned in some excellent spells for Gloucestershire, after joining us in 1976.

Tom Graveney, Worcestershire's captain, playing against his former county, declared, leaving us to score 211 in two hours twenty minutes. Tom had pulled a hamstring and had handed over to Norman Gifford for our tense final innings.

It was a match when Alan Ormrod and Ron Nicholls had got hundreds. Now, however, it was an old-fashioned run chase. Worse, Procky was unwell and hadn't batted at all in the first innings. He staggered out and made no more than half a dozen in the second. By now it was raining and no-one was at all sure the game would run its course. I don't want to sound melodramatic but I really did grit my teeth. Coldwell was bowling his huge in-swingers and in no time had taken five wickets. That was no way for a fellow-Devonian to behave! I suppose I should have known that a lad from the south of the county, Newton Abbot, wouldn't have too much natural sympathy for one from Bideford.

The rain worsened and one of the umpires, Syd Buller, probably assumed we'd be coming off. He asked me and I shook my head emphatically. Seven wickets might be down but I argued we could reach the target. Syd talked to Giff. He, too, wanted to stay on – umbrellas or not. The match was delicately poised.

David Allen was batting with me and we exchanged many determined glances. We kept an eye on the scoreboard – and the clock. He hit the winning run off the first ball of the final over. I was 114 not out and knew I'd completed a good day's work. Tony Brown was delighted: 'Can't tell you how relieved I was, Shep. It was really pissing down when the last runs were scored. You won't get a better hundred or a more valuable one for us.' Every county cricketer is entitled to bask in a spot of immodesty on occasions like that. I secretly knew I'd earned my corn.

As we came off the field, Syd Buller said: 'Absolutely ridiculous playing in conditions like that.' He didn't convince me. I'd have played in a snow blizzard to achieve that kind of victory. Browny came over to me as I unstrapped my pads and told me I'd be awarded my county cap on the strength of my innings.

The award of a cap gives every player a lift. Some cricketers of exceptional ability – and I'm thinking especially of overseas newcomers – receive their caps almost as soon as they play their first match for the county, and rightly so. For others, like David Robert Shepherd, they have to be patient. Then the award is frequently clinched with a personal feat. My match-winning century at Worcester did the trick for me.

That season, Tony Brown's first as captain, was our best since 1959, when we were also runners-up. Yet we tailed away when it mattered. It hardly helped our cause by losing twice to Glamorgan, Tony Lewis's highly efficient team which went through the championship season unbeaten. At Sophia Gardens in July Glamorgan appeared ominously to bat all the way down the order. There were half-centuries from 'Speedy' Cordle and Malcolm Nash at Nos. 8 and 9. Our top score of the match (46) also came from a No. 9, Morty. The trouble was no-one above him had made any significant runs.

I'm pretty sure it was in this match that Speedy Cordle, going for a bold drive, unintentionally introduced an innovation for the batting manual. You could call it the *vertical drive*. The ball went more or less straight up. I've certainly never seen it go higher and thought it would soon be lost in the clouds. The question was who would be under it as it came down? I was fielding at mid-off and Ron Nicholls was at mid-on. It had to be one of us, though on reflection I imagine that our wicket-keeper, Barrie Meyer, would have time to light a cigarette and stroll down the pitch for a token catch in his big gloves. I decided it would be nearer Ron than me. He had plenty of time to position himself for the descent. Although Ron was a goalkeeper by trade in the winter months, it was a different proposition getting under a small ball as it came down from the sky. He looked nervous and, to our shame, we chuckled as he visibly pondered various options. And yes, he dropped the catch: the missile bounced off his chest on to the ground. Cordle, his experiment in orbiting the earth over, survived. Next man in was Don Shepherd. He possessed a compassionate nature: 'Don't worry, Ron,' he said, 'it didn't carry!'

Cordle was a popular player in Cardiff. In that same match he took six for 21. He had Procter, Brown and Mortimore for ducks. I was another victim. The following month we played Glamorgan again, this time at Cheltenham. Cordle had to be satisfied with a couple of wickets, though Gloucestershire batted just as badly, not in any sense like championship aspirants. Brown, a positive skipper, went to the crease with a set expression intended to mask any inward signs of panic. The county, minus Shepherd on that occasion, were all out for 73 in their first innings. Brown was top scorer with 17. We lost by an innings and hopes back in Bristol were fading.

Whenever anyone asks me what was my greatest disappointment as a professional cricketer I reply that it was my county's inability to win the County Championship. We twice went tantalisingly close while I was a player. That title, I assure you, remains the pinnacle of ambition for most of us.

I mentioned the contrasting emotions I experienced that season. At least we finished one from top, having in fact lost only one match more than the champions from Wales. Yet in double-quick time, in 1970, we ended on the bottom. No real excuses, although we'd have liked Mike Procter to be available more than he was. One of our three wins was against Somerset and that is always some kind of consolation. This was the match when Tom Cartwright bowled me for ... 111. Not the most pleasant of memories. Recently I was checking the records of that match and amazingly seven of the players went on to stand alongside me as first-class umpires.

We needed reinforcements in those early seventies: Roger Knight arrived from Surrey; Sadiq and Zaheer would soon be following. Knight proved a timely acquisition as an all-rounder. Our memories can be quirkily selective, however, and I'm always ready to applaud first of all one great catch he took at mid-wicket. Maybe I should add that I was the bowler. The record books can be decidedly ungenerous over some things. For instance, they fail to give me more than a fleeting mention as a bowler. Weren't the editors aware of my prowess, on those occasions I was summoned to take the ball, as a guileful off-spinner who might switch at any given moment to deceptive little seamers?

It's funny how well batsmen can recite their deeds as bowler – and vice versa, of course. In one match, a dead one, it has to be admitted, against Northamptonshire at the Wagon Works ground, Gloucester, I was thrown the ball. The invitation came as a surprise. I removed my sweater with businesslike intent and paced my short run. The batsman was Michael Kettle. My first delivery was encouragingly on a length and he played it with relaxed confidence. I'm not going to get this fellow out. It calls for a cunning plan, I told myself. Baldrick would have been proud of me. My next ball was just outside the leg stump and was turned away for a single. Haydn Sully was now facing me. The same Haydn Sully who came from Sampford Brett in West Somerset, not far from the Devon border, the same Haydn who played for Devon after me. He was an off-spinner so I stuck to my seamers, assuming he was familiar with the arcane tricks of my itching fingers. I sent down an uncomplicated straight one – and bowled him. So ... three balls, 1 run, one wicket. It was the end of the Northants innings and as we came in I accepted the congratulations of my team-mates with good grace. 'Leave it there, Shep. Never bowl again.' Thanks, Morty.

But I did. It was at Old Trafford in the days when over rates were important. The match was going nowhere and, with the wisdom one would expect from an astute skipper, Browny called me up. To take some wickets, I imagined. Well, not quite: the idea was to pep up the over rate. 'Get through the over as fast as you can. Don't bother with too much of a run-up.' I can't think it was the kind of instruction that Jim Laker was ever given. Talk about professional pride.

The batsman was Kenny Snellgrove, another West Countryman and someone I knew quite well. I looked down the track at this fellow from Shepton Mallet. Don't take any liberties, I implied with a kindly smile. I bowled four overs and with great control held one back. Kenny un-wisely tried to take advantage. He hit it hard and high in the direction of mid-wicket, where I had placed my tallest fielder, Roger Knight, who took the catch high above his head.

There were no more wickets for Shepherd, D.R. One could accurately say, I accept, that my bowling career went downhill after my short, triumphant spell at Old Trafford. I fancy Kenny Snellgrove gave me an odd look as he made his way back to the pavilion. It's possible that he, like Haydn Sully, heard my stage whisper: 'That one would have bowled God!'

It was against Lancashire that we played the famous, or infamous, Gillette Cup semi-final in 1971. The memory remains as fresh – or acrid – as ever. It was the match when you needed candles to see the closing overs. And it was the match that was cruelly decided by Yozzer Hughes as he hammered 24 runs, including two sixes and two fours, off poor John Mortimore. Morty probably still has nightmares. I have every sympathy for him, as we were only in contention because he'd dismissed Clive Lloyd, Farokh Engineer and Jack Simmons in a great spell of bowling.

However painful it is, I feel I must run over the pattern of this semi-final. We'd got there by beating Surrey at Bristol in the quarter-finals. Knight had won the man of the match award against his previous county. He had been brought back into the attack to take five for 16 in six overs. Now it was Lancashire. Formidable on paper, but we were up for it.

What an atmosphere: a crowd of more than 25,000. The game was televised and a hundred radio stations seemed to be doing their partisan commentaries. We batted first and leaned on Procky and Ron to take us to 229 for 7. It hadn't helped that there was an hour's interruption for rain. Then it was Lancashire's turn. My Tavistock mate Jack Davey was the most economical of our bowlers while Procter and Brown pegged the scoring, though the Lankies appeared for some time to have wickets in hand. As the light deteriorated alarmingly, the match hung in the balance.

Tony Brown was confronted with the most difficult of all decisions. His instincts told him to bring Davey and Procter back for their final overs. At the same time he realised that the umpires would then call off play for the day and resume next morning. The spectators, many already encroaching on the field of play, wanted a result, so he continued with Morty. And after Hughes's onslaught in the gloom, it was Lancashire who won at four minutes to nine o'clock, taking themselves into the final.

If I'd been either of the umpires, Arthur Jepson and Dickie Bird, I would have been in torment. I think I can say in fairness that it was harder for the fielding side in the half-light. If the ball was coming straight at you, then you had a chance, but it was impossible to anticipate the movement and if the batsmen edged the ball we hadn't a clue where it was going. It was a lottery and one none of us enjoyed.

You can imagine how we felt afterwards. The dressing room was like a morgue. We were pig-sick. No-one was worse than Greeny. For that Gloucestershire team it had to be the grimmest and most surreal experience of our sporting lives. I hated those final overs as we strained our eyes to see what was going on. I could just about make out Yozzer and Jackie Bond, their skipper, at the other end. He was so small, Bondy, that I used to call him 003½, instead of 007. Sadly, that evening in Manchester was no time for nicknames and relaxed humour.

In the cold light of the next morning the Gloucestershire boys maintained their collective sympathy for Morty, who inevitably took much of the flak in the newspaper reports for his side's defeat. Our feelings were mostly conveyed by our eyes, less so by what we said. Cricketers don't welcome fulsome condolences after being bowled first ball or putting down a dolly. For my part, I was more than prepared to forgive him for dubbing me Oggy almost as soon as I arrived at the club. 'Come on, Oggy,' he'd shout, knowing that I came from deep in the South West and deciding to associate me with a Cornish pasty. I ask you, that really was a liberty! Wasn't he aware of the traditional rivalry between Devon and Cornwall?

A few years later we were at Old Trafford again for one of the zonal rounds of the Benson & Hedges Cup. We were ahead when the tie was called off for the day. The weather was so bad that it was impossible to play at all the next day, so we won with a faster scoring rate. I gazed out from the balcony across the virtually empty ground. 'Just imagine it's packed and we've beaten them at last,' I said to my team-mates.

For those still crying in their beer over that Gillette Cup fiasco, there was the chance of a three-week tour to Zambia that October. Grahame Parker came as our manager and I guess the logistics were a bit of a problem – just as had been the sorting out of the financial arrangements in advance. We played three 'Test' matches and won all of them, to the delight of the ex-pat element on the boundary. Our playing guests included the Glamorgan pair Don Shepherd and Roger Davis, and they did us proud. Our party of thirteen was depleted after the opening match by the illness of Tony Brown, who was carted off to the maternity wing of the local Livingstone Hospital, where he lost a stone in weight. His replacement was Zaheer Abbas, who flew in from Karachi to join us, impressing everyone with his elegant upright stance and generous backlift. Then immediately after the last match he left to join the Rest of the World party in Adelaide. We simply knew this emerging Pakistan star was going to make a lot of runs for us. As yet, he had a decidedly limited English vocabulary, but before too long he, like me, would be taken under Tom Hennessy's wing at the Robin Hood. Strictly for orange juice in Zed's case, of course.

It was quite a hectic tour. We crammed in sightseeing and spent a night in the bush at the Kalala Safari Camp. We flew from Lusaka to Kitwe for the second 'Test'. In the early days we had a few problems with the heat and altitude, but the hospitality was generous, if once or twice a trifle untimely on the evening of a match. Graham Wiltshire supervised our exercises; he also found time to coach some of the young locals, displaying a homely skill in which he's probably unsurpassed.

During out visit to Zambia, I was close to taking Holy Orders. The Zambian publicity which had preceded our arrival had got me mixed up with that more illustrious David Sheppard, twenty-two times an England player and at that time the Bishop Suffragan of Woolwich and soon to be Bishop of Liverpool. I'm a little overawed by such comparisons and had better leave the story to Jack Davey.

When we landed we were met by an enthusiastic reception committee, including some church dignitaries and civic leaders. It was the confusion over Shep's identity that appealed to us. It was far too good to be wasted, so we decided to carry on with the charade. Someone got hold of a dog collar and with difficulty fitted it around our 'reverend' cricketer's neck. We even held a mock-marriage ceremony in the grounds of one of our hosts' houses. We did it properly. Julian Shackleton, Derek's son and himself a Gloucestershire player through most of the seventies, was the appointed bridegroom. We found a pretty local young lady to be his 'wife'. With suitable solemnity, Shep conducted the ceremony.

I'm not sure it fooled many people, but it was fun, as were the songs that I led in true South Molton RFC style. Just a few, who had read the wrong pre-tour publicity and wanted to believe I really was bishop material, remained a little inhibited in my company.

There was one reflective postscript on that Zambian tour. It was the first time I'd ever flown. The journey out was quite a frightening experience for me and I was glad that I was fairly well tanked-up before the plane took off. I needed that extra bit of courage. I was so unsophisticated and unworldly then that the first time the aircraft banked, I shot up from my seat on the dubious logic that my weight would allow it to tilt the other way. It took me several years to be completely composed when flying in jets. This admission sounds all the more amazing when I pause to consider the thousands of miles I've flown as an international umpire.

The old Wagon Works ground, known by various names and latterly as Tuffley Park, keeps turning up in my story. No-one would say it ranks with the prettiest venues around the country; it's not as picturesque, for instance, as Archdeacon Meadow, the King's School ground in Gloucester, where more recent county games have been staged. But the Wagon Works – as most long-standing Gloucestershire fans continue defiantly to call it – was seen by some, not so many years ago, as the alternative site for the county club's headquarters. It's where, as everyone tells me, the great Wally Hammond saved Tom Goddard's benefit from ruin by scoring a triple hundred on a pitch they said couldn't possibly last. And it's where I turned up late for a match.

Jack Davey and myself were picked up in Bristol to be driven to the Gloucester ground by David Allen. Away we went in plenty of time –

enjoying a leisurely journey and a chat about our opponents, Hampshire. In Jack's case that meant speculating on how he – honest, uncomplicated left-arm quickish – could dislodge their outstanding opening batsmen, Barry Richards and Gordon Greenidge.

All was going well until we spotted the red light flashing on DA's dashboard. The fanbelt had gone. We were near to the Michael Wood service station on the M5 and David said he'd try to buy another to put on himself. Looking at his watch, he added, 'You two had better walk down the slope in case you recognise anyone going to the match and can hitch a lift.'

We had no luck at all. Nor was there any sign of DA. So we walked back to have a look for him. As we wandered round, trying to discover if he'd found a mechanic or at least a new fanbelt, we somehow missed him. He said later he sorted out his problem, saw no sign of us waiting for a lift, and assumed we were on our way to the ground.

Time was getting on. By now we were quite concerned and phoned the Tuffley club from the service station. They sent a car to collect us, but the game had started by the time we arrived. Gloucestershire were already in the field – with two substitutes.

That morning we weren't the most popular members of the county team. Jack had been needed for the opening overs and we received a few stony glares. We anticipated an official rebuke for late arrival. As for the subs ... I was told later that when Hampshire were asked if we could borrow a couple until Jack and I turned up, Barry Richards picked up an extra sweater, stuffed it under his own to give himself a bulky tummy and said, 'I'll be Shep.' Cheeky. I didn't fully show my gratitude: I held on to a catch to dismiss Barry off Roger Knight's bowling. Jack took four second-innings wickets, and we won the match. It was the only time I was late for a game, although I once cut it very late at Taunton. I'd gone home to see my family and then got held up badly in the traffic on the way to the Somerset ground. My breathless phone call forewarned Gloucestershire. I drove into the car park with a few minutes to spare and was doing up my laces as I hurried on to the field.

I think that was the same year as our service station adventure. If it was, we were all out for 94 first time. We did rather better in the second innings with 484 for 7. Everyone down to Tony Brown at No. 8 scored runs. It hardly pleased Somerset. Brian Close, who'd scored a hundred, made his point by using TEN bowlers in an inevitably drawn match.

As a worrier by nature, just like Dickie Bird, I'm usually a reliable time-keeper. Once I became pretty fraught as I lost my way en route to the Harrogate ground. I had Bert Avery with me and one or two other players. 'Stop and ask someone, Shep. We're going round in circles.' I wound down my window: 'Can you tell me where the Harrogate cricket ground is, please?' There was much scratching of the face as the man thought about my simple question. 'Ee, I wouldn't start from here.' Classic Yorkshire logic.

Fast-forward to my umpiring days. The Test was at Headingley and I'd gone to the ground the day before to park my car. Next morning I walked the short distance from my hotel to Headingley and was stopped at the entrance I'd used in my car.

'Where do you think you're going?'

'To the match.'

'You can't come in here. This gate is for cars only and you haven't got a car.'

'But that's my car over there.'

The gateman wasn't giving way. 'You'll have to go and use the pedestrians' entrance.'

It was beginning to look like a comedy sketch. He had his orders and wasn't prepared to listen to me or hear my explanations. I'm grateful to Joe Lister, the Yorkshire secretary, who turned up at that moment, saw my predicament and ordered: 'Let him in. Don't you recognise him? He's the umpire.'

Man of the Match

In 1973 I played at Lord's in the final of the Gillette Cup. We beat Sussex by 40 runs. It was the first major trophy for Gloucestershire in ninety-seven years.

That appearance has to be one of the imperishable highlights of my cricketing career. It wasn't just the victory but so much else – the build up, the team talks, the collective ecstasy inside the dressing room, the overall euphoria, and later the rides around the county in the open-topped bus. I had no idea we could whip up so much vocal and emotional support. It hadn't always been too much in evidence around the boundaries at Bristol's Nevil Road.

Our progress to the final is for me cast in stone. The first round had been at Sophia Gardens, where Roger Knight held our innings together and won another of his man of the match awards. I remember, too, that we held our catches. David Graveney, not yet even dreaming of his elevated status as chairman of Test selectors, dived at square-leg and brilliantly held on to Majid's pull. There were memorable boundary catches by Mortimore and Sadiq. And there were Roy Swetman's footballing skills.

He hadn't long been at Gloucestershire, his third county after Surrey and Notts, and was a small, tidy, chirpy wicket-keeper who played in eleven Tests. He had a Londoner's sharp skill of repartee. Once when we were playing Essex at Westcliff-on-Sea in a championship match which started on the Saturday we were expected to hurtle off to Derby for a John Player League fixture on the Sunday. It was the kind of weekend chase-around that none of us enjoyed. 'Where are we playing tomorrow?' asked Swets. 'Derby,' he was told. 'My God, we might as well go across the Channel to Calais – it's nearer.'

The relatively short journey across the bridge from Bristol to Cardiff in the Gillette Cup had been more to his liking. His running-out of Eifion Jones with the kind of calculated kick that would have earned him a trial at Ninian Park took its place among the relished features of that game.

I think Swets saw himself as a more dashing figure than the seemingly staid D.R. Shepherd. My first car had been a Morris Minor and I stuck with them for a time, naming them 'Betsy' Marks 1, 2 and 3. Once I found myself driving the wicket-keeper for a match at Cambridge. 'Enjoy the journey, Swets?' I asked. His reply stabbed at my vanity. 'D'you know, Shep, that's the first time I've played at Cambridge – and the first time I've been in the slow lane of a motorway.'

The second round was against Surrey in Bristol. I hope I'll be excused for pausing and reliving a tie that I suppose we should have lost. In my fifteen-year playing career I won only two man of the match awards. This was one of them. The other was in the year we won the Benson & Hedges final. Team-mates used to nominate them as my two best innings. They may have been away from the heady atmosphere of Lord's but they helped to ensure that we would twice reach headquarters. To me, every early round, every quarter- and semi-final took on the importance of a final. Against Surrey we had a greenish wicket invitingly made for Procter. The trouble was that John Edrich won the toss and put us in. Geoff Arnold doubtless said thanks very much. In no time we'd lost five wickets for 24. Nicholls, Knight, Zaheer and Procter had all gone to Arnold. The crowd were silent and in despair. You should have seen our dressing room. 'Might as well pack up and go home' was the unspoken verdict.

Devonians have a cussed streak, and not just when they are playing bowls on Plymouth Hoe. I immediately got my head down: no flashing outside the off stump; in fact, no risk-taking at all. Quietly, at first nervously and agonisingly, I built my score. Time was no problem; our lack of runs was.

Tony Brown came in to join me. I saw those familiar big strides as he approached the crease. He could often look severe with flashing eyes when things were going badly and they couldn't have been worse than they were now. I walked down the track to him.

'Not looking too good is it, Skipper?'

'You know what you've got to do, Shep. Just stay there and bat out sixty overs.'

Basic advice. Not easy to carry out, however, when Surrey had their tails up. I thought they made a tactical mistake in taking off Arnold after eight overs: he'd only given away 17 runs and was firing as if he could run through the rest of us.

Browny doggedly demonstrated a straight bat for a time. Then in came David Graveney, not long out of Millfield and in his second season with the county. The family credentials were undeniably good: Ken was his dad and Tom his uncle. He was in the team mainly as a slow bowler, but we were still aware that he could bat, just as he could hang on to his catches in the gully.

At the end of the sixtieth over, we had pretty miraculously taken the score to 169. Grav was out in the last over. I was 72 not out. We had created an eighth-wicket record for the Gillette Cup.

Long before I'd discovered something about cricket: games are not necessarily won by blazing batting and mountainous scores. Defiance, uphill fights, performances out of character can also bring victory. No bookie would for a moment have anticipated that the two Davids, from the depths of the Gloucestershire innings, would keep us in the cup. Frankly it didn't appear that our modest total was anything like enough. Surrey must have felt the same for they started at their own leisurely pace, showing considerable respect for all our bowlers. Not till Younis and Roope got to work in the middle order did the match seem to be slipping away from us. I remember Morty fearlessly flighting. I remember how tight Procter, Davey, Brown and Knight were. Yet when Younis belted a six, I sensed that Surrey were ready to step up the scoring rate. Younis should have known better than to take that liberty with Morty. The following over the batsman was brilliantly run-out by Morty with a direct hit from more than fifty yards. That was it. We won by 19 runs. Bill Edrich, one of my childhood heroes, was the adjudicator and I received my award from him.

The relief among the Gloucestershire players was almost tangible. Surrey had mismanaged badly. They had been left a highly attainable target. Early on they had us on the run. Arnold had been unplayable and some of our more cynical supporters feared the match might be over by lunchtime, at which time there were more red faces than bats in our dressing room. We'd virtually handed Surrey their passage into the quarter-finals. I don't want to take anything from our bowlers, but Surrey should never have collapsed in the manner they did. To our astonishment, they were all out with nearly six overs left. It was a joyful evening for us. If anyone insists on asking how I personally celebrated, that was the night when I lost my shoes and had to be put to bed.

Next stop Chelmsford, in the quarter-finals. I could tell a score of stories about Essex, many of them inevitably about Ray East. My favourite is of the day I wasn't playing for Gloucestershire but had looked in to watch some play at Cheltenham. Jack van Geloven was the umpire (funny how I remember the names of the umpires, isn't it?) and he gave East out, LBW, in the last over before tea. When play resumed after the interval there were one or two balls remaining of the over. Jack was forced to do a double-take: 'Hey, haven't I seen you somewhere before?' It was Easty back again, padded-up and ready to continue. He didn't get away with that one. The joke, one of so many from him, wasn't lost on the umpire, the fielders or eventually the spectators.

That prompts another memory of a game against Essex. I am thinking of the time Brian 'Tonker' Taylor was caught in an unmentionable part of the lower body by a prodigious swinger from Procky. Down the batsman went. A group of anxious sympathisers gathered round him. Keith Fletcher was at the other end. With an expression to suggest he'd taken the blow himself, Fletch walked down the pitch, gazed down at the stricken Tonker and asked, 'Are you all right, Skipper.' Tonker was in no state to evaluate the extent of his injury or graciously accept such sympathy. All he knew was that he was doubled-up in pain. He offered no more than a half-glance at Fletch: 'Course I'm f—g not!' Keith, a country boy, considerate and caring by nature, realised it was an untimely question and tactfully retreated.

Fletch was smaller than Taylor, but our keeper Swetman was even smaller. It was now his turn. He hovered over Tonker. Knowing of Taylor's days as a Brentford footballer, Swets said, 'Think it might be a good idea for you to go on the wing for half an hour!'

Cricket is full of droll wit. I've eavesdropped on dozens of exchanges or throwaway lines that are better than anything I see on the television. For instance, Leicestershire's Gordon Parsons was once beating the bat repeatedly without any of the success he deserved. In exasperation he walked down the wicket in some despair to ask the fortunate batsman, 'Do you think if I bowled you a piano, you could play that?'

The 1973 quarter-final allowed neither levity from East nor understandable oaths from Tonker. We won by 30 runs, no thanks to me. I had my front foot in the wrong place as I played defensively to Brian Edmeades. We relied on Knight, always a valuable one-day player, Sadiq and Zaheer for the runs; and Jack Davey for the wickets.

For the semi-final we went to New Road and won the toss for the first time that season in the competition. We squeezed through by 5 runs and had Procter to thank for it. He scored a hundred and followed up with three wickets, including that of Worcestershire's century-maker, Glenn Turner. Who could ask for more? Mind you, Proc was dropped in the slips off the first ball he received and soon after by the wicket-keeper. Then he settled down to treat a bulging crowd of 10,000 to a wonderful exhibition of stroke-play. The gates had opened at eight o'clock in the morning and it was a terrific match.

I wish I'd contributed more to our narrow success. Imran Khan, who'd gone to the local Royal Grammar School and was now playing for Worcestershire, at the beginning of his illustrious career, didn't have a great match. His one wicket cost him 50 runs, but it was a valuable one – mine. Yes, LBW again.

A gruelling championship match at Dean Park, Bournemouth, wasn't ideal preparation for our appearance in the final at Lord's. Hampshire beat us by five wickets; I scored a half-century and a duck; Procter was bowled before he was off the mark. The only decent batting, 170 runs in total, came from Sadiq. As for the rest of us, our minds were on other things.

After the match we piled into our cars and headed for London. Jack Davey remembers half a dozen of us sitting on a wall on the Edgware Road, eating spare ribs and chips. It wasn't quite what you would have expected from county cricketers on the eve of what was for many of them the biggest game in their careers. We weren't going to be embarrassed by a surfeit of glamour, I can tell you. Times, schedules and the extent to which players are pampered have changed, of course. And remember that, win or lose, champagne or lager, we were due to drive to Chesterfield for a John Player League game the following day. I'm out of breath even thinking of our commitments.

By the time we arrived at Lord's on the morning of the final, the hallowed place was heaving with throaty West Country voices. I was told the M4 had been bumper to bumper, coaches and private cars. Our supporters were also pouring off the trains at Paddington. Who said cricket was the poor relation in professional sport? This was as I imagined Wembley was like on FA Cup Final day. I was stunned by the marked contrast with what we were used to in many of the championship matches – the lonely knots of anoraks, the comparatively few ever-faithful pensioners, the acres of empty seats, the almost apologetic whimper of atmosphere.

It was impossible not to be nervous. We had gone over our tactics and knew what we had to do. So did Sussex and their towering, highly competitive captain, Tony Greig; he planned to give us no favours. The dressing room was stacked with good-luck messages and telegrams, some from my pals in Devon. One of them suggested: 'Treat it just like a game at Instow.' As if I could!

The pattern of the match is still faithfully recited by every Gloucestershire supporter. We won by 40 runs. Tony Brown, at his very best and most positive, deservedly won the man of the match award, handed over by Alec Bedser. Browny took over from Procter with an undefeated innings of 77, of which 46 came in the last eight overs. Then, as Sussex batted, his captaincy was sharp and intuitive. Procter played a succession of great shots and was caught in the deep as he hunted for the six that would have given him his hundred. He received a standing ovation. So did his captain and ally. So, to be honest, did all of us.

There were monumental individual feats by a number of Gloucestershire players that day. Let no-one omit the name of Jim Foat from our roll of honour. He went in at No. 8 and received thunderous applause when he was out, bowled by John Snow. Foat had scored 7, hardly a statistic to earn such adulation, you'd have thought, so it calls for closer study. He came to us by way of Millfield and played 91 first-class matches for us over eight seasons. He scored five first-class centuries and could look a most attractive bat. There was no doubting his basic ability, although the big innings didn't come as often as they should have. He was, however, a wonderful fielder, one of the finest in the county's history. He lurked in the covers, ready to pounce and save us hundreds of runs. He was probably the fastest runner in the club. The temptation was always to use him as our twelfth man, but opposing skippers were inclined to be suspicious when he made timely arrivals on to the field. Jim was an obvious asset for one-day games. Never was that more evident than in the Gillette Cup Final. Forget the piffling number of runs he scored. He partnered his captain at a crucial stage of the innings, running daring singles, sprinting with exquisite judgement to the danger end. 'Foaty's in the wrong game,' his many admirers used to shout. 'He should be an Olympic sprinter.' So he should have been. Only his team-mates fully appreciated the extent of his headline-lacking value to our team.

His work was far from over after he chased up and down with such timing and zest while Tony plundered late runs. We had been worried about Greig in the middle order, but we dismissed him without scoring. Or rather Jim Foat did. Our skipper sensed that Greig was anxious to get away from Procter who, with shirt-tails again flying, was generating a fearsome pace. Procky glanced towards Foat at square cover: 'Come in a bit, Jim.' When the ball rebounded off Greig's pads he was ready to go for a single and anxiously set off. Graves sent him back. It was one of the most tense moments of the match. Jim didn't risk an erratic throw, though one could never remember one from him. He chased in, the ball tightly in his hands, to break the stumps. He had the exceptional speed to do that.

There was a great deal of celebrating in London that night – by the players as well as their supporters. 'Oh Christ, none of us is going to be fit to travel to Chesterfield.' It was a reasonable comment. I think we got to the ground initially with eight players. Morty began as captain; Jack Davey, who could barely walk because of an injury aggravated at Lord's, hobbled on to the field as a sub. We didn't do badly, all things considered, losing, for the record, by 12 runs. Procter went for 46 without taking a wicket. Brown, his drinking chum, was our top scorer, having coped with the strains of logistics that followed our Lord's triumph. Strains, did I say? Here comes Davey with a strictly unauthorised version. I may be forced to take legal action if he goes on like this.

I roomed with Shep but when I woke in the morning of our Chesterfield match there was no sign of my companion. The bed hadn't been slept in. I went down to breakfast at our hotel. He wasn't to be seen. By this time I was getting more than a little worried. I hurried back to the pub on the Edgware Road where we'd been for a few beers the night before.

It was still early and I'd had to wake up the landlord. He wasn't too happy. Nor had he seen Shep. Back at the hotel, our captain wasn't too impressed when I told him we were a man short. I went back for a final search along the corridors of our hotel. And suddenly I spotted Shep. There was his head peeping out of a door, looking left and then right. Very sheepish. This little red face. He was coming out of Jenny's room.

'Come on, Shep, for God's sake. I've been looking every-bloody-where for you. We're late – we've to get to Chesterfield.'

I bundled him into the kit van that I was driving. There was no time for explanations. They'd have to wait. In truth, he never uttered a word about his nocturnal adventures.

As I was saying, that's Jack's account. Always was a bit of a joker, especially if it was at my expense. All I'm prepared to say is that all the Gloucestershire boys had a skinful, as surely they had every right to, after winning the final. Events become a little bit confused as the night went on. And, well, I overslept . . .

This seems like the best moment to introduce Jenny. She applied in that 1973 year for the job as Grahame Parker's secretary. He was the county's secretary-manager, a former rugby international who played for Gloucestershire as an amateur and was talented enough to score a double hundred for us. He went on to become the club president in the late eighties. During the mid-fifties he made some appearances for Devon in the Minor Counties. Jenny had no particular interest in cricket. Coincidentally she was from North Devon but had come to Bristol to work, just like me.

In the language of the gossip columnists we've been an item since 1973. As I mentioned, she looked after me when I had that severe attack of dehydration during the game with Worcestershire and a few of my tongue-in-cheek team-mates were talking of the last rites. Our friendship grew and fellow-players, seeing us chatting in confidential tones around the offices of the county ground, suspected that something was going on.

Jenny and I have much in common, including a similar sense of humour. She is a steadying influence on me and is as honest as the day is long. Our shared affection for our part of Devon didn't need to be spelled out: we just knew that was where we'd end up, back there. While I was still playing we bought a house in Patchway, Bristol. And, of course, we're still together, living in Instow. She ran a fabrics shop in Bideford for a time and I used to go in, a little self-consciously, to help out. She keeps an eye on me, watches my diet – she's a good cook – and makes sure we take plenty of walks. With us goes Skipper, the dog, a most lovable collie cross. He's very much part of the family.

The obvious question: why have I never married Jenny? I suppose I've been influenced by the depressing fact that there are so many separations and divorces in professional cricket, probably more than in any other sport. The trouble is that husbands and wives are often apart for so long. For half the summer the players are away from home, and for the international cricketers it can also be half the winter. It's the same with the umpires, especially those who live far from the main cricket centres. In my case I sometimes find myself away from home for six or seven weeks at a time, or even longer. This is no recipe for a settled, conventional home life. These absences can put a terrible strain on relationships. My phone bill is huge because I like to keep in touch with Jenny every evening. But I try to offer some kind of compensation by taking her with me on a number of my overseas assignments. She's been to Australia and New Zealand, South Africa, the West Indies, India and Zimbabwe. She's usually well looked after by her hosts and enjoys the sightseeing. Only on one occasion was the experience painful for her – in the literal sense.

She was sitting in the pavilion at the Recreation ground, St John's, Antigua, before the start of play one morning in a Test match. Richie Richardson was having a knock-up nearby and one of his drives came straight through the door and hit Jenny in the eye, cracking her cheekbone. Concern was immediately shown. Dennis Waight, who was in charge of the West Indians' fitness then, was on hand with advice on how to control the swelling. Jenny's instructions, I discovered later, were: 'Don't you dare tell Shep.' She knew I was a worrier and always had enough on my mind before play began. The kindness and concern shown by the catering staff (supplying ice continually during the whole day) and the general public were much appreciated. For the first time Jenny was more recognised than me. People in the streets were shouting out next day: 'How's your face, Jenny?'

Jenny remains no cricket fanatic and that is no bad thing. If she's home alone, she may casually switch on to see what is happening in the current Test and when she worked in the office at the county ground in Bristol she would sit in the sun with one or two of the other girls for a few overs, but she was never remotely a cricket groupie. We seldom talk about the match or my contribution. At the same time, she built up, unconsciously, a sound working knowledge of the game. She's particularly good on the psychology involved and says she knows immediately when I'm building up for my next Test.

It's a bonus when I can take her with me to distant parts of the world. We have been fortunate in having friends prepared to look after that third member of our family, Skipper, who so affectionately joined us from the National Canine Defence League more than six years ago. No matter what sort of a day we've had – maybe one of those my mother used to talk so quaintly about – or how far we've been away from home, we know we're guaranteed the warmest of wagging greetings and a 'smile'. In the winter months when I've been out delivering the newspapers for my brother, my unfailing ritual is then to set off with Skipper. We'll go down through the sandhills and across the cricket ground to the beach. That's where he demands to chase a ball. The routine doesn't change much. I'm a man of habit. Most umpires are, you know. After Skipper has done his chasing, faster even than Jim Foat, I make a call on Bill Davies's chalet for a cup of tea, a Bonio for Skipper and a chat and gossip with Bill and his mate, John Huxtable. Bill used to like to go down to the beach collecting shellfish.

Because of that, I nicknamed him Cockle Bill – and it stuck. He's a Welshman, just like my dad, and an ardent rugby follower, so we always have a row when England play Wales. As for John, my 'team-mate' from Mutton Hill Sunday mornings, he's nuts about Plymouth Argyle, and for years travelled down to Home Park for every home game. So you can imagine our conversation is a good old sporting mix. Cricket is seldom ignored for long. And that means we've reminisced about that magical Gillette Cup a hundred times. Not necessarily, however, about the thick head I shared with the majority of the Gloucestershire team – or those slanderous rumours emanating from Tavistock's Jolly Jack. I may even be tempted one day to spill a few beans at *his* expense,

A Hundred with Viv

There are some seasons that counties would willingly obliterate from the records. In 1974 the weather was dreadful and all round the country the crowds were down. Test match receipts suffered – and so did we, as a result. That proposal to sell our ground to the corporation and switch to Gloucester hadn't come to anything but there remained an air of uncertainty about the place. Gloucestershire were in a bad way financially – no new thing – and the public, affected by economic gloom and the three-day working week, were apt to stay away. The club was disappointed that we failed to capitalise on our Gillette Cup success and what had been the mood of animation in the dressing room.

On top of that we seemed to have more injuries than ever before. Les Bardsley, no stranger to the pressures of an overcrowded treatment room at Bristol City's Ashton Gate, was now fully occupied tending our aches and pains. One bonus was that younger players were given their chance. I'm thinking of Andy Stovold, Andy Brassington and Alistair Hignell. Still at Cambridge, Higgy would soon be selected for the England rugby squad, bound for Australia, a terrific achievement at his age. We were encouraged in that he liked cricket just as much, and we saw him as a long-term asset.

Our form was at times as uninspiring as the weather. We didn't finish on the bottom, but we weren't far off.

One useful thing about writing a book, I've discovered, is that I can be shrewdly selective. I can discreetly overlook my failures. The temptation for any sporting author is to treat it rather like those televised highlights of a cricket match. The viewer sees all the excitement, the best shots and boundaries, the wicket-taking and spectacular catches, which go to give the undeniable impression that it was a great match. Those who attend, watching the whole day's cricket, so often know different.

So what did I do of note in that pretty miserable 1974? Well, I got a pair at Dover. Doesn't that show that I'm going through the motions of being objective? We lost by an innings and never really sniffed anything better. The most attractive of the batting came from Colin Cowdrey with an undefeated hundred, scored at his own pace on a track that wasn't easy. When it was my turn, I barely had time to take guard; Derek Underwood was the bowler, twice. It was the only occasion I played at Dover. The pitch was wet and, of course, there was no bowler in the world who was more impossible to handle in those conditions. Alan Knott was the perfect ally for him and that lethal combination accounted for me, in the blink of an eye, in the first innings.

I used often to scan the cricket scores in the morning papers. I'd be sure to see that familiar and eloquent line 'c Knott b Underwood'. They were altogether too good for most of the opposition. Some years after my Dover misery I was talking to Alan about Underwood, a bowler I admired so much. 'Do you know how many catches I've taken off his bowling this season?' asked Knotty. I shook my head. 'Not a single one,' said the wicket-keeper. By then the pitches were being covered. Nothing more graphically illustrates the difference.

Just as I rated Derek Underwood very high among the bowlers I faced, I continue to place Knott at the top of the list of keepers. I have never seen a better one, although I've always retained a very high regard for Australia's Ian Healy. Nearer home, the quirky and technical brilliance of Jack Russell, especially when he stands up to the medium-pacers, has left me in no doubt that he takes his place among Gloucestershire's finest. That is no small compliment as the county has a long, distinguished line of keepers, including Test players Jack Board, Harry Smith, Andy Wilson, Peter Rochford and my long-time team-mate Barrie Meyer. WG would have insisted on including Arthur Bush, but 'Frizzie' was his best man, after all.

All of which has deflected me from pondering my nondescript form at Dover. Such lows – and frankly you can't get lower than that – were offset by a couple of tons.

We went to Swansea and, under the St Helen's rugby posts, beat Glamorgan by an innings. I felt sorry in that match for Len Hill, better known across the Bridge as a footballer for Swansea and Newport County. In Glamorgan's second innings he was 96 not out, his career best, when he ran out of partners. I opened in that match with Arthur Milton. Geoffrey Ellis didn't take many wickets – he turned from professional cricket to schoolteaching – but he took mine that day: out for 100. Roger Knight went 44 runs better. It invariably seemed to me that the most exhausting part of any match at Swansea was climbing all those steps back to the pavilion after an innings. Wasn't that where they lined up to cheer in Viv Richards after his match-winning debut performance for Somerset? Brian Close led the applause.

My other hundred was against Somerset. Viv was one century-maker in that Bristol fixture; I was the other. I wouldn't presume to bracket myself with him in any other way than the statistical coincidence. An emerging Ian Botham, his talents already as evident as his self-confidence, didn't have a great match against us. He scored 2 and 1 and his fourteen overs went for 51 runs. Believe me, though, most of us sensed his potential. He'd do a great deal better against us, we simply knew.

We beat Somerset twice that year, though at Weston-super-Mare in late August it was a near thing. I liked going to Clarence Park, whatever the unreliability of the track, as it reminded me of home. The kids would come in off the beach, buckets and spades in their hands, to join their parents. The Weston Festival was something of an annual ritual: cricket lovers, some from the Midlands and deprived of seaside resorts, would arrange their holidays to coincide with it. The facilities may have been restricted for the players but there was seldom a lack of atmosphere.

For that return match, Closey declared his second innings and invited us to chase 227 in about three hours. It was a day for the spinners, Brian Langford, Dennis Breakwell and Closey himself. We soon lost three wickets and by then nearly everyone around the ground resigned themselves to a draw. Knight didn't; nor did I. By North Devon and village standards, I reckoned the game was still on. It helped when I decided it might be my lucky day; Richards, one of the finest fielders in the country, dropped me. He made amends with a boundary catch but by then I'd made 93 and was able to leave the final formalities to Tony Brown as we won by five wickets. It's true I enjoyed myself. I rode my luck again when I survived a skier, but the fours and sixes mounted as I went after the slow bowlers. It was Brian Close who enticed me in the end to give that boundary catch.

During my playing career of peaks and troughs I knew well enough what it was like to be dropped from the team. I also knew the value of a word in the ear. This one came from Jim Foat, who was playing alongside me for the 2nd XI against Hampshire at Bristol. There was a general discussion about the strength of the opposition. 'Well, they've got this guy,' Jim began, 'his name is Alderson Montgomery Everton Roberts – and I'm telling you, he can let them go.' Foaty had already come up against the Antiguan fast bowler in an under-19s game.

So this new man was fast, was he? I pondered the words of warning. Foat was young, alert, able to take evasive action, not scared of a quickie in any case. He went in first and was rolled over by Roberts in the opening over. Wow! Yes, he was fast. I was at No. 3 and walked out apprehensively. I noticed that the bowler had quite an aggressive look about him. No sooner had I taken guard than he had one flying past my head. I said anxiously to myself: 'Beware, Shep old son, if that last ball had been a bit straighter, you'd never have got out of the way.'

In that match Andy Roberts put three of our lads into hospital. I argued that it wasn't a time for hanging around too long and scored a hundred, but don't ask me how. Mostly off the bowler at the other end,

I should say. I took many a sideways glance at Andy in that 2nd XI game. He didn't have much to say for himself. He carried a brooding expression. I remember saying good morning to him and he looked straight through me. Perhaps he didn't hear me. It's a fact that as I got to know him better, there was more of a two-way communication. Taciturn by nature he may have been, but he could certainly make the ball whistle.

It's a useful moment to pause and try to answer the layman question about how a young batsman, say new to the professional game, copes with sheer speed. When the ball may be hurtling towards him at nearly 90 m.p.h., how much can he rely on eyesight and reflexes? Well, clearly, good eyesight is important. Viv Richards used to say he could look round the ground between overs and identify his friends, tucked away in big Test crowds. My eyes also served me pretty well, although facing a truly quick bowler demands more than that. Incessant practice in the nets helps; it teaches us how to pick up the trajectory and direction of the ball as early as possible.

I arrived at Bristol at the same time as Mike Procter. Initially, as I've said, he wasn't regarded too seriously as a bowler, but of course we soon had to adjust our opinions about that. There was no place for faint hearts in the Gloucestershire nets when Procter, even off a few yards, was flexing his muscles. I can't think of a better apprenticeship. That was the testing time, when coaches and senior pros watched with critical concentration. Any hint of cowardice would condemn you in the eyes of your peers. There is always an element of rivalry between the batsmen and the bowlers at the net sessions. When a team-mate, who you'll soon be sharing a cordial pint with, makes a practice ball whistle past your ribcage, you suspect there is a touch of (good-natured) sadism in the look he exchanges with you.

Some would never have suggested that David Smith or even Tony Brown were among the fastest bowlers in the country. In the case of 'Smudge', I didn't allow that short, amiable, run-up to fool me. He was fast all right, as the Test selectors eventually acknowledged. The action was whippy, the wastage minimal: you had to play him. Bill Alley, that canny old Aussie, once said to me, 'I don't know where he gets his bloody pace from, off those few yards.' As for Browny, I still wince as I recall my net experiences against his bowling. For three seasons on the trot he whacked me on the toe with an in-swinger. He could be awkward and decidedly painful to face. And he did take 1,230 first-class wickets, after all.

The hours of practice, including the knocks, and the willing help and advice from the coach and senior professionals, combined to make us better able to pick up the flight of the Truemans and the Stathams – and to know instinctively when to leave well alone. Yet against the great speed merchants batsmen are allowed no more than an instant glimpse of the ball rifling towards them. Don't forget the umpires either. They, too, are given only fleeting vision of that little red missile. When the no-ball law was changed, determined by front-foot rather than back-foot landing, the umpire had even less time to pick up the flight. I've been on the receiving end as both a batsman and an umpire; and, believe me, the really fast bowlers are an eternal challenge.

Back in the championship side, I found Ron Nicholls wandering up to me and saying, 'Everyone's talking about this Andy Roberts, Shep. You've seen him. How quick is he?'

'Very quick.' You couldn't give a team-mate a more accurate assessment than that.

Roberts, still brooding, was up from Hampshire's 2nd XI. One gathered he didn't have a great affection for batsmen. He liked to send their stumps flying or have them ducking out of trouble.

Ron had a nice range of correct shots, some of which he used far too sparingly, in my opinion; one of these was an attractive, well-timed hook. So when Roberts dug one in short, our batsman leaned back and elegantly put it away between mid-wicket and square-leg. The audacious four won roars of approval around the ground. I was slightly less enthusiastic. 'Now this Andy Roberts', I said to myself, 'has two kinds of bouncers – the slow one and the fast one. So look out, Ron!' Andy

A long-time friend and one of the men I would pick out as an inspiration and profound influence on my umpiring career, Barrie Meyer. This is at Bristol back in 1985, before umpires were sponsored!

1990 and I congratulate Sir Richard Hadlee on his knighthood as he leads the New Zealand team at Lord's. In my opinion, Hadlee is the finest New Zealand bowler ever. Add to that his skill as a batsman and it's clear just what a special cricketer he is.

'There are six balls in an over, Shep!' Another extraordinary all-rounder, Ian Botham. Whether playing against him or umpiring a game in which he was playing, he was one of the most entertaining and exciting cricketers I've known.

Alec Stewart looks on as South African bowler Fanie De Villiers jokingly gives me a bite on the ear after I turned down several typically enthusiastic appeals from him on 5 August 1994. I've always felt that good humour is a vital part of even the most hotly fought competitive games.

It's not always possible to keep the smiles on everyone's faces, though. There was a certain amount of tension on show here in the 4th Test between Australia and the West Indies at Adelaide at the beginning of 1997.

We may have had different styles but my long-standing partnership with Dickie Bird became something of a feature of cricket in the 1980s.

So much so that the Oval Test between England and India in 1990 was played under this advert draped across one of the landmark gasholders. It's perhaps worth pointing out, in these days of judgement by the television cameras, just how far back Jack Russell and the slip fielders are standing from the batting crease in this photograph. The camera always shortens the apparent distances involved.

Another of cricket's great characters, Steve 'Slow Death' Bucknor. Steve has earned his nickname from the intense and unhurried deliberation he makes before giving a batsman out. Here we're at Old Trafford in 1997 for the World Cup match between India and Pakistan. Steve has officiated in more than 50 Test matches. Only Dickie and I have officiated in more.

In some quarters I have my own nickname, 'the dancing umpire' because of the little jump I simply have to do when the score reaches Nelson (111). It's a long-standing superstition of mine. One of many this particular Devonshire boy has.

So you can imagine my shock when I saw this photograph of a road sign in British Columbia. Thank goodness Canada don't play Test cricket!

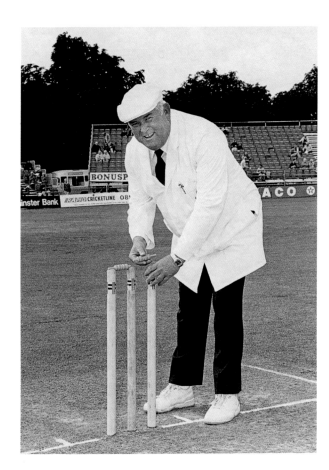

Setting up the wicket back in 1992. Now, of course, the middle stump would probably have a camera in it.

My proudest moment was being awarded the MBE in 1997 for services to cricket.

In 2000 I passed a half century that took marginally longer to get to than any of the half centuries I made at the crease – 50 Test matches as an umpire. My 50th Test was between India and South Africa in Mumbal.

I may not be smiling on the front cover but I hope this is a more typical shot of me.

Still a fine figure
of a man!

Before a test match . . .

And after! This is in 1998 after the one-
off test between England and Sri Lanka at
the Oval.

And you thought I looked good in white! Here I am making one of my appearances in the Instow W.I. Christmas pantomime. At least I had a pair of white shoes to go with the dresses! These ones have seen plenty of service on the cricket pitch.

Here I am again at the Instow pantomime in 1989.

I always come back to Devon and to Instow. Whether for a friendly get-together at our pavilion . . .

Or to help out Bill at the post office as I am here back in 1992 . . .

Or to take a walk on the beach with Skipper. Some players have suggested that I should get a white stick and a dog. So I thought I'd meet them halfway and get a dog! Whatever I'm up to, Instow always takes me a world away from the rigours of cricket.

didn't believe in taking prisoners. The next ball was incredibly fiery and Ron had no time to get out of the way. He was hit on the head and toppled to the ground. To give you some indication of what kind of delivery it was – the ball bounced off Ron's head and reached cover point.

Umpire Lloyd Budd, himself a Hampshire man, was worried. He hurried down the track with some smelling salts. It looked like a serious injury. I was next in, so got up and pensively put on my gloves. I think I was wishing that I was back in Instow delivering the papers. But to everyone's surprise Ron climbed to his feet, rubbed his bruised head, thanked everyone for their concern and insisted that he'd stay on the field. I gratefully took off my gloves.

Ron's knocks weren't over: later he was hit on the neck and then on the wrist. The umpires and some of the Hampshire players advised him to go off. But he'd gone down often enough at the feet of marauding centre-forwards and could hold his own in a congested goalmouth full of beefy opponents. No fast bowler was going to make him quake. At the close of that day's play he was 50 not out. He'd seen off Roberts. In the dressing room I was waiting for him, lit a cigarette and gave it to him.

'Ron, no bullshit, that was the bravest knock I've ever seen.'

He gave me one of his long, meaningful grins. 'You're right about one thing, Shep. Yes, he is fast!'

Soon it would be a strange dressing room: without Nicholls, without Mortimore, without Milton and without Swetman. Allen had already gone. Knight would soon be on his way to Sussex. Procter was missing for a time because of a second operation on his knee.

Zaheer and Sadiq, with their distinctive styles and talents, headed the batting averages in 1975. They were the only two to top 1,000 runs in championship matches. During 1976, when the sun kept shining and the fields were parched in a way I'd not seen before, these two fine Pakistani batsmen were in their element. They rarely seemed to be away from the crease. Zed, all wristy Asian elegance, passed 2,500 runs.

In that sun-drenched summer he three times scored a double century and a century in the same match. No fewer than eight times in his rich career he reached two hundreds in a match. I used to watch him and wish that I had half of his ability. Off the field he was quiet but friendly.

The two Pakistanis used to travel together. There are countless stories, some no doubt embroidered, of their navigational skills. One classic was of the time they got hopelessly lost for a Sunday fixture against Sussex at Arundel. We'd been playing at Edgbaston on the Saturday. Sadiq was the driver and he discovered that Arundel was a tortuous route from the Midlands. Sadiq and Zed, after many stops for directions, not always easily absorbed, arrived at the delightful ground. It was just about the time that the Gloucestershire team was going out to bowl. Zed, flustered and sheepish, took over from a sub. Poor old Sadiq, who as the driver took the brunt of his skipper's blame, was left out. His protestations were in vain. It had been a long and hazardous car ride in a foreign country only to find you were dropped.

My cherished memory of the two is of a match against Glamorgan, captained then by Majid Khan, himself to be sixty-three times a Test player for Pakistan. I had good reason to remember this early season fixture at Cardiff because I was making the first of my few appearances in charge of Gloucestershire. Brown and Procter were both injured, and I was by this time the senior pro. It wasn't, I have to tell you, a very good pitch. Some drains had been laid across the square and the ball was bouncing at varying heights in all directions. Glamorgan had a Barbadian fast bowler called Greg Armstrong who, even if he failed to make too much of an impression for the Welsh county, appeared very hostile indeed against us. He had several deliveries flying around Zed's head, and earlier Sadiq had been subjected to a similar barrage.

The Gloucestershire boys suddenly heard a babble of animated conversation, entirely in Urdu. It featured Majid, Sadiq and Zaheer. It intrigued us and we wondered what was going on. Soon it became clear when Armstrong was withdrawn from the attack. The Pakistani contingent, representing both teams at Sophia Gardens, had come to the conclusion, it seemed, that Armstrong's belligerence with the ball wasn't the ideal preparation for two star batsmen when the World Cup was near at hand.

I was proud of my elevated status as senior pro. In May 1977 I was nominated to lead the county in the match with Oxford. No strings; this time I wasn't standing in for someone. I can still remember walking out at The Parks, a trifle self-consciously, to toss up with Vic Marks, the Somerset farmer's son from Middle Chinnock. Two ex-Gloucestershire players, Jack Crapp and Peter Rochford, were the umpires. They didn't let me get away with it, but good-natured mickey-taking has never bothered me. The university team included David Gurr, a fast bowler with a lovely action, of whom much was expected. He joined Somerset, but made only twenty-four appearances in an unfulfilled county career.

Our game was ruined by the weather. My side, I should add, included a young fellow by the name of Allan Border. He'd been playing club cricket for Downend and this was his only first-class match for Gloucestershire. I put him at No. 5 in the order, one below me. Ah well, I had no idea that he'd become Australia's captain. I was also to skipper him in several 2nd XI games for the county. In those fledgling days, he struck me as a very capable cricketer, though not an exceptional one.

That same summer we played at New Road. On paper, Worcestershire had the stronger team. Halfway through the game, Procter was sick and had to leave the field: 'I'll have to ask you to take over, Shep.' I didn't let him down on that occasion. We beat Worcestershire in two days, and we didn't often do that. Brian Brain was fired up against his former employers and took three wickets in each innings. Basil D'Oliveira was often the stumbling block, so I was particularly pleased to contribute to his dismissal, holding on at mid-wicket to a catch off Brian. Maybe captaincy brought an added alertness to my fielding. I also got rid of Phil Neale with a decent catch off John Childs, another

Devonian. John, or Charlie as we all knew him, was a quiet, popular left-arm spinner, who later moved on to Essex – at Bristol he was competing directly with David Graveney – and played in two Tests, to the delight of his West Country friends.

Returning to Zed, he went on to become, of course, only the second batsman to score his hundredth hundred in a Test match. I can't repeat too often what a privilege it was to play alongside great overseas cricketers. Procter was the greatest of them all. What an all-rounder. What a match-winner. What an inspiration. Never was there a more fearsome sight, at least for the opposing batsman, than when Procky steamed in off that long run. The run was terrifying enough, but add to that his highly personalised delivery action. Did he really bowl off the wrong foot? In his early days with us we were playing Worcestershire. Ron Nicholls saw Ron Headley having trouble trying to read the new-comer because of his disconcerting action as well as the sheer speed.

'What do you make of him, Ron?' asked Nicholls, a smile in his voice.

'Just can't work him out. First he arrives and then the ball does.'

Very soon after, Headley had been seen off by Procter. He passed Nicholls on the way back to the pavilion and was told: 'I think you got that the wrong way round!'

Procter, who took over from Brown as captain, had a convivial nature and he could probably tell as many stories about us as we do about him. One post-match calamity we all light-heartedly shared was after a testimonial match at Basingstoke. A champagne reception in one of the tents was a prelude to a darts match in a local pub. Dutifully the Gloucestershire players set off in convoy from the ground. There were three of us in my car, which for some reason led the way. I wasn't wholly sure of the directions so went at a cautious speed. Some would say I always did.

The incident that took place en route to the darts match has gone down in our dressing-room folklore, though I have to say it has been exaggerated over the years. I had to brake suddenly – and the consequences were more comic than frightening. Tony Brown, in the second car, went into my bumper. Camp follower Tom Hennessy, in car number three, collided with the back of our captain's vehicle. That wasn't the end of it. Mike Procter maintained the chain reaction by going into Tom's car, and Roy Swetman, bringing up the rear, completed the comedy of errors. We got out solemnly to inspect the damage and I fancy there were a few withering comments about my driving. Then we continued the journey.

There can be a permanent tension among the players in professional cricket. Much is at stake, not least our own contracts. The dressing room tends to be claustrophobic and it is easy for factions to form. I found that we needed the light relief that came in the evening. Visits to hospitality tents and showing our faces to the sponsors are parts of the game. Sometimes, it's true to say, this is the last thing a player wants after a tiring day in the field; he's ready to get back to the team hotel as quickly as possible. Some players are better than others when it comes to going through the PR motions. Zaheer didn't much enjoy them. In his autobiography, *Another Day Another Match*, Brian Brain criticised him for not attending one of the sponsors' tents at Folkestone, having been asked to do so. Zed in turn gave his explanation in his own book: he went out of his way to say he was showing no discourtesy to the sponsors and he regretted that Brian had made the incident so public. At the same time he argued that his job was to make runs for the county rather than be seen in a promotional role. He wrote: 'At Cheltenham, for instance, I went to sponsorship events a large number of times. The attitude of some non-cricketing people present bothered me. I do hope it doesn't sound arrogant to say that the cricketers often walked around unrecognised. I remember occasions when guests in the tents didn't even know Mike Procter. It made me think at times: whatever is the point?' Knowing Zaheer's background and personality I could understand how he felt. But I looked on those sponsorship appearances, even after the most exacting of days, as part of the job of representing Gloucestershire.

While we're talking of the players' role in public relations, the county had no-one to touch Graham Wiltshire. He went off to speak at cricket clubs' annual dinners at a minute's notice. His style was homely and anecdotal, and he usually took a few amusing visual aids with him, demonstrating the lack of facilities in some corners of the world. The voice never strayed far from Chipping Sodbury. Nothing much surprised him, but the telegram that arrived at the county ground in Bristol all the way from Zambia must surely have caused him to catch his breath. It requested him to speak at the Nkana Cricket Club dinner a week or so later. 'Well, I'm damned – ten thousand miles just to speak at a dinner,' he said in that slow, good-humoured delivery. No question of turning it down. He'd already proved himself something of a cult figure on the county's tour to Zambia and this time he was equally popular. He told the locals all his favourite stories about cricket in the West Country – of the schoolboys he coached on their climb to county cricket, and of the famous players with whom he'd shared a dressing room. He had a captive audience and he needed no persuading to remain in Zambia for a few days' coaching.

In those mid-seventies, Gloucestershire yo-yoed with a strange inconsistency that must have caused consternation one year and quiet satisfaction the next to the supporters. For instance, we were one from the bottom in 1975 and third from top in 1976. Our improvement was a timely counterbalance to the chastening admission by the new chairman, Ken Graveney, that he and his predecessor, Frank Twiselton, had been perilously close to giving their personal guarantees to the bank for the payment of our wages.

As a county inclined to be unfashionable, out of favour with the Test selectors and with a large rather soulless ground dominated by grey Victorian orphanages, Gloucestershire was given a lift by being invited to host a Test trial. Dennis Amiss scored a century; Mike Brearley skippered The Rest. The only West Country player on view was Somerset's wicket-keeper, Derek Taylor (that is if we're going to overlook the other keeper, Devon's Roger Tolchard, then with Leicestershire).

Winning the B&H

We retained third place in the next season, but we should have won the title. The last time Gloucestershire had finished on top was in 1877. Now we were so agonisingly close and everything rested on the final game. Our defeat by Hampshire remains perhaps the bitterest disappointment in my sporting life.

What we did win that year was the Benson & Hedges Cup. Again I must pause for reflection. I think back to some of the great players who represented the county: Wally Hammond, Charlie Parker, Tom Goddard, Tom Graveney and many others. They gave great service to Gloucestershire, yet in their time the county won no title. It makes me feel all the more lucky that I've appeared in two finals at Lord's and been on the winning side in both.

That season I'd got off to a slow start, not for the first time. John Snow had blown me away twice at Hove. That yearly contract appeared as uncertain as ever. My weight was still a problem: acceptably down to fifteen stones when I was chasing around most, it worried me, and my well-meaning advisers, when it soared nearer to eighteen.

By my fluctuating standards I was comparatively trim for the Benson & Hedges quarter-finals against Middlesex in Bristol. Middlesex had been first and second in the championship table over the previous two years. For their visit they had Mike Gatting at No. 6. Needless to say, there was plenty of batting strength. Plenty of bowling, too. Wayne Daniel rapidly knocked over Sadiq's stumps and Procter was out before he'd scored. I was more nervous than usual. 'Stay out there and give Zed some company. Get your head down,' said Procky as we crossed. His face was clouded: it was pretty obvious what he was thinking about the LBW decision just given against him.

No sportsman can be completely objective about his own performances, but I honestly consider my 60 runs against Middlesex rank with my best, along with, say, my Gillette Cup innings against Surrey. I've never grafted harder, many of my runs coming in singles. It was straight from the coaching manual: eye on the ball, forward defensive; no wanton slogging. Geoffrey Boycott would have nodded in approval. In front of the Jessop Tavern, where support was apt to be noisy and bold, attacking shots were advocated relentlessly, and my old mates were unusually quiet. But they knew that too many wickets had gone down. It was important for us to bat through.

I liked a chat and a smile when I played cricket. That kind of approach was something I acquired in the villages around Instow or when I was skipping my geography lectures for a quickfire 50 at St Luke's. But it was no laughing matter in the quarter-finals with Middlesex. There was too much riding on the result because, as I told you, every match leading up to a final was as vital as Lord's itself in my mind. I came off undefeated, glancing anxiously at the board and wondering whether we had enough. I wondered, too, whether the captain would criticise me for being as studied and cautious as I was. He congratulated me. Everyone told me the innings had given us a real chance. Ultimately it was Procter who determined the result, a win for us by 18 runs, when he came back, fired up as only he could be, to destroy the Middlesex tail.

This is beginning to read like a biography of Procter! Yet it is impossible to devalue his massive contribution to the county. As an all-rounder I believe he can be mentioned in the same breath as Gary Sobers. How much more could he have achieved but for the political climate in his homeland?

We were paired with Hampshire in the semi-final. Victory for us was narrower this time, by a mere 7 runs. Only Sadiq and Stovold, at the top of the order, scored any significant runs for us. Who won the match for us, then? Predictably, it was Procter. No wonder the cynics were dubbing us Proctershire. It frequently seemed to me that he was in a different league from players like myself.

'What did you think of Procky as a bloke?' spectators would sometimes ask me.

'A good leader, a nice guy, one of the boys … but not quite as sentimental as you might believe.'

The semi-final was the perfect example. He and Barry Richards were great friends. They had shared schoolboy cricket and teenage adventures. Before they arrived in Bristol together for those early trials, they were firm friends. But he produced one of his most wicked deliveries, almost unplayable, to trap Richards. Then he went on to dismiss Trevor Jesty and John Rice. He had already accounted for Gordon Greenidge. And all the drama was seen on television. It was more than a memorable hat-trick; it was four wickets in five balls. He finished with six for 13. Brain, as tight and ungenerous as ever to the batsmen, took another three. But it was still a close-run thing. Close-run, did I say? You should have seen my run-out: I was scampering like one of those Dartmoor ponies.

By any standards, Procter was a remarkable cricketer. Some of us were in awe of him, though he was an easygoing and unaffected companion in the dressing room. I think of Procky, and later Courtney Walsh, and realise how fortunate the county has been in its choice of overseas players. Both played their hearts out for Gloucestershire.

Procter smoked (he brought over a regular supply of cigarettes from what was still Rhodesia) and he drank. His drinking capacity earned the admiration of colleagues like David Green – that was praise indeed from someone who always had a cordial relationship with the brewery trade. Procter's performance as a fast bowler never to my knowledge suffered because of a few jars the night before. If there was ever the occasional thick head, he didn't show it. He was naturally a very fit man, carrying no surplus weight, and ruggedly muscled. In the South African tradition he was competitive and dispensed no favours to opposing batsmen. It's true that at times he seemed to carry us, setting the kind of standard which left one or two of us with an understandable feeling of team guilt. Opponents were ceaselessly trying to detect any hint of a flaw in his cricketing make-up.

'He bowls off the wrong foot, for heaven's sake,' a few adversaries whispered. If he heard anyone suggest this, his denial was rapid. In any case, what did his unorthodox delivery matter if he was rolling over opposing counties with ludicrous ease. He undeniably frightened the life out of some batsmen, and he was a fearsome sight as he steamed in. Then when it was his turn at the crease, he was a genuine and thrilling stroke-maker. The short boundary at Cheltenham was made for him. Sometimes I used to think that the patients in the hospital just across the road were in most danger from a Procter pull. Up on the balcony of the college gym, on the other side of the ground, the occupants developed an adept facility for ducking and diving.

The odd pundit on the circuit dared to come up with the theory that Procter didn't always like facing fiery bowling himself. Such a view was sensibly voiced out of the great all-rounder's hearing. I can only say I saw precious little evidence of trepidation from him and I did witness many instances when he went after the quickies, surely disproving that particular notion. Like most outstanding players he could do most things on the field. I had a high regard for his off-spinners and know that he took nine wickets in one match with them at home. Spinners mostly have long, dextrous fingers; Tom Goddard, our tall, lugubrious exponent of off-break, was an obvious example of that. Procter had small but immensely strong fingers.

Now here we were, off to play Kent in the final. They'd won the Benson & Hedges Cup the previous year and were strong favourites. Kent may have had the 'feel' of Lord's, but our captain got us to the ground early. We'd had a gentle net, done our exercises and gone back to the pavilion to relax before we clapped eyes on our opposition. It was the ideal way to absorb the atmosphere at cricket's most famous ground. I gazed around the ground and saw the hundreds taking their seats. As we'd come in from our warm-up, I'd heard West Country accents on all sides of me.

We remember the final as the one when Andy Stovold won the gold award. He was a small, sturdy player who probably suffered because of the incessant pressures – later experienced by Alec Stewart – of combining the onerous duties of wicket-keeping and opening the innings. I can only say Andy did both brilliantly that day at Lord's. First he rattled away with early runs as Kent's bowlers searched for a length. His 71, and Zaheer's 70, gave us the edge we never let go. Apart from Bob Woolmer and John Shepherd, Kent always struggled to keep up with the rate. It was a brave, fighting innings by my namesake and I was pleased to see him later join Gloucestershire. I fancy Kent's tactics would have been to show care against Procter and Brain and then get stuck into our more fragile support bowling. It didn't work out like that. Brain had a terrific spell: his three for 9 in seven and a half overs must surely have been another factor in the triumph.

Alan Knott, I recall, was generous to us. He was much impressed with Stovold's keeping. So he was later, of course, with that of Jack Russell, and for several years became the little Stroud man's mentor. Andy Stovold's younger brother, Martin, also came to the county and made twenty-five appearances. The two of them were known as Bubble and Squeak.

That 1977 summer ended for me in bitter-sweet style. My 142 not out at Taunton meant little to me because we lost the match. Like most professional cricketers, I like to think I value a team success higher than an individual one. But when our livelihoods depend on what we achieve, it's difficult not to become preoccupied at times with our own performances. Self-interest is inevitable. As I cracked my second-innings century against Somerset, I was reflecting on both myself and my team. We only picked up six points, but we were still riding high. Off we went to Cardiff, this time winning for twenty points.

Now the championship depended on the last match, at home against Hampshire. We were on the top, although Kent and Middlesex were breathing down our necks. We needed to win, but we didn't.

We still can't quite work out what went wrong. Certainly not century-maker Procter or newcomer Phil Bainbridge, who batted well in the first innings, or Alastair Hignell – who'd just won the third of his four Cambridge blues – in the second innings with a fighting 92. Gordon Greenidge was put down at mid-off and that was significant. He blazed his way to 94 after that. For once, the exhausted, wholehearted Procter had no petrol left in the tank. His twenty-two overs were fruitless and that was rare indeed for him.

Hampshire won by six wickets. We trudged off the field, hardly consoled by the warmth of the big crowd's applause for a season well done. The captain scooped up a child in his arms. Competitive he may have been by nature but that evening in Nevil Road he was generous in defeat. There were no excuses, no scapegoats.

We all knew that the Greenidge let-off was crucial. He was a terrific player, one I admired enormously, and opponents could simply grant him no favours. The West Indies had so many fabulous cricketers in those days – and Gordon was right up there with the best. I think back to all his plentiful partnerships with Desmond Haynes. Just to see those two walking out at the start of a Test innings must have demoralised the other side. What a technique he had at the crease. What a square cut. You couldn't better it. English coaches used to say to their pupils: 'If you want to know how to play that shot perfectly, just watch Greenidge.' Some of his team-mates implied that he was quite an introspective person and that he wasn't always completely at ease in the West Indies dressing room. If he was a man of moods – and come to that, aren't we all – he was wonderfully constant at the wicket.

Do you realise that he nearly ended up playing for England? He'd come over from Barbados with his parents when he was twelve and from that point grew up in Guildford. Ray Illingworth, in particular, liked what he saw and I am told he pencilled in Gordon as a future England Test opener. We could have done with him, of course. I suspect that he may have been torn in terms of ambition. By then he was well versed in the English way of life and St Peter, Barbados, must have seemed a long way away. But the native pull, in the emotional sense, would have been strong. His decision was the right one. After all, he went on to play 108 Tests.

I loved watching him. It wasn't just those square cuts; it was all the beautifully timed shots through the 'V' between mid-off and mid-on; it was also the vicious pulls and hooks. He didn't believe in letting the bowler get on top. In 1976, on the West Indies' tour of this country, he had a fantastic match at Old Trafford. The pitch wasn't easy but you would never have known. Spectators and his Test colleagues contend it was his finest performance. He made 134 in the first innings and 101 in the second. And he went on to score another hundred in the next Test at Headingley.

Gordon was to suffer increasingly from injury. It was wholly genuine and certainly at times had an effect on his agility and co-ordination, but I have to tell you we dreaded it when he started to limp. It invariably meant he was on his way to a big score. At Lord's, I even heard it said: 'Look out, Gordon's limping.' He was probably in pain, so was ready to go after the bowling more than usual, as quickly as he could, and then rest the troublesome knee.

More recently, he's been the official coach for Bangladesh. After stepping down, he was invited back to watch a Test last winter. I was one of the umpires and travelled from Dubai airport with Gordon, Steve Bucknor, the other umpire, and Raman Subba Row, the referee. There was plenty about which to reminisce, although I don't believe we got on to that reprieve for Greenidge in the crucial Bristol match. I mentioned his lethal pairing with Haynes for the West Indies; just as engrossing could be the manner he and Barry Richards did their stylish stuff for Hampshire. Not once was Gordon overshadowed by his partner, who was one of the most sublime batsmen I ever saw. That shows my admiration for the Barbadian, who could gobble up slip catches, more than 500 in total, as adeptly as he penetrated the arc of off-side fielders. He scored ninety-two hundreds and was tantalisingly close to another in that match in 1977 when the championship pennant was snatched away from Gloucestershire.

I stuffed my kit in the coffin, wondering how much first-class cricket I had left in me. It was good to see players like Hignell and Bainbridge stepping into the side. I admired Higgy for his rugby as well as his cricketing skills. I should perhaps have been wary of his athleticism: once he ran me out when he was acting as my runner!

It was in a Sunday game at Old Trafford: I was buzzing along nicely in the middle order when I stroked the ball to mid-off and called for a single. I put my head down and charged, my favoured method of getting to the other end in a John Player League fixture. On this occasion, it was my downfall. Colin Croft, a towering opponent, came striding in to field the ball. He hurled it at the bowler's end. Unfortunately I was in mid-air as he attempted to brake. Too late, alas. We collided, all arms and legs, and plenty of muscle between us. As the Gloucestershire boys said later, 'There was this long, thin, black body and a short, fat white one – all over the place!' In the physical confusion, the umpire Arthur Jepson felt he was in no position to make a decision so he gave me not out. My team-mates, watching from a safe distance and chuckling away at my discomfort, suspected I was well out.

It was obvious that I was incapacitated. No more short singles could be contemplated. After the hold-up, Alastair was sent out as my runner. I should say that, like Foat, Hignell was a phenomenal sprinter between the stumps. He was, I'll admit under cross-examination, an improvement on me. There should have been scope for a sudden upsurge in my scoring rate, but it didn't quite work out like that. I was at square-leg, leaning on my bat and still recovering from my breathless collision with Croft, when Higgy was called for a risky one and was run-out. Or rather I was. We meandered back to the pavilion, me limping and Alastair apologising.

I liked him, admiring his brilliance and courage as a fielder. At the crease, he had his own way of playing and was not maybe the best of technicians. He still scored eleven centuries. One sympathised with the injuries that restricted his playing career. He went on to become a teacher and then a broadcaster. In 2000 it was revealed that he was suffering from multiple sclerosis.

Reaping the Benefit

Every county cricketer hopes for a benefit. It's the reward that comes for loyalty. The system has its faults and too easily the modest performers suffer in comparison with the star names who can lean on their powerful organising committees, agents and all the material advantages of corporate hospitality and sponsorship. We can all think of players who did their best over a number of years, never quite sure of a regular place, and were then denied a benefit.

Mine came in 1978, along with Jack Davey's. The two Devon boys had been lumped together. It left us shrugging – and disappointed. Obviously we'd have liked separate benefits. If we were surprised, so were our past and present colleagues. David Allen was among those who regretted the county's decision. 'I don't know what Gloucestershire's circumstances were at the time but I think it was wrong that two such wholehearted players should have to share,' he said. It was even sadder when, around the country, we saw overseas stars being awarded two benefits.

Jack and I made the best of it. Our team-mates were determined that we should do well, which, in truth, we did in the context of the times. We had a marvellous committee. Gerry Collis ran a cricket 'sixes' in the Bristol area. More than a hundred pubs took part, no doubt attracted by the fact that the final was to be played on the county ground. It was, I know, pretty complicated to organise – even more than the early rounds of the NatWest Trophy! We had the presence of mind to insure the final against rain. It poured, although we were able to reschedule it a fortnight later. Grateful smiles all round, except from the insurance company. As the two beneficiaries, we worked tirelessly, dropping off hundreds of pontoon boxes in pubs. Devon, as you might expect, did us proud. The routine of delivering and then returning to collect the boxes put miles on the clock but was never a chore. Not with all those free drinks.

Fred Trueman and the late Leslie Crowther, always so generous with his time when it came to cricket, were the speakers for our launch dinner at the Grand Hotel in Bristol. We had a South Devon tour in May (in deference to Jack) and a North Devon one in September, for me. All were wonderful occasions, I know, for our hosts as well as ourselves. Devon is starved of first-class cricket and here was the chance to rectify that. The locals saw Procter enjoying himself again at grass-roots level, coming in considerately off a less intimidating run than usual. Jim Foat and Andy Brassington, invariably among our most chirpy and extrovert players, were unfailingly in good social form.

Many of my old friends turned up when we played at Instow and at Westward Ho!, Bideford's ground, with its pebble ridge and sea just on the other side. Nothing was more fun or more rustic than when we had a third match, on that tour, at Hatherleigh. We adjourned – before and after the match, I should report – to the Half Moon at nearby Sheepwash. We sat on straw bales with our pints of cider and beer – the gravel square had been specially raked for us. Two brothers, Charlie and Benji Innis, kept the Half Moon, and they had helped to create a tremendous old-English atmosphere. I can't imagine a more enjoyable benefit match. Don't ask me how the game went, it wasn't that important. Here, I honestly feel, was public relations at its best. I only wish the pragmatic accountants and county officials obsessed with balancing the books even if it means losing all the out grounds could have peeped over the straw bales and seen that cordial scene. The soul of the game is to be found as much in a small village in Devon as at Lord's. I honestly believe that.

A less happy picture of rural life came more recently when Hatherleigh, like a number of parishes in my part of the country, suffered from the dreadful effects of the foot and mouth epidemic. There were farmers and farm workers in the cricket teams. Some of the grounds had to be placed out-of-bounds and a number of the teams were forced to make temporary plans, as everyone down here in Devon, a severely hit county, waited anxiously to discover whether the disease had peaked. The Devon League, for its part, suspended promotion and relegation because some clubs might have been unfairly penalised.

I've always been conscious that Devon is a county heavily reliant on agriculture. When foot and mouth raged at its worst, and widespread culling was being carried out, there was a feeling of concern and depression in the streets and local shops of a kind I hadn't experienced before. The disease had come so suddenly, bringing with it such brutal repercussions. Small hill farmers in Devon have had to scratch for a modest living for years. Their added hardship now puts into perspective the fact that some village cricket clubs have for the time being missed out on promotion.

I didn't make too many runs in that benefit season and ended with an average of less than 20. A visit to Cardiff, where as a timeless tribute to my father I often think of the red shirts and the Arms Park, provided me with my best memory. In one of the most exciting John Player League matches I ever played in I scored my only hundred in the competition. I was out for 111, so half expected the ultimate disappointment of defeat, and indeed we did lose – Glamorgan beating us with two balls to spare. It's funny how little a century means when you lose the game.

This was still a cracking match. Zaheer was at his most fluent and I believed that between us we'd scored enough. Alan Jones, with some assistance from Gwyn Richards, had very different ideas. I doubt if there was a more attractive and assertive century at Sophia Gardens that season. Procky couldn't get over it: 'Why isn't this chap in the England side – I don't know of a more accomplished opener in the country.' Most of Wales would have said amen to that. Like Procter, I couldn't understand why Jones was overlooked so often. The Glamorgan batsman's only recognition came in the unofficial Test against the Rest of the World, whose line-up included Procter.

As a batsman, there was nothing memorable from me. We went to Old Trafford again in the second round of the Gillette Cup – by then, most of us were heartily sick of the place – and lost again. The Lloyds, David and Clive, clobbered us. Tavistock Jack, Nick Finan and Graveney all suffered.

After all the benefit commitments, the chasing around, the impromptu speeches, the social obligations, Pro Am golf and donkey derbies, Jack and I were ready for a break. The Malawi tour in October couldn't have been more welcome. A supporter living out there had set it up. The local cricket club was financing it, as well as organising the travel arrangements and accommodation. All we had to do was play seven matches and take ample advantage of our hosts' generous hospitality. In addition, we knew that Graham Wiltshire would supervise a coaching session whenever he was asked. He was asked many times.

Nigel Cowley, the Hampshire off-spinner, widely known as Dougal, joined our tour party and came up with several useful performances. I've already told you how, having lost count of my score on the Indian Sports Club ground, I was reckless enough to get myself out on 111. Young Chris Broad reached a hundred in another match and Foat, chasing an impossible single, was dismissed for 99.

We won six of the games, as indeed we should have done, and drew the other. Mostly we played on matting wickets. It was in every sense a happy, relaxed tour. We also beat the locals at darts, snooker and soccer. The last of these followed a challenge from the Blantyre Sports Club. Dougal played like Charlie George and we won 5–1. Tony Brown says he retains visions of Jack and me vocally holding forth with 'You'll Never Walk Alone'. I can't say I remember it, but the song repertoire was always extensive. Gloucestershire was a county club in good voice: it was Bill Athey, I think, who said when he joined the club that he had never heard a county which sang so well and so often. Everyone in the team, as well as the chairman, officials and loyal camp followers, was expected to do a party piece. Some were more tuneful than others, some had lyrics more suitable for a rugby club than a cricket one, but all were urged on. Songs accompanied our joy after victory, as Frank Twiselton climbed on to the table to conduct. Songs, like strong ale, could drown the sorrows of cruel defeat. After losing one of our one-day games in Manchester, we went back to the Queen's Hotel for something to eat . . . and then to sing. One after another the players went into their song, led by Higgy and his 'Teapot' rendition. In the next bar were Jim Laker and Peter West, their broadcasting stint over. Laker turned to his companion and asked, 'If they do this when they lose, what the hell happens when they win?'

By 1979 I had less reason to sing, I suppose. I was coming to the end of my career. The timing and maybe the confidence were beginning to go. I was left out of the side more frequently and captained the 2nd XI instead. After a dozen yearly contracts, I accepted that there was unlikely to be another one. In short, I'd got the message.

I played in eight first-class matches and cobbled together 223 runs. My best, pleasantly, was at Lord's, where on my playing farewell there I got to 70 before being bowled by John Emburey. He did me again in the second innings almost as soon as I'd reached the wicket. Is there no heart left in the game, Embers? Didn't you realise that your fat friend was bidding his leave?

I liked my role in the 2nd XI, seeing new talent emerging, offering what I hoped were kindly and encouraging words. The left-hander Allan Border, from New South Wales and more recently Downend CC (just across the road from WG's birthplace), was never likely to finish up with us because we had a full complement of overseas players, but the county still wanted a close look at him. As I said earlier, I honestly didn't think him then too great a player, even though his famous determination and application were already clear for all to see. Shaun Graf, the Victorian, also played in the 2nd XI under me.

I'm not sure that the psychological turmoil that a professional sportsman goes through as he comes reluctantly, grudgingly, sadly towards the end of his career is fully appreciated. He has to start thinking of the future and the abrupt change of course that will ensue. There's the grim realisation that he is on the decline, that the fluency of drives come less easily and that the physical commitment of fielding all day is increasingly a grind. He senses, unless he's either insensitive or consumed with bitterness, that the supporters know he is on the way out. The draughty exit door is already ajar. In the bar the sentiments are unspoken.

As I captained the 2nd XI, I continued to check on how the championship team was doing. Sadiq, Zaheer and Stovold were full of runs. Broad was coming along very nicely indeed, to the delight of his mentor at Colston's School, Reg Sinfield, with a maiden hundred against Northants. There were two centuries each for Hignell and Foat, who overall promised more than he'd delivered, unless it was pouncing brilliantly on the ball in the covers. With eight hundreds, the little left-hander Sadiq never seemed to leave the crease. He kept batting well, in his own gritty style, just as he had during that sunny 1976. Mind you, he'd been playing first-class cricket since the age of fourteen. He and Zed still had many more runs in them, and I sadly contrasted that with my own diminishing returns. I wasn't making comparisons, just coming to terms with my looming departure from the game as a player.

I wished that I'd been around more often to see the mastery of Procter. That's also something you miss, the skill of your team-mates. In Procter's case the skill was exceptional that year. He had a summer of superb heights. In his most majestic manner he was usually in a hurry. Against Warwickshire he slammed 50 in twenty-one minutes. In the next game, when Northants came to Bristol, he scored the fastest hundred of the season: it took him fifty-seven minutes, with the last 50 coming in sixteen minutes. Dickie Bird stood in both games and I've no doubt he had to demonstrate his nimblest form in getting out of the way of Procter's straight drives.

The batting was only half of it. Again in successive fixtures, this time against Leicestershire and Yorkshire, he took a hat-trick. Against Yorkshire, at Cheltenham, all his victims went LBW. They were Bill Athey, John Hampshire and Kevin Sharp. It was the second time Procky had completed an LBW hat-trick.

Procter was probably the fastest bowler around, but Imran Khan, a fabulous cricketer and good captain of Pakistan, could also be distinctly nippy. He'd gone from Worcestershire to Sussex and comprised with Garth Le Roux a pretty unfriendly new-ball attack. On one occasion I was sitting in the Hove pavilion, pads on, watching Imran pounding down the slope. From the pavilion there you have a side-on view, giving the impression of even more speed. He dug one in short and it zipped up like a rocket to hit Zaheer on the head. Imran's Pakistan colleague collapsed and was helped from the field. The bowler was meanwhile showing great concern; Zed was not wearing a helmet, of course. At this point I had started to accept that my career was coming to an end. As I saw Zaheer staggering off, a bandage to his head, I thought to myself: If Imran can hit a batsman as proficient as Zed, he can certainly hit me. From that day at Hove, I decided to wear a helmet. I discussed it with Jenny who said, 'It's the cheapest form of insurance, Shep!'

Ian Crawford, our 2nd XI off-spinner, had come back from Australia with a helmet and I asked if I could borrow it. I resolved to wear it in the next championship match, which was against Essex at Gloucester. The advice I was given was that if I'd definitely decided to use a helmet in future, I should put it on every time I walked to the wicket. That would give me the necessary sense of balance.

What followed was seen, for the time, as slightly farcical. The Wagon Works ground was the slowest and lowest you can imagine, and I found myself immediately facing the belligerent combination of David Acfield and Ray East, in truth two decidedly slow bowlers who relied more on affable cunning, mischief and laughing eyes than on any semblance of venomous intent. There were titters around the ground and my complexion was even redder than usual. 'Hey, Shep,' I could see East saying, 'leave the humour to me.' I looked at the startled fielders and bowlers. Defensively, I said, 'Mark my words, lads, very soon every nine, ten, jack will be wearing one of these.' And, of course, I was right.

My borrowed helmet became something of a talking point. I discovered that, because of the visor, it was virtually impossible to have a smoke immediately before I went out to bat. That cigarette had become an obligatory part of my nervous ritual and I missed it, but Les Bardsley came up with the perfect solution, as so often was the case: one day he handed me a cigarette holder. It allowed me to have a smoke by pushing the holder through a slit in the visor.

Cricket, as I accepted years ago when the ball went for the ribcage in my village cricket on natural wickets, is a dangerous game. It's all very well for the odd genius like Viv Richards to spurn protection, but the average county cricketer isn't blessed with such reflexes. I saw Essex's Gordon Barker get carried off when injured by a Procter bouncer. He also laid out his South African bosom chum, Barry Richards. If these superior batsmen couldn't get out of the way in time, what chance had I?

The decision not to renew my contract was predictable. I think I read it first in the local paper, but that was nothing new. Jack Davey had already left to manage a pub and rest his aching limbs. Gloucestershire's first manager, Grahame Parker, had gone off, also back to Devon, to write the county's history. New players were coming through. Time to go.

Perhaps I can be allowed to quote Ken Graveney, the club chairman. In the *Year Book*, he wrote: 'It is with some sadness that we look towards a new season without the genial shape of Shep casting his warm and gentle shadow on all. We will remember his contributions in our Gillette and Benson victories, as one who produced the goods when the going was tough.'

In his book Procter warmly described me as a team man and I would wish for no other tribute. I scored only 10,672 runs at an average of

24.47. I reached 1,000 runs in a season only twice. I set no beacons alight and should have done a little better. But within my limitations I always tried my best. I played with a big tum and a smile on my face, and I hated factions, did what my skipper demanded and integrated with enthusiasm in the dressing room. I never ceased to be a schoolboy, happiest when striking the ball firmly and chasing the runs as I once did with natural intent, playing for my grammar school.

There was much I was going to miss, though not necessarily the preseason exercises devised annually with fiendish invention and lack of consideration for the human frame. I'd miss the banter, the friendships, Bert Avery's company on the drives to distant towns and the grounds of opposing teams, his tales of Shirehampton CC, the confidences we shared, his copperplate handwriting, his unavailing attempts to book me into Room 111.

When I was told my fate as a player, Tony Brown, as the secretary, had a chat with me. 'We could offer you a coaching job with us. Think about it.' The intention was for me to assist Graham Wiltshire and to continue captaining the 2nd XI. It didn't much appeal to me. I don't think I was cut out to be a coach.

My decision to break my links with Gloucestershire probably surprised the secretary as he suspected how much I wanted to stay in the game, in some form or another. But umpiring rather than coaching had caught my eye. Bill Alley and David Halfyard both encouraged me: 'You could do our job, Shep.' They knew how keenly I read the game. I applied to Lord's to be taken on to the first-class list and was unsuccessful, but it was suggested that I should go on the reserve list. In the meantime I was advised to do as much umpiring as I could. During the summer of 1980 I did some coaching at Downside School in Somerset. The arrangement couldn't have been better for me; the school released me for reserve-list umpiring commitments, including a week at Oxford, where the university was playing Leicestershire. There were also stints standing in 2nd XI matches for Gloucestershire and I found I liked it – the concentration wasn't a problem and it was good to remain involved in the game, even if a few steps removed from the players' changing rooms.

At Oxford I found myself standing with John Langridge.

'What are you going to count with, Shep?'

It was such a basic question yet I hadn't really a clue. 'Oh, erm, I've got some two-pence pieces in my pocket.'

John shook his head. 'Here are some little red barrels. Why not use them? They've been lucky for me and maybe they'll be just as lucky for you.'

The barrels were symbols of a popular drink in those days. It's possible the experienced and kindly Langridge was aware that I had a healthy thirst. I accepted them with thanks – and I still use them.

To be honest, my baptism wasn't exactly onerous. There was no play at all on the first and third days. Only two and a half hours of cricket were possible on the second, so I was left with plenty of time to talk, or rather listen and learn my first lesson. Over lunch on that second day, John said, 'Have you got the ball?' I was aghast – no I hadn't. Quietly, helpfully and with just the merest suggestion of a smile, he pointed out that the umpire who would be at the bowler's end after the break took possession of the ball.

I had the feeling there were going to be so many things like that to remember. Here was my first first-class match, one in which I'd spent much of my time in the pavilion waiting for the rain to stop, and I'd forgotten the ball. The kindly Langridge must have known I was nervous as he methodically went through the routine of what I needed to take on to the field with me. He told me to keep a record of who had bowled the last over before the interval, and which batsman would be facing afterwards. All simple stuff but very important.

This early advice served me well. I can think at once of a Test between England and the West Indies at Leeds some years later. At the start of play on the second morning Graham Gooch, according to my notes, had to be at the non-striker's end, but he wasn't. 'Graham, shouldn't you be down here?' He seemed equally emphatic that I'd got it wrong. It worried me for a moment, then I looked towards the scorebox and dear old Ted Lester gave me the reassuring nod that the batsmen had to switch ends. I'm not sure Goochie was absolutely convinced.

I got through my Oxford–Leicestershire fixture without any serious mishaps. We chatted to David Gower, the Leicestershire captain. We made our regular visits to the square to discover how well it was drying out. There seemed to be an awful lot of hanging around. Now it was just a matter of making a sufficient impression to earn my place on the first-class list.

Some felt Gloucestershire had been too inflexible in their final dealings with me. They were surprised when I rejected that somewhat vague post as assistant coach in order to try my luck as an applicant for first-class umpiring. When I didn't succeed, one might have thought my county would renew their original offer, but they chose not to and went on record as saying they weren't prepared to come back to me a second time. I retain a faded cutting from the *Bristol Evening Post*: 'If he had really wanted to stay with us, he would have accepted our offer ... He wouldn't have earned quite so much as he did as a player but it would have been a worthwhile job for someone who wanted to stay in cricket.' In print it sounds cold and impersonal. That same article quoted my reaction. 'I was disappointed. The job back with Gloucestershire was never actually defined and no salary was mentioned. It would have been nice to get back because after fifteen years with the county it is going to be a wrench packing up cricket.'

I was coming up to thirty-nine and not by any means certain that my next umpiring application would be any more successful. There were days when my fundamental insecurity, the plague of so many professional cricketers as their playing careers come to an end, would surface and nag me. Had I been too hasty in not taking up that coaching post? Had Gloucestershire decided to make me suffer because I hadn't put them first? They seemed to be taking an unforgiving stance. I pondered the options and came to the conclusion that I'd rather be an umpire than a coach of unspecified status. I took a risk, and was patient (and frequently anxious) for twelve months. The decision I took was the correct one for me and my relationship with Gloucestershire has remained warm.

My professional playing career was over, that much was clear. The front-foot aggression, the lofted drives over mid-off, the puffing and panting were to be relegated to the memory. From now on, it would be no more than one or two club matches. Wistfully I gave most of my kit away, some to local clubs in North Devon.

For some time I made a happy, if nominal, appearance in Tavistock's last match of the season. It was something I did for twenty years. Brother Bill and my chum Bill Walter always played too and it was an annual ritual to which we looked forward. We were selected for the President's XI against the club side, would arrive at the ground together and were known as the Three Musketeers. More appropriately, I used to think, we were like Compo, Clegg and Foggy from *The Last of the Summer Wine*. The three of us liked to make a day of it, complete with a morning round of golf. Bill and I would then crack a few nostalgic fours. His left-arm slows were, as ever, on a length. This was the spirit of the game in which we'd both been steeped. Fifteen years' travelling around the country as a Gloucestershire pro may have refined my batting disciplines, it had taught me how to dodge an Andy Roberts bouncer and to adjust my scoring rate according to the needs of the match, but the essence of cricket had, for me, never drifted too far from Devon's buttercup outfields and the distractions of cows strolling home at milking-time beyond the bowler's arm.

One final memory of those Tavistock friendlies. We were playing for the President's XI and after half an hour or so someone said he had the distinct impression that the pitch was too long; bowlers were having trouble with their length. Conscientiously we paced out the pitch and discovered, to both our horror and then mirth, that it was twenty-three yards in length, a whole yard more than it should have been. By now I was on the first-class list as an umpire, so the players consulted me: 'What the hell do we do, Shep?'

I pondered this unlikely dilemma. 'Leave it as it is. It's the same for both sides. And it's only a fun match, after all.'

When it was our turn to bat and I was at the crease, I played the ball and called for one. That was a salutary lesson for me: I learned the hard way that there's no such thing as a short single on a twenty-three-yard pitch. I was run-out, much to everyone's amusement. Back in the bar we decided collectively it was that mate of mine, Stuart Munday's fault. He had got his measurements wrong. Somehow I don't think I'll ever have that particular problem in a Test match.

Second Attempt

At the end of 1980 I applied again to be accepted as a first-class umpire. There were three vacancies and this time I was successful. The other newcomers were Yorkshire's Barrie Leadbeater, and Peter Eele, destined as a player to be Somerset's second-choice wicket-keeper and someone who went on to play some cricket for Devon. For me, this was it, I was on the list. It never remotely crossed my mind that one day I might end up as a Test umpire.

Like every player who had reached the stage of giving away his bats, I began to think increasingly about the game. Were the changes and innovations going to lead to improvement? Would the imaginative, or frantic, attempts to woo back the crowds and boost the bank balances work? Might the unrelenting demands for, and subsequent commitments to, sponsorship take a disquieting amount from the spirit of this most tradition-bound and quaintly charming of summer pastimes?

It is worth making the point that when I applied to Lord's to be considered as an umpire, the monetary inducements were hardly excessive. In other words, we wouldn't be doing it just for the money; non-financial factors were far more important. The prospect of staying in the first-class game was tremendously appealing. Almost all the umpires were retired players and it struck me that it was a great advantage to have played the game at county level. At the same time, I didn't see this as a necessity, and, plucked from my experience, I could nominate excellent first-class umpires who never played the game at a high level.

Let's revert to village cricket for a moment. Umpiring standards have tightened up and improved with the introduction of league structures. Before that, they could be pretty appalling. Hastily recruited umpires who came and went in rotation during the match often showed an abysmal lack of knowledge of the laws, as well as outrageous bias. We had some classic cases in the Devon and Cornish byways. Yet – dare I say it? – it was an accepted part of the Saturday afternoon ritual. We would have a little moan and forget our unjust dismissal half an hour later, certainly when it was time for a mutual pint. In any case, the bloomers seemed to balance themselves out, and we laughed about them later.

Then there were the good, no, the priceless, umpires. Perhaps they were a retired headmaster, the elderly village parson, disabled pensioners who gave you guard by pointing one of their crutches in the direction of middle-and-leg. I can remember wonderful local umpires who gave their time willingly and never seemed to make a mistake. They had an affection and an instinct for the game, and yet some of them had probably never picked up a bat in their lives. The point I am trying to make is that it isn't essential for an umpire to have played the game. But I am sure it can help . . .

Sometimes I'm asked whether I needed to take exams before I was accepted for the first-class list. The honest answer is that I haven't taken a single one. Nor has Dickie Bird or any of the best-known umpires of our day. It just didn't happen then. You could say that we were judged instead in a more practical way – on the job, if you like. We were initially given 2nd XI matches and reports were submitted on us by the respective captains. Maybe it's my West Country background, but I am a great advocate of *practical* training. I learned to be a better umpire by making the odd blunder in the line of fire, by listening to the wise words of my seniors at the other end, and by gradually having more confidence in my own judgement. I learned not to be browbeaten and bullied, or influenced by the foxy wiles of old campaigners in the field, who thought they could manipulate me. 'Listen, my old dear, I wasn't bloody well born yesterday.' I have had to say that more than once. They don't try it on so much nowadays. I'm not sure if that's because one or two of them have become older and wiser or because they have a bit more respect for me. I'd like to think it's both!

These days the introduction to umpiring is more theoretically comprehensive and rigorous. There are preparations, under training officers, for exams. Great emphasis is rightly placed on the constantly evolving laws.

About the time that my playing career with Gloucestershire was ending, I was asked by one of the weekly papers in North Devon to write my reflections for them. I gave it some thought and studiously made my assessment of professional cricket as it moved into the eighties. I looked back and forward. The other day I came across the yellowing cutting. My considered observations, taken within the context of my transition, are of some interest:

With all this new-found wealth in the game, I think we enjoyed the actual playing of cricket much more when I first started than players do today. We played in a more friendly atmosphere then and lasting friendships were made with opposing players. Don't get me wrong – the game was played in a very competitive spirit but it was played *honestly*. With so many knockout and league matches being played now, and a lot more pressures put on the players, they are tempted – like everyone else – to get away with what they can. Some even resort to what, years ago, we would have called cheating.

With these attitudes being shown at the top levels of the sport, is it any wonder that we now see players trying to cheat in local club matches?

In my early days as a player, the umpire's job was probably the easiest in the world. All he had to do was count up to six and call 'over'. If a batsman thought he was out, he left the crease and often the umpire would not be called on to make a decision. How frequently does this happen now?

147

Behaviour standards have declined. The antics of some of the world's most talented players in the last Test series in Australia were, I thought, deplorable. When such behaviour is televised all over the world and apparently goes unpunished, can we blame youngsters who try to emulate their heroes? We can and we must. I feel certain that had those incidents occurred in this country, action would have been taken and players would have been banned from the game – and rightly so.

More than twenty years later I see no reason to revise my opinions. It was what I sincerely felt at the time and the majority of my views remain just as relevant today. This is particularly true in the way club cricketers are apt to ape the bad behaviour and excesses of international players. Never has there been a greater need for role-models. All too often I see top cricketers around the world showing dissent, appealing for leg-before every time the ball raps the pads, or trying to hoodwink umpires with outrageous claims for catches behind. Their misplaced examples are followed by copy-cat players on village greens. It depresses me: it's alien to the pleasant, pastoral world in which I was nurtured and even the hard-fought county matches of my early career.

My progress as an umpire, from county to international status, should be accepted by me as a considerable compliment. In truth it has surprised me. More than that, it has frightened the life out of me. When I was first upgraded, I confided my apprehension to one of my best friends, fellow-umpire Barrie Meyer. We'd trained together for Gloucestershire, now stood together in county and one-day internationals. I'd seen him blaze shots just over the bar for Bristol Rovers and sadly missed his hat-tricks against Fulham and Derby County. We shared many confidences. 'I'm not sure, Barrie, whether I've got enough experience as an umpire behind me for international matches.' His reply couldn't have been more reassuring: 'Listen, Shep, if they didn't think you could do the job, they wouldn't ask you.' Devon lads, as I've admitted more than once, are not by nature boosted by a surfeit of self-confidence. BJ's words helped.

He lives these days in South Africa. His links with the republic probably go back to when Dr Ali Bacher asked him to fly over and, in his own words, sort out a few umpiring problems. I'm not sure what exactly they were but Barrie was their man. In all, he stood in twenty-six Tests and twenty-three one-day internationals. He had what I always reckoned were the ideal qualities, the right blend of authority and accessibility. His old soccer mates at Eastville, Bristol, where the rose borders behind the goals used to contrast with the ugly gaso-meters, would say he also had a lovely dry sense of humour. Mind you, that ready grin helped if you played football for both Rovers and City in Bristol. The tribal zealots didn't easily forgive that kind of defection. He'd joined Rovers in the first place because his dad had been in the army with Brough Fletcher, who was then the manager at the club. Barrie didn't take his cricket too seriously: he used to field in the slips at Sleepy Hollow, the nicely named ground of Stapleton CC, on the edge of the city. Then he and some of his Rovers team-mates were asked to sell scorecards and help the Gloucestershire CCC groundstaff in the summer months. He found himself playing in 'Club and Ground' and 2nd XI fixtures and, almost certainly to his surprise, taking over from Bobby Etheridge – when he went off on a soccer tour with Bristol City, ironically – as wicket-keeper. Barrie never claimed to be a natural, yet he worked so hard at it that he turned into an excellent stumper.

I was now on the list proper and Oxford (yes, The Parks again) against Glamorgan was to be my first game of the 1981 season. Nice and relaxing, I thought – and, even better, Barrie was going to be at the other end. We stayed at a bed and breakfast on the outskirts of the town. It was late April and once more it poured. The match was drawn after only four hours' play.

We were at Oxford for a week, surrounded by undergraduates with preoccupied studious expressions. The next match there was against Somerset, who went on to win by an innings. Frankly, Oxford's batting was inclined to be dire, causing all those old arguments about whether

149

Oxford and Cambridge should be dropped discreetly from the first-class list to resurface. They were dreadful: all out for 63 in the first innings. That Barbadian charmer Hallam Moseley, who spent so much time talking to the kids and their grandparents at Taunton that he should have been paid as a public relations officer, took four for 6 in one spell. He was an orthodox seam bowler with a good style, and he might have made the West Indies' Test team in another era. Dennis Breakwell, perhaps not the biggest spinner in the business, took six wickets in the second innings.

B.J. Meyer and D.R. Shepherd were together again in July when Surrey came west to play Somerset. I fancy the best of the batting was paraded by Dasher Denning, straw hair all over the place and as ever rebelliously popular.

'How am I doing, me old mate?' I asked Barrie.

'Fine. You're going to be a good'un. I like your enthusiasm and willingness to listen and I can see you'll have a real rapport with the players.'

That heartened me, not that I shared his predictions for my future. We were quite often to be fellow-umpires, including four one-day internationals. Yet sadly we never once walked out together for a Test match. By contrast, Barrie and Dickie Bird shared a Test seven times.

I was the umpire with Barrie, however, when Gloucestershire played the Australians. Our presence, as two former players for the county, was I think happily stage-managed for this special occasion with a celebration dinner. Diana, Princess of Wales, attended part of the match and then the dinner as the county's patron. She was introduced to the players and then the umpires. We had a very pleasant conversation and she showed a lively interest in the game. Perhaps by then she had become, by sheer practice in attending a wide variety of social events, adept at being a good listener and asking the right questions. I can only say that she was a most attractive principal guest. Barrie described her warmly, I remember, as 'this nice bashful princess'.

Within three years of going on the list I was appointed for World

Cup matches; the following year came my first Test. I've officiated at two World Cup Finals, at the 1985–6 Asia Cup and at tournaments in Dhaka, Sharjah (six times) and Canada. I went on the international panel in 1994. For me, it's all pretty mind-boggling. This kind of elevation is both flattering and intimidating. Just as well I've never been swayed by grandiose ideas. My feet have remained sensibly embedded in the Instow sand. No question, I promise you, of ever getting above myself. I like to think that I was being recognised for doing a decent job at the top level. The marks must have gone in my favour.

Sometimes I wonder whether my comparatively rapid rise has caused a few brows to arch among my colleagues. Human nature reacts in strange ways and I wouldn't be surprised if one or two umpires felt that too much luck was coming my way and perhaps that I was being singled out for special recognition. It would be untrue to say that there isn't a strong element of competition among umpires. I see nothing at all wrong with that, but I hope it doesn't veer towards jealousy. From the time I first took the white coat, I looked on umpiring as a joint operation, a two-man team. I have steadfastly remained friendly, I like to think, with all the other umpires.

So to 1983 and my first World Cup game, Pakistan against Sri Lanka at Swansea. As I gazed out across the bay and came down those count-less steps from the lofty pavilion, I gripped the half-dozen miniature red barrels in my pocket and trusted everything would go smoothly. It was good to have Kenny Palmer at the other end. Our eyes met a few times and he approved of the instant way I turned down some of the more optimistic leg-before appeals. I glanced towards him at square-leg: he was nodding his satisfaction at the assertiveness of my responses.

If Ken helped, at least subconsciously, so did David Constant when I umpired England against the West Indies at Old Trafford. I knew this was going to be the severest test for me so far. Many eyes would be on me; there was no room for error. Whenever anyone asks how I got on in that Texaco Trophy match, I say, 'Connie looked after me.' And so he did. There is nothing so reassuring for a fledgling international umpire as to know that there's a friendly old hand as your partner.

West Indies won the match easily enough – or rather, Viv Richards did. He was quite magnificent in an undefeated innings of 189, including twenty-one fours and five sixes, one of them sailing far out of the ground at the Warwick Road end. How do I know all this? By looking it up. Not till I got home and switched on the video did I realise the extent and glory of Richards's batsmanship. It had been a privilege to see him at his best, and yet I'd not been fully aware of it. That didn't mean I failed to appreciate the brilliance of his aggressive stroke-play. It was simply that I'd detached myself from individual performances, so focused was I on the job in hand. Viv considers that May innings one of the best he ever played and I'm sure it was. His fellow-Antiguan, Eldine Baptiste, was the West Indies' next highest scorer with 26. It leaves me feeling almost guilty that I marvelled fully at Richards's virtues only as I sat in my armchair at home in front of the TV.

That day in Manchester reminded me, not for the first time, just how much we have to shut ourselves off emotionally from the players' deeds. Our pragmatic task is to count the deliveries, respond to appeals and make sure that the laws are adhered to. The degree of concentration is immense.

'But hang on, Shep,' I can hear a few players saying, 'isn't it a fact that you like a chat?' How can I deny that? I don't believe that cricket should be an impersonal business. When a batsman passes 50 or 100, I may well have a quiet word with him and say, 'Well done.' If a bowler is having some trouble with his line or delivery stride, or maybe tending to send down too many short-pitched balls, I'm also inclined to pass on a confidential bit of advice. That would be in county matches, however. At international level I try to pursue snatches of conversation, but only if it's encouraged. I very definitely steer clear of technical counsel!

By the next summer I was being given the nod – again to my surprise

– for my first Test. This time it was against the Australians at Old Trafford. Dickie Bird, who had been umpiring Tests since 1973, was at the other end. It was a drawn game, though England had always appeared more likely to win. One reason they didn't was Allan Border's century and resistance in the second innings. He saved the Aussies. From an umpire's point of view, the match passed without much incident. 'Nothing to it really, is there?' said Dickie. I wasn't so sure.

Any reservations I may have had were underlined when it came to the next Test, the fifth in the series, this time at Edgbaston. David Evans was due to stand with David Constant but was taken ill, and I was called up to take his place. Not bad, you might say: two Tests in my debut season. But it was time for the first serious controversy in my umpiring career. This arrived on a grand scale: Border and his manager were irate – and I was the victim of their wrath. England deservedly won by an innings and the pair seemed to blame me for that. More specifically, they argued that one decision of mine had in effect gifted the match (and therefore the Ashes) to England.

On the final day, as tension mounted, Australia were trying to work out how they could save the Test. They were relying very much on Wayne Phillips, who had doggedly progressed to 59. He'd gone in at No. 6 and was their last realistic hope. Phil Edmonds, slow left-arm, was bowling from my end. The fielders were crowding the bat. England knew the importance of the wicket; their eagerness and body language said it all. Phillips leaned back to crack Edmonds, the ball hit something and flew into the air. England's captain, David Gower, one of the close-in fielders, snatched the ball triumphantly. There was a loud collective appeal. Unfortunately for me, my view was completely obstructed by the bowler. I hadn't a clue what exactly had happened, what the ball had hit on its diverted route into Gower's hands. There was only one thing for it. Solemnly I walked across to my colleague, David Constant, at square-leg.

'Look, Connie, I was obscured. Did you have a good view?'

'Yes.'

'All I need to know is whether the ball hit the ground before ending up in Gower's hands.'

'It didn't – it came off Allan Lamb's foot. So he's out.'

I returned to my end and gave Phillips out. To be honest, I was a little concerned when I was told the ball bounced off Lamb's foot, but any doubts disappeared when I realised he was jumping, taking evasive action, at the time and was well off the ground.

After the game the Australians wasted little time in letting me know what they thought of my decision. 'There was no way you could have given Wayne out,' said the exceedingly angry Border.

David Constant cut in: 'Forget about Shep. I gave him out and I take full responsibility.'

It's another example of how vital it is for umpires to work as a team, to assist each other at difficult moments.

Border wasn't going to be placated. 'I've watched it on television and there's no doubt about it. Wayne wasn't out.' I hadn't, of course, had the advantage of a close-up look on TV. It was all the more heartening, then, to see Jim Laker as he left his broadcasting box. 'Just listen to what I say on tonight's highlights,' he said. 'You got it right, lads.'

I've always valued the interdependence and mutual loyalty that exist between umpires. My regard for David Constant will be evident from several incidents I relate in this book. When, in the summer of 2000, he was given a bad time by the Sussex captain, Chris Adams, I rang Connie to commiserate and give him my backing. We have a duty to support one another.

I can't let that famous Gower catch go without delaying briefly to discuss the bowler: Philippe Henri Edmonds. He played in forty-one Tests and it should probably have been more. Some of his colleagues would have said he was a victim of his temperament. Henri was a man of strong views and he expressed them forcibly, not always with the approval of Mike Brearley or Mike Gatting. You always knew when Edmonds was playing. His withering or dogmatic opinions, fearlessly voiced, left you in no doubt that here was the definitive independent spirit.

He was a fine cricketer, an orthodox left-arm spinner who could win matches for Middlesex. His father was English, his mother Belgian; he was born and grew up in the old Northern Rhodesia. Over here, he skippered Cambridge in 1973 and was on his impressive way towards 1,185 first-class wickets. There were many stories about him, told usually with a degree of affection. The best known and most often repeated concerned his habit of walking backwards to his mark, ball in hand.

'Why do you do that?' he was asked.

'So that bloody Gatting can't change the field while my back is turned.'

There were also tongue-in-cheek tales about how he'd place all his black colleagues in the team on one side of the field, and the rest on the other, and then say, in those pre-politically correct days, 'Come on lads, over the border,' as he made an adjustment.

He was a person of whims. Kenny Palmer told me of one match when Henri was playing against the New Zealander Richard Hadlee, who used to bowl wearing wrist bands. Edmonds asked Hadlee to remove them because they were putting him off. Later in the match, the positions were amusingly reversed. Edmonds liked to keep on his wristwatch as he played. Hadlee turned to Kenny and said, 'Excuse me, Mr Umpire. Will you ask him to take off his wristwatch. It's distracting me!'

Kenny's retort: 'Oh, we're playing silly buggers, are we?'

For Edmonds, as I well remember, the watch was an almost obligatory part of his cricketing dress. Team-mates would pass him in the field and regularly ask him for the time.

John Holder and Bob 'Knocker' White were the umpires when Middlesex played Somerset during the Bath Festival in 1987. It was at a time when Henri had business dealings on his mind and was often on his mobile phone. He was even keen to select which fixtures he appeared in, a suggestion of his which met with minimal approval in the committee room. When he asked Gatt if he could leave the field because he needed to make a phone call, he was told pointedly that he couldn't. Shortly afterwards he asked one of the umpires for permission to go off, ostensibly to change his boots. His captain was far from pleased, and even less so when on Henri's return he misfielded and took his time about returning the ball. Gatting roared angrily at him to hurry up about it, a public rebuke in front of a large crowd. Edmonds's response was an inaccurate return, appearing to be aimed at Gatt rather than the wicket-keeper. Somerset ran 2 on the overthrow. The row between Edmonds and his skipper which followed was highly embarrassing: play was delayed; the press went to town; Gatting was unforgiving; back at headquarters, the Middlesex officials were equally so.

Now I go back to my favoured theme of umpires working in tandem. I like to think that, just as Connie gave me that timely moral support, I've willingly done the same for my colleagues. Self-doubts go with the job, especially in the early years. In his second season as an umpire Graham Burgess was standing in a Warwickshire–Notts match at Edgbaston. Allan Donald was the bowler, decidedly nippy and invariably awkward to counter in those days. He let go of one at Kevin Evans, a full toss at least waist high. The ball flew off the bat and there was a fantastic catch in the slips by Dominic Ostler. Budgie gave him out and then, in his own words, was consumed with doubt. Tim Robinson, the Nottinghamshire captain, who was the non-striker, turned to the umpire and said, 'Shouldn't that have been a no-ball?' Budgie was uneasy. He wandered down to square-leg to discuss the relevant law with me, and I did my best to reassure him. (The law states that any full toss above waist height is a no-ball. If it comes from a fast bowler then he also receives a warning for intimidatory bowling.)

Something similar happened when Barrie Meyer stood with me in the final of the Benson & Hedges Cup in 1993. It was a tense match which Derbyshire won against Lancashire by just 6 runs, their first triumph in the competition. But it's true to say that the mood of this highly dramatic meeting was set less than a fortnight before. They'd met in the championship and there wasn't much love lost. It was apparently an incredible match at Derby, full of runs and hundreds by Mike Atherton, Wasim Akram, Kim Barnett and John Morris. Then things went decidedly sour on the last afternoon. Wasim Akram suddenly transformed the game. In forty-nine deliveries he took six for 11. In the context of a fixture that had seen an abundance of runs, it was an amazing display. Vanburn Holder and George Sharp, the umpires, were kept busy scrutinsing the ball. Derbyshire went further: they sent it to Lord's for official inspection. No action was taken.

The final was inevitably preceded by bad feeling. Whispers of ball-tampering may not have been borne out by the TCCB response, but it was clearly not going to be a day of unmitigated cordiality at Lord's. Lancashire were the firm favourites; Derbyshire, eyes glinting, had other ideas. Their sense of vengeance took on increased passion when Chris Adams was struck on the back of his shoulder as he tried to get out of the way of a full toss from ... Wasim Akram.

I was standing at square-leg and Barrie was at Wasim's end. It was a painful blow and the Derbyshire partisans around the ground were beginning to erupt. My fellow-umpire and long-time mate walked across to me. 'Shep, I've already given a no-ball for the beamer, and a warning. But I'm wondering if it was deliberate.' That meant only one thing – Wasim would have to be taken out of the attack.

'Listen, Barrie, there's only one person on this ground who knows for sure whether it was an intentional beamer. And that's the bowler.'

BJ strolled reflectively back to his position as Adams received treatment. He decided to let the bowler continue. Not that it did Wasim much good: he finished with one for 65 and Dominic Cork took him to the cleaners with an undefeated 92. It was a smashing innings, well supported by Tim O'Gorman and Karl Krikken.

Meyer told me later how close he was to banning the Pakistani fast bowler. 'Do you know, Shep, there was no remorse from him at all. I'd have liked at least to hear him say, "Sorry."' I can only say there were a few sheepish expressions among the Lancashire fielders. Neil

Fairbrother had turned to Barrie: 'He didn't really mean to do that.' From the bowler, according to my partner, not a word.

It's necessary to be positive. There's nothing more disconcerting than a dithering umpire. If he appears uncertain, visibly in torment over a decision, it only makes the batsman more disgruntled. Any advice I was given on the subject was put into practice with singular enthusiasm by me in my debut season. I'll leave Ray Julian to take up the story: 'It was Surrey against Sussex at Guildford. Some claimed I had a bit of a reputation for giving LBWs. In this match nine batsmen went that way. And seven of them were shot out by Shep.' During my career I don't feel I've ever been in the front row of trigger-happy umpires. Inexperienced I may have been at Guildford, but I had no serious misgivings about any of my decisions there.

Once I received a phone call from Ken Palmer. We had strong West Country links and were good mates, often travelling to meetings in the same car. It was 1988 and Ken was in a bad way: he'd just lost his wife, Joy, and although he had been appointed to stand with me in the second Test against the West Indies at Lord's, he said he didn't feel in any suitable state to carry out his duties. The death had hit him hard. 'Shep,' he said, 'you'll have to bear with me and hold my hand. Can I rely on you?'

My immediate reply was: 'I'd be honoured to do that, Kenny.'

We drove to London together, a fairly quiet, meaningful journey. I knew what he was thinking about and I tried to relax him so that he was in the right mental attitude for a match which was always liable to generate tensions and judgements that needed steel nerves. Kenny had a good Test, even though controversy didn't elude him completely. Not by any means. In England's second innings David Gower was facing Pat Patterson. The West Indies had a wide arc of slips and gullies for the anticipated flash from the left-hander. This is how Kenny remembers the incident:

Martyn Moxon was at the non-striker's end and I asked him if he'd move slightly to give me a better view of the ring of fielders. Then

Gower got a nick and the ball was taken low down by Richie Richardson. But, oh dear, Moxon still partly obstructed my view. I just froze. A full house at Lord's and I wasn't sure about the catch.

As I hesitated, Viv Richards, who was captaining the West Indies, said, 'Come on, Kenny man, he nicked it. He's out.'

Summoning up all my composure, I walked across to David Shepherd. 'Did it carry, Shep?'

'Go back and give him out. It was a fair catch.'

I can still see Kenny walking back to his end and sending Gower back to the pavilion. He told me the batsman, out for a single, said, 'Thank you, Mr Palmer,' as he left the crease. No doubt those few cryptic words were as near as this fine, elegant batsman ever got to dissent.

Ken Palmer, burdened by grief, was glad to get that particular Test out of the way. He did well to get through it and if, as he says, I gave him the support he desperately needed, I'm pleased. Many didn't even know of his wife's death. I do recall, however, that as the two of us booked in at the hotel, we saw Derek Pringle coming down the stairs. He came straight across and offered his condolences and said how pleased he was to see Palmer back in action. That kind of sincere, considerate remark meant a great deal to an umpire who at that moment was probably thinking he should have stayed at home.

Four years later I was to stand with Ken's younger brother, Roy, in the third Test against Pakistan, at Old Trafford. There was much to enjoy, like Aamir Sohail's memorable double hundred. It was also the occasion when Gower played his 115th Test, to beat Colin Cowdrey's record, and when he went past Geoffrey Boycott's record England aggregate of 8,114 Test runs. And it was the match when Ian Botham and Allan Lamb were dropped. You see there were many reasons to recall that Manchester Test, but the saddest was what happened late on the fourth day. Roy Palmer, standing in the first of his two Tests, must have hated the mood of the match that argumentative early evening. I certainly did.

Clyde Walcott, the match referee, given dispensation to leave so that he could attend an ICC meeting, would have been glad to miss what went on. His deputy, the late Conrad Hunte, found himself bang in the middle of what had become a thoroughly bad-tempered match. He was to be kept busy handing out the fines. Aqib Javed came off worst, forfeiting half his match fee, but the Pakistan manager was severely reprimanded, too, for his part in the acrimony. Aqib had been warned by Roy for intimidating bowling against England's last man, Devon Malcolm. From square-leg I was bothered by the bowler's hostility and privately approved of Roy's rebuke. When it came to the end of the over it was alleged that the bowler's sweater was returned to him in less than friendly fashion. That was the cue for Javed Miandad, the Pakistan captain, to become involved. As *Wisden* rather neatly put it: 'Palmer retained the dignity of a patient policeman watching a family squabble.'

Roy Palmer called it an 'awkward' Test. I know what he means, but, based on that fourth-evening contretemps, I'd put it a little stronger than that: ugly and uncomfortable, maybe. The match was drawn. Intikhab Alam continued to seethe and refused to apologise for what he'd said publicly. The Pakistani players left the ground in what I imagine was high dudgeon – on top of everything else, they had been fined for their slow over rate.

Pakistani cricketers are frequently excitable. They can be noisy; some of their appealing has taken their exuberance into the realms of extreme optimism, fantasy and gamesmanship. The game's history, over recent decades, shows they are not by any means the only guilty parties. When Test cricket loses its charm and ability to smile at itself – even within the context of hard-edged competition – as it did at Old Trafford, life becomes so much less enjoyable for the crowds ... and the umpires. Roy and I knew this only too well as we came off the field and quietly pondered the high drama that had gone before.

Two-Man Team

There's something particularly comforting when you hear your peers say they can't think of anyone they would rather have at the other end. Perhaps, in my case, that ruddy apple face and substantial girth are factors. It was said to me by the highly regarded Nigel Plews when, in his last big game before retirement, we walked out together for the NatWest Cup Final in 1999. We sustained a genuine rapport. At my invitation he came to Instow to talk to our local umpires. A decade earlier we had umpired the fifth Test against Australia at Trent Bridge. England lost by an innings and Mike Atherton was out second ball on his Test debut. Nigel's memories are not solely of Australia's superiority, of that extraordinary record-breaking opening stand of 329 by Mark Taylor and Geoff (Swampy) Marsh, or Robin Smith's brave century retort. As he says:

It was also the moment when Geoff Lawson was bowling to Eddie Hemmings, batting in front of his home crowd. Steve Waugh in the gully claimed a catch and I wasn't quite sure if it had carried. I looked towards Shep and he shook his head. That was all I needed – it confirmed my own view. In those days there were no visual or electronic aids to assist the decision. But I didn't need to talk to my partner. Just a glance was all that was required. We were utterly on the same wavelength. Allan Border, the captain, was at mid-on and I can vividly remember his query.

'Here, Nige, what's wrong with that?'

'It didn't carry to Steve Waugh.'

Border was far from satisfied. He pointed towards David Shepherd. 'What about your mate, then? What does he think?'

Shep probably overheard the conversation. The Australia captain looked in his direction. My colleague was in no doubt and shook his head. That was it. Border got on with the game.

Let no-one come to the conclusion that, in my case, moral support from one umpire to the other is always one-way. I badly needed David Constant to be around during my first slightly tentative season. I needed my Bristol chum Barrie Meyer to build my confidence and say, 'They chose you for big games because they know you can do it.' When Mervyn Kitchen was on the point of going on to the field, for his debut Test as an umpire against New Zealand at Lord's, he turned to me and asked, 'Do you get nervous, Shep? I'm in a hell of a state.' I nodded.

As we sat down for lunch on that opening day, I said to him, 'That's one down and fourteen to go.' This apparently mystified him and he asked me to explain. 'One session gone and another fourteen to go.' I continued the count for the duration of the match ... 'Going well, Merv: seven gone, eight left,' and so on.

Alan Whitehead is a fine, unbending umpire. He isn't everyone's cup of tea because he fervently believes in adhering to the letter of the law. He's fearless in the way he administers it and isn't cowed by reputations. There was his much-quoted difference of opinion with Ian Botham which appeared to bring a premature end to Alan's Test career of five matches. He is another who has noticed how nervous I can be.

We were travelling together from the West for a one-day international at the Oval. But we ran into very bad traffic and realised we were running late. We'd motored up in the morning and needed to be at the ground at least an hour and a half before the start. I looked at

Shep and the sweat was pouring off him. He was beginning to panic and I was pretty anxious myself.

I put the window down to give him some air. I told him to stick with me and I'd get him there. And we did, although too close for comfort.

It's time to rid myself of any semblance of self-righteousness. Some accolades and compliments have come my way. For instance, I was tremendously proud to receive a card from Sir Colin Cowdrey, telling me how well he felt I had handled top games like those in the World Cup. But any tendency towards self-congratulation is rapidly offset by knowledge of the mistakes I have made. Umpiring is a human function: we do our best, relying on our eyes, our technical knowledge of the game and our instincts. On occasion they let us down. I consider it is only right to list some of my more fallible moments. One would find it hard to imagine a more public arena than at Lord's for a World Cup Final. I was being watched in all corners of the world. Every TV viewer was given a close-up analysis. There seemed to be more pundits than spectators at the ground. And there it was I dropped my clanger, even if it was a completely honest judgement on my part. Confronted with an identical set of circumstances, I suspect I'd make the same mistake again.

As you may remember, it wasn't much of a match. Australia and Pakistan were in theory the perfect pairing. The two sides were laden with elegance and talent, not to mention hard-nosed aggression from the Aussies. Before the final started, I heard some of the announcements in Urdu, intended for the Pakistani spectators. Snatches brought back to me memories of listening in bewilderment to Zaheer and Sadiq chattering away at great speed and high decibels in their Gloucestershire days. As for the game, it embarrassingly lacked the competitive edge demanded by the occasion. There were only about four and a half hours of cricket. Australia cantered to victory in slightly more than twenty overs. No-one enjoys a game as one-sided as that, certainly not in a much-hyped World Cup Final. However, there were still memorable aspects to the game, such as some wonderful bowling by Shane Warne, man of the match with his four for 33, reinforced by the general opinion that he is a timelessly great leg-break and googly exponent.

In the Pakistan dressing room there was communal dejection and disbelief. The dismissal of Inzamam-ul-Haq was no doubt prominent among their miscellany of explanations, excuses if you like, for the ignominious defeat. So I'd better tell you how it went.

Paul Reiffel came steaming in, from my end, and beat Inzamam as he stretched forward. I was convinced the batsman got a touch, Adam Gilchrist took the catch and my finger went up. From Inzamam's demeanour and then his slow, pensive and patently unhappy walk back to the pavilion I sensed that I had got it wrong. So it proved when I later saw the reruns and bit my lip in anguish. The Australian fielders had gone up as one for the 'catch' and I hope they didn't influence me in any way.

That was a mistake with which I had to live. In that same season, again at Lord's – I seem to reveal my occasional human flaws on the grand stage – I was the subject of some gentle criticism (at least I thought it was gentle) for giving out the Somerset captain, Jamie Cox. It was in the NatWest all-West Country Final. St John's Wood Road had been given a welcome rustic feel, very much to my liking. Some MCC and establishment diehards took a slightly patronising view of the proceedings. How dare a couple of counties from the sticks claim they were the most proficient one-day performers in the country and take over Lord's to demonstrate it? they seemed to be saying. I think some of the players sensed this and resented it. They had my sympathy entirely on that.

The talented Tasmanian Jamie Cox had arrived in Taunton that summer to captain Somerset and to open their batting. He'd proved an inspired, if initially surprising, choice. Somerset have always had this knack of coming up with exceptional overseas players: Viv Richards,

Joel Garner, Martin Crowe, Sunil Gavaskar, Steve Waugh, Jimmy Cook and Mushtaq Ahmed, and one or two others, make up a pretty impressive list.

Cox's arrival gladdened Mendip and Blackdown hearts. In that 1999 season he scored five championship centuries, headed the batting averages by some distance and led the county with a quiet and positive authority. His batting was tidy, invariably attractive and orthodox. He became something of an instant hero for those who watched. Many decided his skills were the crucial factor in what could be a Somerset win. Somerset lost – and Cox was dismissed for 1. The records tell us he was LBW to Mike Smith, but the playbacks gave a different version: he had nicked the ball and in any case it was too high for LBW.

I don't suppose the Somerset supporters ever forgave me. Cox, an intelligent, courteous man not in any way given to shows of dissent, left the crease in eloquent silence. He said nothing to me later, yet I sensed that he might have held it against me. There's a remarkable sensitivity at times in the relationship between players and umpires. My decision against him was a grim, untimely reverse for Somerset. They never really looked like recovering.

Before I move on from Lord's, I must mention the second Test there in 1997 between England and Australia. You'll remember it: England all out for 77 in the first innings, and eight wickets for Glenn McGrath. Graham Thorpe was top scorer with 21 and he was nearly out before he was off the mark. There was a confident, collective appeal (they always are) for a catch behind the wicket by Ian Healy. Oh dear, I wasn't absolutely certain that it had carried. My duty was plain – I set off to consult Umpire Ventataraghavan at square-leg.

On my way there Healy ran up to me: 'The other guys all thought it was out, Shep, but I wasn't sure.' That, to me, was a particularly honest thing to do, contrasting as it does with so many of the so-called 'professional' attitudes of the present day. The wicket-keeper's words helped me no end and I gave Thorpe not out. Spontaneously I applauded Healy's action and I understand it was picked up on the TV cameras. I'm glad of that. The public should always be made aware of integrity, especially at Test-match level. Too much rain fell in London and the match was drawn. For me, Healy provided a timeless ray of sunshine.

I have other good memories of him. It was the third Test between India and Australia, at Bangalore in 1998, when Darren Lehmann made his debut. Both sides reached 400 in their first innings; Sachin Tendulkar and Mark Waugh were the century-makers. Anil Kumble bowled well for his six wickets, though one of them was assisted arguably by my generosity. I gave Healy out caught behind. The body language told me that my decision should perhaps have gone the other way.

Next morning I asked him, 'Did I get it wrong, Ian?'

'Yes, but don't worry about it. You didn't do it on purpose.'

Just a simple friendly exchange. There were some players, famous names among them, with whom I couldn't have had that kind of confidential conversation.

The previous evening Healy was invited for a meal at the home of the Indian wicket-keeper, Nayan Mongia. Fellow-players have often remarked, with affection, that Mongia is something of a split personality. It would be hard to think of a wicket-keeper more noisy and unfailing in his appeals. This could quickly irritate opponents, his impulsive, aggressive approach leading him into trouble; he was given a suspended one-match sentence for dissent during the Australasia Cup in Sharjah. The ICC referees were apt to home in on him. Yet off the field, as we all found, he was a person of much charm. He loved talking cricket and on that evening when he acted as dinner host to Healy, he quickly asked, 'Did you hit the ball when Shep gave you out?'

'You know I didn't.'

'I didn't think you did.'

That's Healy's memory of what was said of his contentious dismissal. The two went on to have a pleasant and civilised night together.

I offer no comment, other than to record that Mongia had appealed with vociferous enthusiasm for the catch. Maybe he genuinely believed, as an instant reaction, that it was a legitimate dismissal. At the same time, if those who cherish old-fashioned standards and a minimum of unrealistic appealing become increasingly cynical, who am I to blame them?

In the Oval Test against the West Indies in 2000, I must hold up my hands and say I was guilty of a marginal injustice against Brian Lara. It was a match when he was having problems with his sunglasses and I told him that I would hold them for him. Soon after I gave him out LBW, though the replay showed that the ball had pitched outside leg stump. On reflection, perhaps he felt that I really needed those glasses. The following winter, during a one-day series in Kenya, I reminded him that I still had his sunglasses. 'Keep them as a keepsake,' he joked. He is not a player to harbour a grievance or make an issue of a suspect decision.

One can't always be so sure how players will react. Not long ago, in a county match at Edgbaston, I gave Nottinghamshire's Paul Johnson out LBW. At the close of play I went for a drink in one of the bars at the ground. 'Come on, Shep,' said Johnno, 'can I get you a pint?'

'Yes, please.'

'And what about your dog?'

The good-natured dig about a blind man's companion didn't in any way trouble me. I have a feeling that one or two umpires of a more sensitive disposition might have been less enamoured, bristling at the Notts batsman's lack of tact.

I don't know what some of them would have made of the kind of abuse directed by Shane Warne at the South African opener Andrew Hudson. This tirade of bad language occurred in 1994 at the Johannesburg ground. It was the first Test and a few players were bearing grudges, I understand, from the previous series between these two countries. I was standing in that emotive Test and I promise you that, though I'm in no sense a prude or normally bothered by what professional sportsmen are apt to say in moments of tension, I was shocked by Warne's comments. It was really terrible. With the agreement of my fellow-umpire, I called the Australian captain, Allan Border, over to discuss the young leg-spinner's appalling lapse. Warne had just bowled Hudson round his legs and had given the departing batsman what I can only describe as the soldier's farewell.

Border admitted that Warne had gone way over the top this time but qualified this with 'He's had a lot to put up with, going back to our last clash with South Africa.'

'Well, that's nothing at all to do with this series,' I told him, making it clear that the bowler could be in serious trouble.

It was the early days of Test-match referees. Donald Carr was the referee at Johannesburg and we had a meeting with him afterwards. He handed out a slap on the wrist, not a hefty fine by any means, to Warne, and to Merv Hughes, who was also judged to have misbehaved, abusing a batsman and showing aggression to a spectator. (I always liked Hughes, very much a character and one of the game's most wholehearted players.) What pleased me was the intervention of the Australian Cricket Board, who stepped in and registered their disapproval of the two players' behaviour. They imposed fines in keeping with the extent of the offences.

If you would like to know how challenging an umpire's duties and judgements are, let me take you back to the third Test with Pakistan at Headingley in 1987. Imran Khan was the bowler, Chris Broad, briefly my Gloucestershire team-mate in Bristol, the batsman. The ball came off Broad's glove, to be taken by Salim Yousuf. It seemed plain enough to me, even though the batsman appeared less than happy. I turned to Broad's county colleague at Notts, Tim Robinson, at my end. 'What's wrong with Broady. Not much doubt about it, was there?'

'That was a big glove.'

'And that's how I saw it.'

All the same, we were both wrong. The replays revealed by a camera at third-man, illustrated that the relevant glove wasn't gripping the bat at the time; Broad's hand was off the bat at the moment of impact.

Later in the match I discussed the incident again with Robinson. He found it hard to believe that we had both been deceived: 'As we saw it from our end, he had to be out.'

'I hope you told him so,' I said. Robinson added that he'd also told Mike Gatting, the England captain.

There was another incident in that Leeds match which sticks in the memory. Salim Yousuf claimed a catch, anything but a clean one, to dismiss Ian Botham. The batsman had turned to see exactly what had happened and he viewed the exuberant appeal for a catch behind as mischievous fantasy, or worse. I certainly had no qualms about rejecting the appeal. As for Botham, he moved towards the wicket-keeper. I truly believed we were poised for a punch-up. My partner, Ken Palmer, wasted no time. He chased in from square-leg to quieten things down. Here was yet another instance of umpires working in tandem. I dread to think what might have taken place if the confrontation hadn't been broken up.

'May your God Go with You'

Whenever I walk on to the field at the start of a match, county or Test, I turn to my partner and say, 'Good luck – may your God go with you.' It's something I first picked up from the Irish comedian Dave Allen. In my case, you could put it down to another strand of Devon superstition. My abiding wish for the match itself is simple: like that of almost every umpire – on village green or Test enclosure – it is to avoid controversy and make the right decisions. I don't want headlines and reporters knocking on my hotel door.

Umpires vary in character: some are naturally gregarious; a few enjoy or even seek a high profile; one or two relish controversy. For all the crowds and the daily banter, umpiring is fundamentally a lonely life: we spend hours on the motorways or seated alone on jets; during a match we're very conscious that we are on our own. Questioning eyes turn in our direction every time there is an appeal and the expectation is unswervingly high. Socially, some umpires move in pairs, spending their evenings together. A high proportion, however, return alone to the guest houses or small hotels – let's forget the luxury of Test scheduling for the moment – for a shower and then to flop on their beds. We are tired physically and certainly mentally. We twiddle the knobs on the job-lot television set and dwell needlessly on the bat–pad dilemma that faced us in the last over before tea. It's over and done with and we should be able to shut it from our minds, but it isn't as straightforward as that.

My philosophy has always been that if I can wake up in the morning, look in my hotel-room mirror and know that every verdict has been an honest one, it's a job well done. I've evolved my own style: it involves a smile, and an informal and accessible approach. There are no barriers: if players want me to share a drink with them at the close of play, I accept, provided the invitation has come from them. If a batsman thinks he has been wronged, unjustly given out by me, I'm prepared to talk about it. We do that in private, in a perfectly friendly manner. Umpires know the players who are inclined to be argumentative or have outsized chips on their shoulders. Discreetly we keep our distance from them. I hate players to bear a grudge; I like to end on good terms. Cricketers are well aware when they have had a good match. So are umpires.

None of this means that I am necessarily a soft touch. I wasn't too inhibited once at Edgbaston to tick off Mike Atherton. As a fielder he seemed to be sledging Sachin Tendulkar about something or other and I found myself saying, with a distinct reprimand in my voice, 'Hey, Mike, it's nothing to do with you.' I also needed to give a word of censure to Prasad during the World Cup in Bangalore. He and Sohail were having a little difference of opinion and I felt something needed to be said. Prasad was most apologetic to me afterwards and I fancy I was unduly hard on him, having missed Sohail's gesture the previous ball. Personal taunts and vendettas are commonplace and often the public know nothing of the background.

Thankfully there are shafts of humour, never too far away, to lighten the mood and encourage laughter from the players and spectators. That brings me to the case of the streaker in May 1989. We made the front page of the *Sun* on the strength of it.

It was a one-day match at Lord's against Australia. Everything was blissfully incident-free. Dickie Bird wasn't there so we had no fear of rain. It was a lovely sunny day and, as I used to say, God was in his heaven. Then suddenly there was a roar from the crowd. I hadn't a clue what was going on but when I looked in the direction of the Nursery

171

End ... there she was in all her glory, naked as the day she was born. And, oh dear me, she was heading straight for Umpire Shepherd. Ian Botham was near by but I was the focus of this nubile apparition's intentions. I suppose you could say I was in a state of confusion. This was a new experience for me, at Lord's of all places, with all the TV cameras there to record my brief skirmish with a curvy stranger I'd never had the pleasure of meeting formally. Various thoughts raced through my head. One carried a hint of warning – Mum would be watching back in Instow. She wouldn't have approved of this kind of brazen overture made to her younger son. When the streaker reached me she did a cartwheel. I wasn't quite sure what to do so I shielded my eyes. The girl was eventually escorted from the field and, fleshly distractions over, we got on with the cricket. Next day my reaction of affected embarrassment was reproduced on the front page. 'Did you ever meet Sheila Nicholls again?' I was asked more than once. 'Unfortunately no' was my reply.

The amiable Barbadian John Holder was the other umpire when, the following month, it was time for the opening Test against Australia at Leeds. He offers this postscript.

Streaking was becoming rather too fashionable, in rugby as well as cricket. We'd arrived on the Wednesday, Shep, Roy Palmer, the third umpire, and myself, for the normal briefing, and it was obvious that Yorkshire's then secretary, Joe Lister, was determined to avoid any displays of female nudity or anything else he saw as unseemly. In fact, he said he would be employing his fittest stewards for that purpose. On the Saturday, a streaker attempt was nipped in the bud. Then, on the last day, with England heading for defeat, an uninhibited girl streaker chased on to the field. Her target appeared to be Shep. She was brought down by a couple of stewards with a rugby tackle. That was the cue for an exchange of dialogue between the two umpires. Shep passed a message, via one of the Australian fielders, that the girl should have headed for me because of my supposed sexual prowess. I sent back a message that she knew she was safe with him!

I hope John was flattered by my assessment of his virility. Streaking was initially good fun and harmless enough. Afterwards it became too repetitive and predictable. These interruptions from curvaceous young ladies and boozy, boring men became irritating to the organisers. The originality had been part of the appeal of the diversion but drunken blokes with pot bellies, craving a few seconds of televised exposure (it seems the most appropriate word), had no appeal at all.

I have mentioned Dickie Bird. He is, of course, the subject of many stories, most of them emanating from the umpires' room. He's famed for his emotional nature and his mannerisms. In recent years he has doubtless become a wealthy man from his books. Over the seasons I have come to know him well, and to accept his eccentricities. When he retired the game lost a character and someone who usually got it right from twenty-two yards. At the same time I was very conscious that there was both a private and a public Dickie. For all his endearing traits, he gave the impression of often being a loner. Many who love and practise the game of cricket are.

In the early years of international cricket in Sharjah, Dickie and I were frequently invited to umpire matches. We were there, standing for a final between Pakistan and the West Indies, in sweltering heat. After a meal break we had returned to the field for the second innings. I was about to start play when I glanced across to square-leg. Dickie had collapsed. The fielders crowded round him; everyone was making a fuss of him; and I hurried across to see what the trouble was. A few cynics would say there was often an aura of drama surrounding Dickie. I can only say that this was a genuine case of dehydration – something on which I was an expert, based on past experience as a panting batsman running an outrageous five with Tony Brown in that game long ago against Worcestershire in Bristol – and now it was my fellow-umpire being helped from the ground.

At that point, I took charge from both ends. It was a taxing exercise in concentration. With that and the intense heat I was glad when it came to the close of play. By the time I got back to the pavilion Dickie had recovered and we shared a meal. As he pointed out, the climate was very different from what he was used to in Barnsley.

My favourite story of Dickie Bird, and one to which I was a witness, came during the World Cup in India. We were staying at the Taj Hotel in Delhi and Dickie was ill, so ill in fact that he was confined to his room. It happened that the England team were passing through, with a stop-over at the same hotel. I was concerned that my colleague was suffering from the occupational hazard, turbulent tummy, and was desperately trying to think of a way to cheer him up. Then I spotted Allan Lamb, renowned as a joker. I went over to him: 'Your mate Dickie isn't at all well. See what you can do to make him laugh.' I gave Lamby the number of the room.

Allan went up in the lift, with me following. In the corridor on Dickie's floor were a number of men with rifles. This wasn't unusual; it was the hotel security. Lamb knocked on the door and a pale, fragile Dickie eventually answered it. Lamb had by then lined up a row of armed guards. Now he officiously marched them in, positioning them at the end of the bed, into which the startled Dickie had retreated. 'Take aim!' bellowed Sergeant-Major Lamb and the rifles were ominously raised. I suppose the implication was that it was time to put Dickie out of his misery. It was a practical joke that couldn't be sustained for long. The military charade had its effect, however: the bedridden Bird broke into laughter and he admitted the unscheduled visit did him more good than the prescribed tablets.

On another occasion, at the close of play in Bristol, Dickie was seated in the Hammond bar, reading a newspaper. The impish Lamb couldn't let the opportunity go – he set light to the paper, to the poor chap's consternation. More than once, Dickie was the victim of practical jokes.

Dickie has a complex personality. There is the withdrawn, private, maybe at times lonely man and then there is the extrovert, loved by the public. The two of us once had to fly to Lahore for a World Cup semi-final between Pakistan and Australia. The hype and advance publicity had been considerable and as we stepped off the plane, along with the Australian team, an assembled local band struck up a tune of welcome. It seemed that the presence of 'Mr Dickie Bird' was of as much interest as that of the players. It was a moment for him to savour. He walked up to the band, took the baton from a mildly surprised conductor, and proceeded to lead the musicians in their chosen repertoire. I've been round the world with him, so know most of his quirks. It used to be said that some of Dickie's contemporaries had a few reservations about him, though not based on his technical ability or intimate knowledge of the game. Maybe it was this facility for self-publicity that irked his contemporaries more than anything. He certainly liked an audience.

I got on well with him in a pleasant, casual, rather than a personal, way. He made himself into something of a cult figure, relishing a chat-show appearance and a superficial peep into the glitzy showbiz world. To his credit, he retained that down-to-earth, unsophisticated, self-contained Barnsley appeal. He doubtless enjoys the trappings of fame but at the same time it's never going to change too drastically his simple, homespun way of life. I'm pretty sure his favourite meal is fish and chips, and not just in Leeds or Scarborough. I've seen him go up to the chef in an Indian hotel and ask: 'Got a bit of fish?'

When Dickie was still umpiring, he was constantly a talking point among his peers. Some of them were possibly jealous of the attention he continually commanded. All observed his nervous energy and listened to his quaint commentary on the human scene. Some even reckoned they could write a book about him. But, of course, he beat them to it, proving himself a publisher's dream as a salesman and making himself a rich man in the process.

He's renowned for his time-keeping. I thought that as an ex-newspaper delivery boy, still doing the rounds when I am at home, I was an early riser, but Dickie seems to wake before any of us and is frequently the first to arrive at the ground. I don't know how reliable this tale is, but I've heard that there was no-one about once when he turned up, probably not long after dawn, for a Test at the Oval. Impatient for entry, he is said to have tried to climb over the iron gates.

As he had every right to, he could stand on his dignity. I recall graphically what happened during a match between the West Indies and Sri Lanka in Sharjah. The organisers had been short of a scorer and a local man was recruited. After the game, according to him and gleefully reported in the regional papers, Courtney Walsh had bowled 10.2 overs. In other words the umpires, Dickie and I, had got it wrong. Bird was irate and demanded to see the senior match official. He went bananas, the only time I've seen him like that. Reasonably enough, he didn't like to be shown up publicly for making a mistake – especially when he hadn't!

But cricket rarely leads to such anger. Much more often it leads to smiles and laughter. I think back to a Test at Johannesburg, where I was standing with Cyril Mitchley, himself a South African. On the boundary were half a dozen Alsatians and their handlers, in position to keep back the crowd. The ball was hit in the direction of third-man and Pat Symcox set off in an attempt to save the four. His eye was on the ball and he so nearly ran into one of the big dogs. When Symcox came back to the middle, my fellow-umpire said to him: 'You were in no danger, you know, Pat. The Alsatians wouldn't have bitten you – they'd have been afraid of catching rabies!' I have to put that down to a South African sense of humour.

I must say that in these modern times, when cricket has been besmirched by almost unthinkable allegations of bribery and corruption, a sense of humour among the umpires has helped enormously. The jokes have occasionally taken on a black hue and I can fully understand why. I recall a conversation 'Knocker' White had with Nigel Plews just before the latter's retirement. It was when new laws were being introduced and there were all sorts of unsubstantiated rumours of match-fixing.

'Do you realise, Plewsy, that the authorities have missed a wonderful opportunity to change the nature of an appeal during a game?'

'What do you mean, Knocker?'

'Well it shouldn't be "How's that?" any longer. It should be "How much?"'

Is that an unsuitable subject for humour? I don't think so – it's just a way of dealing with disturbing news stories. While we're touching on what should and shouldn't be turned into comedy, it's worth rewinding cricket history back four or five decades. There are plenty of tales about Arthur Jepson, the former Nottinghamshire fast bowler who went on to stand as umpire in four Test matches. He was umpiring in a match between Glamorgan and Gloucestershire on a slow wicket at the Steel Company of Wales ground in Margam, Port Talbot, where some county fixtures were played in the early sixties. Jim Presdee became impatient and started giving Tony Brown the charge. This didn't often happen to Browny. Jepson said to the Gloucestershire bowler, 'I wouldn't stand for that.'

'Well, I'm not quick enough to bounce it, Jeppo,' replied Browny.

Jepson gave him an old-fashioned look: 'Who's saying anything about bouncing 'im.'

Tony was left to interpret the umpire's words in any way he wished. It was probably just a passing joke, but it could have been sentiments dredged up from the fast bowler's spiky, down-to-earth culture of former years. That happened a year or two before I became a county player, still immersed as I was in the endearing innocence of local club cricket.

So we have the black humour; then there is the dry variety, very much to my liking. Mike Smedley appeared more than 350 times for Notts and skippered the county for five seasons. Smedley was a cricketer with distinct theories on the game. One, which he'd developed and persuasively argued, was that if you batted in a certain way you could never legitimately be given out LBW. Alas, it didn't work in one game and the umpire, Fred Jakeman, a fellow-Yorkie who had gone on to play for Northamptonshire himself, was in no doubt. He raised his finger. In the bar later Smedley brought up his pet subject and said to Jakeman that he was surprised to be given out. Fred, dry as ever an ex-pro from Holmfirth could be, gave a slow smile and explained, 'Mike, I'm a practical man myself.' In other words it was no good for theorist Mike to try to blind him with science.

Much more recently I was standing at Cardiff for the visit of the West Indians. Suddenly I was aware of consternation on the field. The tourists were in a state of alarm and were diving for cover. They'd seen, no doubt for the first time, a swarm of bees coming across Sophia Gardens. It was a new experience for me, too – and a frightening one. I imagine the sight was rather similar to the famous shot at Lord's during wartime when all the fielders and the batsmen, including Wally Hammond, threw themselves on the ground as a doodlebug approached.

I have always contended that there is more genuine fun in cricket than any other game. When it becomes so glum and impersonal that it is geared only to the whims of the accountant I won't want any part of it.

I understand that at times I have been seen as a genuine figure of fun. That's fine with me. I take my duties very seriously and know well enough when they are no laughing matter. To counter that, I can laugh with others back in the bar or hotel, about my superstitions, my comfortable size and the fact that I share a name – if not quite the spelling – with Bishop Sheppard. Taking the last point first, David Allen has continued to call me 'Rev', going back to that pseudo-religious charade the Gloucestershire boys put on during a tour of Zambia. As for my size, this is positively my last word on the subject, or rather the last word from recently retired umpire John Harris: 'We were standing together at Worcester for a county match, and staying at the Shakespeare pub. Well, we started the evening with a few beers – several for Shep, one for me. Then he suggested something to eat. We went along to the corner where he had a double McDonald's burger. Out we came and he questioned what we were going to have for the main course. And off we went for cod and chips. Yes, he has a healthy appetite.' I don't remember that gastronomic sortie in downtown Worcester but, yes, I liked a decent meal. My eating habits have been quite drastically restricted in the last year or so by diabetes. I fancy, all the same, that John thoroughly exaggerated the story.

Before I move on from the subject of umpiring with a smile – and, I like to feel, a rejection of self-importance – I'm tempted to mention an amusing aside when I was in South Africa, umpiring them against the West Indies. Simultaneously England were in Australia being given a fearful hammering, and that meant I was receiving plenty of stick. An invitation came from Peter Van der Merwe, an ex-ICC referee and captain of his country, to the other umpire, Ranjan Madugalle, the match referee and myself to watch England's rugby game with South Africa, televised from Twickenham. I found I was the only Englishman in the group and felt quite lonely and defensive. The British national anthem was played and I immediately stood up. This struck some of my hosts as a little odd and they exchanged smiles at my outward sign of patriotism. It was at a time when the South African rugby players were on the crest of a wave. Their confidence had soared and I sank lower into my chair as the stylish visitors scored a try in the corner. It was converted and the course of the game seemed predetermined. My hosts, for their part, became noisier in their mood of premature celebration. I think they were even beginning to feel sorry for me. It was a misplaced, if affected, sympathy. England came storming back into the match. Now it was my turn to make my presence felt. Ranjan looked severely in my direction, accusing me of being a soccer hooligan, but I had every reason for my spiralling exuberance. England went on to win – and the rest of the gathering went significantly quiet. As the final whistle sounded, I jumped to my feet: 'My name's Shep and I'm from Devon ... England thirteen, South Africa *seven*.' The Springboks aren't famed as good losers. At least Ranjan laughed; I'm not so sure about the others.

As I've indicated more than once, international cricket can be riven with antipathy and lack of grace, so I'm glad that sentimental moments can also surface. Typical of this was the way the English players lined up at the Oval to honour those great West Indian Test bowlers Courtney Walsh and Curtly Ambrose on their final appearances for their team in England. It was, I'm told, a spontaneous gesture. The pair were taken by surprise, and moved. After the ovation from the big crowd, I turned to my fellow-umpire, the Australian Daryl Harper and said: 'Of course you know they did this for Don Bradman on his last appearance here.'

'What happened?' asked Daryl.

'Eric Hollies bowled him second ball.'

As Courtney took guard, Harper told him what had happened to the Don. Maybe he didn't treat it sufficiently as an omen. Dominic Cork dismissed Walsh ... second ball. Mind you, Bradman was a rather better batsman.

The first time I saw Walsh in action was in 1984 when I umpired the West Indies against Somerset at Taunton. He was twenty-one, and what I noticed about him most of all was his physique. He looked young and diffident, but it was his height that caught my attention. And I'd never seen a bowler so thin. In that match the winds howled and the tourists shivered under their sweaters. Walsh still looked skinny under three layers. Speed merchants usually had thick thighs like Fred Trueman, or iron constitutions like our own Syd Lawrence, who had made his debut for Gloucestershire only three years before.

Many in this country hadn't heard of Courtney before his name was announced for the tour party, and many hadn't heard of him later, as he didn't play in any of the Texaco Trophy matches or the Tests that summer. He'd been brought over to absorb the atmosphere at the highest level. None of us really had a clue about his enormous potential. Well, on reflection, possibly one or two at Gloucestershire detected the rustle of excitement whenever his name was mentioned.

I don't suppose he imagined he would have much chance of early elevation on that 1984 tour. The West Indies had bowlers like Malcolm Marshall, Joel Garner, Michael Holding and Eldine Baptiste ahead of him. This wide-eyed beanpole from Jamaica was there to observe, learn and perhaps occasionally take out the drinks.

A few days after the Taunton game I was talking to David Graveney and he surprised me by telling me his county had signed Courtney. 'You've seen him, Shep. What do you think?'

'Looks useful to me. But he's so slim. I don't know what to say about his stamina.'

How wrong could I be? Stamina wasn't ever a problem for Walsh. He'd keep going as long as his successive Gloucestershire captains asked him. He would say, if asked, that he always bowled within himself, that his physical control enabled him to ping away for over after over, longer than was customary for a fast bowler.

Against Somerset on those windy days in May he bowled Vic Marks in the first innings and trapped Brian Rose LBW in the second. They were his only wickets in the match. During the tour his appearances were limited and he took fourteen wickets in all at a relatively expensive 39.79. In the years that followed I monitored his career with increasing interest. Wasn't he one of us, as an adopted West Countryman, after all? I later found him more talkative than Curtly Ambrose, though hardly an animated companion. Some claimed he had a comparatively easygoing temperament in the Test match battle-field. Mostly, but not wholly true: many of us remember his uncharacteristic blasting of Devon Malcolm on one occasion. The fuse wasn't often short, but it could be ignited occasionally, to the detriment of an opponent. In the best, most fearsome, West Indian tradition, he could give the stare to the batsman. It can be a psychological weapon every bit as intimidating as the bouncer.

I must say I liked him, marvelled at his monumental wicket-taking Test record, and regretted his abrupt departure from the county we jointly represented. I dropped him a line when he finally retired: 'Watch your front foot – you're getting close!' He'd come off the field at the Oval, on his farewell, with an arm around my shoulders.

He was a polite cricketer in his relationship with umpires. If a player hands me his sweater at the start of an over, I automatically thank him. I expect him to be equally civil when it's handed back. A few times, in county matches, the sweater has been snatched from me without a word. 'Hey,' I say, the disapproval in my eyes.

It was during the Oval Test that I heard a shout of 'Shep, Shep!' from high up in the pavilion as I walked out after lunch with Daryl Harper. Whoever could that be? I turned and peered up at the committee balcony. There proudly stood Dickie Bird with John Major. I felt it was my turn for a gentle dig. Smiling at my umpiring companion, I asked, 'Who's that with Dickie Bird?'

I relish the privilege of being a worldwide umpire. Invariably I'm well looked after by my host country. There's a liaison officer to do our bidding and a doctor at hand if we're feeling peaky. Sometimes a stray thought crosses my mind: are we equally good with our hospitality when foreign umpires come on duty to England? I see exotic countries and sublime cricket grounds, with Adelaide my unchallengeable favourite. Every ground is different – in atmosphere as well as pitch conditions.

It's our practice to visit the ground the day before the Test starts. For a match when the West Indies were playing Australia, at the Queen's Park Oval, Port-of-Spain, Trinidad, I spent longer than usual surveying the pitch. The Oval is generally considered to be set in a landscape as delightful as you'll find anywhere. It's also a particularly large arena with space for 25,000 spectators. But it wasn't the hills of the Northern Range or the ambience that delayed my departure. The simple fact was that I'd never before seen so much grass on a pitch prepared for a top-class match. One could only conclude that the grass had been left on for the West Indian seamers. The groundsmen and officials must have seen the face I was pulling. 'I know my name's Shepherd,' I blurted out, 'but I haven't brought my sheep for grazing.'

It was a Test I'm not likely to forget. The grass on the pitch was almost an inch long. I'm sure Curtly Ambrose couldn't believe his luck; he proceeded to take nine wickets. In every sense it was a crucial match: Australia had gone one up and the West Indies needed to level. Now Steve Waugh, a fabulous cricketer, was batting and he was the one opponent the Windies desperately wanted to dismiss. The rest of the batsmen were disappearing in understandable haste. Not Waugh; indeed, he was the only player in the Test to make more than 50. Ambrose was well aware of what was needed for his side: he focused on Waugh and let fly a few unpleasant bouncers. The two went eyeball to eyeball. I couldn't hear what was being said, which was maybe just as well. It was a situation which called for me to act and I moved towards the pair. Richie Richardson, the home captain, got there before me and showed admirable authority in pulling them apart. I was full of praise for him. As for Ambrose and Waugh, here were two highly, even dangerously, competitive sportsmen.

For the record, that 1995 Test in Port-of-Spain was won by the West Indies by nine wickets. There was an aftermath of heated debate about the pitch – and many sheepish expressions among the home players and their officials. Australia won the next Test, in Kingston, by an innings . . . and the series.

Jet-setting isn't quite as glamorous as it may appear to some of my relatively home-bound lads back in the West Country. Travel can be tiring, even if not quite as much as for my late father as he sailed the oceans in wave-lashed Merchant Navy ships. 'Lucky devil, Shep,' my mates are apt to say when, just back from Australia, I meet up with them again in a Devon pub or in the Instow CC clubhouse. If only they knew how confusing it can get – not least to a few locals who don't know whether I'm coming or going. Back on my paper rounds for Brother Bill, after one commitment in Sharjah, John Edwards, club cricketer and former headmaster, turned to the sports pages of *The Times* and said: 'Well I'm blowed. Here I am reading a report of an international yesterday in which you were the umpire – and you're home to bring me the paper!'

Umpiring at the highest level, though now well remunerated, comes at a price. I don't know how the other umpires feel before and after, but I'm pretty drained, physically, mentally and emotionally, by the end of the match. It's hard not to be apprehensive beforehand. Will there be any incidents? Shall I be deafened by the cacophony of tin-cans and raucous barracking to the extent of not being able to hear the nick on the bat? What about the sledging and the crude verbals that too readily fly in all directions around the crease – or the whingeing and dissent? Shall I get a vital decision wrong and be roundly criticised for it? From the moment Jenny packs my bag, slipping in a picture of Skipper the dog to remind me of home, I'm utterly focused on the big match coming up. I don't get much notice before matches and my social life suffers. 'Can you come and speak at our dinner, Shep?' . . . 'How about a pantomime comeback?' My reply is invariably the same: 'I'd love to but I just don't know if I'm going to be on the other side of the world.' Are my inoculations in order? Have I mugged-up the latest ICC edicts and done all the paperwork? Do I know which foods to avoid? Is there going to be time for a bit of sightseeing? Too late now to worry. The National Express coach is waiting and will take me all the way to Heathrow. That avoids worries about finding somewhere to park. I find a quiet seat on the coach, look out of the window for a final wave to Jenny and Skipper and go into a shell. My mental preparations start as soon as we're pulling out of Instow: from that point, I cocoon myself mentally.

As the cliché has it, all of us are only as good as our last match. An impeccable umpiring performance may be followed by an example of understandable human fallibility. Yet it's a blunder, witnessed, it seems, by a million eyes. Back in the hotel room I switch on the TV set and relive the agony. On occasion I cringe, accepting that I've marginally gone wrong. Other times I'll nod with satisfaction to myself. That thunderous appeal from the bowler, wicket-keeper and close fielders – and frequently from those nowhere within visual range – has not fooled me. My gut instinct was right.

These are the days of high technology in international cricket. We have the giant TV screens and other visual aids. We have the obvious advantages of third umpires and neutral referees. Many of the innovations have initially brought a little unease and suspicion from the umpires. We first saw it all as Big Brother's omnipresence. Was he there to undermine our authority? In an interview I gave in 1994 I said I'd been won over to the idea of a third umpire: 'It makes for correct line decisions and players have accepted it more readily than I thought. With so much money in the game nowadays, they also want to avoid mistakes.' Then, as an afterthought, I asked: 'Where is it likely to end? Are we going to do away with umpires altogether?'

I asked that question in slightly tongue-in-cheek fashion, but at the same time I was making a serious point. Was the human arbiter being superseded by machines in the computer age?

Since then, umpires have become less suspicious and more ready to accept that the electronic aids and the third umpire have been introduced to help us and ease some of our most demanding responsibilities. Much of the earlier cynicism has disappeared. When we take the field, we carry more than a pen and paper and our counters. We also have our two-way radios, so that we can keep in touch with the other match umpire, the third umpire and, if necessary, the match referee. It allows us to convey to the officials the first sign of trouble. Vastly differing accents on a crackling set can pose their own problems, however. I remember a chat I had with the West Indian Steve Bucknor. I told him I was due to stand in the Sri Lanka Test at the Oval with the Guyanan Ed Nichols. 'Shall I be able to understand Ed when I talk to him on my two-way radio?' I asked, only half joking.

'Listen,' said Steve, 'I'm from Jamaica – and I have difficulty understanding him at times.'

There's a danger of this radio communication being taken to extremes. That was what the outraged authorities thought during the World Cup game at Hove between India and South Africa. When the South Africans came out to field I looked at Hansie Cronje and then did a double-take. What was he doing with what appeared to be a plaster over his ear? I concluded he must have an ear infection or injury and thought no more about it. But, as was later revealed to the accompaniment of much tut-tutting, he had a radio receiver plugged into his ear. It meant that he was able to keep in constant touch with his coach, Bob Woolmer. I think it was John Reid who first worked it out and he contacted the match referee, Talat Ali. Shock, horror – and I suppose rightly so. Woolmer argued that they were doing nothing wrong. He still believes its day will come, and realistically so do I. That departure from the laws, seen variously as an act of daring and cheating, was one controversy when I was present but not involved.

By far the biggest kerfuffle - and one I fear isn't over yet – was the one that came with those amazing allegations of match-fixing and corruption. It has left all of us, and that includes the umpires, looking over our shoulders. Well-known names have been mentioned, along with bookmakers and whistle-blowers. For the good of the game, I can only hope that the majority of the rumours lack substance.

So, you may ask (in fun I trust), have I ever been approached? Back in the winter of 2000 I received a call at my Instow home from one of Sir Paul Condon's anti-corruption unit. In some ways it was a routine part of the inquiries which were being carried out domestically and internationally. Had I ever heard a whisper of murky deeds? It was a confidential conversation and I've no intention of discussing it in print, but I gained the firm impression that Sir Paul was taking the allegations very seriously indeed, as later became apparent when his report was published. One of the inevitable questions, though wrapped up much more tactfully than this, was whether I'd ever been sounded out. No, I hadn't … yet there *had* been that single call to my hotel bedroom in India. I'd just arrived to umpire an India–Australia Test.

'Ah, is that Mr Shepherd, the England umpire?' It was an Asian accent.

'Who's that? Do I know you?'

No, he said, we'd never met, but he wanted to ask me about the match. What did I think of India's prospects? And then the direct question: Who did I believe was going to win? He was particularly effusive, saying how nice it was to have me in their country. The conversation was largely one-way and almost embarrassing in its pleasantries. I was polite enough to the stranger, who never revealed his identity to me. At last, after more generalities from him and questions about the likely outcome which prompted no real replies from me, he hung up. It was a thoroughly odd, even pointless, phone call. Maybe it was completely harmless. I thought no more about it until the allegations surfaced. The memory of his persistence and smarmy charms returned, and my suspicions only came in retrospect. At the time of the call, I wouldn't have been remotely aware of any wrongdoing.

Those covert phone calls seem to have been common, I'm sorry to say. It emerged that the Australian players Adam Gilchrist and Colin Miller were contacted for match information by an anonymous caller while the third Test with India was in progress this March. The pair and then coach John Buchanan were in their various hotel rooms in Chennai when they were phoned and asked for specific information about the state of the pitch and how they thought the match would go. Gilchrist said he was asked whether he felt the wicket would turn, to help Warne and Miller. The Australian Board's chief executive, Malcolm Speed, said the players had been given advice on how to deal with any 'inappropriate approaches'. He had no idea if the mysterious caller was a gambler, a bookie or just a fan, but the incidents had been reported promptly to the team manger. I'm left with the impression that those unsolicited phone calls may have had more sinister intent than the one I received, but I can't be sure ...

When it came to the first Test against Pakistan this May, I phoned Lord's in all innocence. I wanted to offer good luck to the umpires. Would the switchboard put me through to the Umpires' Room? It seemed to be a reasonable enough request. There was a delay at the other end of the line, then, 'Erm, I don't think we can do that, sir. Why do you wish to talk to them?'

'Just to give them my good wishes for the match.'

'Afraid we can't. Will you tell us who you are?'

'I'm David Shepherd, another umpire.'

After some additional screening, and, I felt, hesitation, my call was transferred. I've no idea whether it was monitored, but on reflection I do approve of this increased security. Mind you, they should have recognised the Devon vowels.

My visit from the man with the anti-corruption unit lasted about an hour. He went to pains to make me aware of what the various allegations entailed, and encouraged me to be extremely wary. One piece of advice he gave was for me to avoid incoming phone calls to my hotel room. As a result of that, I have asked hotel receptionists to monitor requests by outsiders who want to be put through to me. The exceptions are those calls from my family and friends or any official messages. Sad, isn't it, that cricket has come to that.

Sad, too, and bewildering to me, when I read what the ex-Essex bowler Don Topley alleged happened: an arrangement over results between his county and Lancashire in 1991. I know it caused some fidgeting as well as denials. People couldn't decide whether Topley was brave or imprudent. Here, for the first time, was the suggestion of misdemeanours on our own patch and it was too close to home to be ignored. It exercised the police and the ECB and there was bated breath in some quarters. In the end the ECB said the allegations were impossible to prove; the chairman of the disciplinary committee, Gerald Elias, announced the police hadn't found enough corroboration for Topley's claims.

That was how it was left. If there were any truth at all in the claims, I can only say how disturbed and horrified I'd be. Just before I broke into county cricket as a player, soccer bribery scandals were being exposed in this country. I remember how two Bristol Rovers players were banned from the game for life after a pathetic attempt to earn themselves a few quid on a fixed-odds scam. Professional football, well, yes, but *never* cricket, surely ...

Earlier this year I was standing in Bombay for India's first Test of the series with Australia. Maybe it was too much to hope that the Wankhede Stadium would be blissfully free of contention. Michael Slater was fielding at mid-wicket and jubilantly claimed a catch, low down, off Rahul Dravid. The batsman was less than convinced about the validity of the catch and stayed put. My colleague, Venkataraghavan, hesitated and called on the third umpire. The verdict was not out. It angered Slater, who took mighty offence that he wasn't believed. He complained bitterly to Venkat before directing his fury on Dravid. His behaviour earned him a reprimand from the match referee, Cammie Smith.

While my back was turned, as you might say, far more histrionic scenes were happening in Galle, during England's opening Test with Sri Lanka. I read the *Daily Telegraph* headline with understandable concern. After all, it isn't a paper renowned for sporting sensationalism: 'UMPIRES PLUMB NEW DEPTHS – WOEFUL MISTAKES IN TEST CONFUSION'. This was above a hard-hitting piece from Simon Hughes, who wrote about what he saw as 'an outbreak of hand and eye disease sweeping through the international umpires' panel'. He claimed that 'the men in white coats are becoming trigger-happy'. The ex-Middlesex bowler, who became an outspoken journalist and TV cricket pundit, was here giving my trade a desperately bad time of it. I wasn't so far from Sri Lanka at the time, but I wasn't at the match and certainly wouldn't comment on the ability of another umpire. That's an unwritten law – and a very good one, too. According to Hughes there were eight LBW decisions given against England, and the TV replays showed that all but one were wrong. Of course, that is a worrying statistic. In that same fiery article, he wrote: 'Looking back at the Galle match, it begs the question how two (supposedly) Test-class umpires make so many errors ... Umpires do not have the advantage of TV replays for LBWs yet, so getting these hairline decisions right requires exceptional eyesight, not to mention some luck. But some of the mistakes in Galle were unpardonable.' That attack, echoed, it has to be said, by other cricket writers, upset me. It's bad for the game, bad for umpires' morale.

The two in charge for that explosive Test were Peter Manuel, a senior executive with a Hong Kong bank in Colombo, and A.V. Jayaprakash. By the second Test they had given way to B.C. Cooray and the South African Rudi Koertzen. Some series are destined to be uncomfortable, and this was clearly one. Craig White was sledged; Graeme Hick not by any means a candidate in anyone's list of troublemakers, earned himself a suspended one-match ban. Someone who came back from the series and was asked about all those decisions that went against England said that what pleased him was the amount of self-restraint demonstrated by the batsmen concerned!

Not that the practice matches were any easier than the Tests, it appears. I'm inevitably thinking of England's fixture with a Colts' XI at Kurenegala. It wasn't, I'm told, in any way a popular commitment. The players had to be up very early and there was a long, tiring journey to the ground. Isn't it sad that we so often remember games for the wrong reason? In this case it was the collision between Darren Gough, the bowler, and Indika de Saram, the batsman. Saram, the non-striker, had gone for a single and Gough claimed he was intentionally impeded as he followed through for what he hoped might be a run-out. We all saw the pictures of the Yorkshire bowler pointing a belligerent finger at the umpire, T.M. Samarasinghe. It seemed to be backed up by some decidedly pointed remarks.

What followed was even more drastic. After a conversation with his captain, Nasser Hussain, Gough left the field. The natural conclusion, not just to the occupants of the press box, was that he'd been sent on his way to cool down. Nasser later rallied to Gough's aid: 'He'd been exemplary on and off the field during this tour and I wish all the players had his attitude ... to say I ordered him off is a total exaggeration.' I can appreciate the loyalty and psychology of an intelligent captain like Nasser. In his diary of the week's hairy events he added: 'If anyone thinks we should have fined him or slapped him on the wrist just four days before a crucial Test, then I feel they have no idea of man-management or how best to treat your leading fast bowler in the build-up to a huge match.'

In my search for balance in the argument, I feel I must quote the calm words of Scyld Berry, a respected, objective cricket writer, in the *Sunday Telegraph*: 'If Gough's behaviour were copied, it would certainly lead to anarchy on the cricket field.' He contended that England's failure to discipline the fast bowler cost his side the moral high ground. It led Berry – a West Country-based scribe, happiest of all essaying his optimistic leg-breaks in village cricket for Hinton Charterhouse – to wonder aloud whether even practice matches, like the one in Kurenegala, needed 'strong umpires, preferably neutral ones and even match referees'. Well, I'm not too sure about the practicalities of that in the case of a game lacking the authority of the ICC, but he makes a thoroughly worthwhile point.

Gough is a popular and undeniably wholehearted player. I've always got on well with him, exchanging light-hearted words. The unfavourable publicity he received from this incident no doubt upset him. He claimed vehemently that there was no suggestion at all of being sent-off (we're getting into the realms of soccer here!) and that he always intended to leave the field at the end of that over for treatment to his troublesome back. Yet it has to be mentioned that he isn't a complete stranger to controversy. Just recall that little dust-up with Rosham Mahanama in Australia the previous year. For someone I much admired as a chirpy and honest quickie, the image of that finger-wagging troubled me. It was too easy to make comparisons, at least pictorially, with Mike Gatting's infamous differences of opinion with the umpire in Faisalabad.

As a former player myself, my heart leads me to look for excuses. The combination of frustrations, the remorseless heat and a nagging back were surely bad for the liver, but ...

Darren is someone I've always admired for his unbridled enthusiasm. He's a jovial chap, uplifting, bubbly by nature, easy to get on with. This little snatch of dialogue is typical.

'Back from your holiday then, Goughie?'

'Had to, didn't I? Needed to be back for the match.' Then the pause, the open Yorkie grin, and the postscript: 'Leeds United's match.'

He's a team man. Before the first Test with Pakistan in 2001 he was liberal in his praise for Andrew Caddick, who has often been his new-ball partner. It was Gough's fiftieth Test and he'd just been handed Vodafone's Player of the Year award. He spoke of the affinity that the two had built up, fast bowlers of different types yet complementing each other: 'Caddy is tall, gets bounce and swings the ball away. Because I'm short it's harder for me in some ways. I try to pitch the ball up, skid it on the batsmen and surprise them with pace.' He went on to say they were also different in character, implying he was more noisy and extrovert, I assume.

I've seen plenty of evidence of how successful they can be as foils for each other. I admire their varying qualities and I've a suspicion that Gough could score more runs than he does. There have been occasions when he has batted most attractively and not seemed too far short of being considered a genuine all-rounder. As for his bowling, the statistics should be truly impressive by the time he retires. I watched the Sunday evening highlights of the Lord's Test against Pakistan when Alec Stewart's catch down the leg side gave Gough his 200th wicket at that exalted level. I shall forever retain the image of sheer joy on his face: it was as much schoolboy as England fast bowler. Lovely to see. The ovation he earned emphasised his popularity and the affection in which he is held, not just in Yorkshire. Outstanding sporting achievement and that kind of heartfelt popularity don't always go together.

It's time for me to attempt to take a detached view of the qualities that an umpire, county or Test, needs in the complicated, over-excitable modern game. Whenever I'm asked how I am, perhaps when I'm taking my dog for a walk or arriving for duty at a famous Test ground, I unfailingly answer: 'Oh, fair to middling – umpires are always fair, you know, or up and down like the pound.'

Fairness really is the operative word. You must have a feel and affection for the game. As I've said, it can be a positive advantage, giving you added insights, if you've played the game at championship level. Arthur Milton once said, 'I could see early on why Shep would make a good umpire. He was always watching the game intently, working it all out. And he was even-tempered.' I value warm compliments like that, especially when they come from someone with such an analytical mind as Arthur's. Yes, for the most part I am blessed with an equable personality; I don't easily get roused. Vic Marks kindly says one of my strengths is in defusing explosive moments. On one occasion, though, during a Test at Lord's when I was staying in the hotel across the road, an irksome spectator wouldn't let go. At a time when I wanted only to relax, he kept plying me with provocative questions. There was a smugness in his voice as he hinted at criticism of the umpires. I stood so much and then let him have it. It was about the only time I became embroiled in an argument of that sort. In the end I counted up to ten and walked away.

Confession time continues. I was playing in a one-day match in Bristol between Gloucestershire and Leicestershire. We had reached slog-time and I carted Ken Higgs to mid-wicket for six. This didn't please him at all. The next ball from him seemed to be coming straight for my head and with some difficulty I got my bat handle on it and sent it down to fine-leg for a single. I trotted down to his end, fully expecting him to apologise. All Ken gave me was a glare. That disappointed me and I gave him a few choice words, but it was soon forgotten and we got on well after that. In that same match, I remember, I overheard one or two racial taunts directed at our Pakistani pair, Zaheer and Sadiq. I imagine that was upsetting to them; we told them to ignore what had been said, but it can't have been easy.

Swearing is pretty commonplace in professional cricket. It's the industrial language of the game. I don't know what had bothered me or whether I'd got out of bed the wrong side one particular day. John Emburey, capable of some pretty colourful language himself, this time heard me swearing under my breath. Between deliveries he gave me a sly, amused look and said, 'Do you know, Shep, that's the first time I've ever heard that from you.' I like to think I can put my moderation of language down to my non-conformist roots in Instow.

How I hate the cheats, and the attitudes of some well-known cricketers. In 1998 I gave an interview to the *Asian Age* in which I said: 'I have been a first-class umpire for the past seventeen years and I notice a tremendous change in the attitude of the players. They are quite aggressive and with so much money coming into the game winning and losing makes a lot of difference to the competing teams. Earlier, the players used to help the umpires in making the decisions but now it is not the case.' I see no reason to change a word.

We've always had an element of gamesmanship. Bristol's own W.G. was a master-craftsman in that black art; some of his contemporaries found it difficult to differentiate between his gamesmanship and cheating. A number of more recent practices, often at international level, leave no such confusion in the mind: they are unmitigated cheating. If the practitioners can get away with murder, by cunning and subterfuge, they'll do so.

Let me tell you of two incidents in which I was involved. I hadn't been in the Gloucestershire team for too long and my eyes were bright with innocence. We were playing against Hampshire, and Mike Bissex was bowling to Peter Sainsbury. Milton was at slip and I was at gully. Sainsbury nicked and Arthur, diving forward, caught the ball. The batsman didn't move; there was no appeal.

'I caught it, Peter,' said Milton.

'I didn't think you did, Art.'

Arthur threw the ball back to Bissex and the over continued. As we came off the field at the close, I asked about the catch.

'Oh, I caught it all right.'

'But why didn't you ask the umpire?'

'It only creates bad feeling, Shep. We have to play them again later in the season.'

Then there was the occasion when I didn't walk. We were playing Derbyshire at Ilkeston and Bob Taylor was keeping wicket. It was late in the day and it was my job to make sure I wasn't out. A short ball glanced off my glove to Bob but no-one appealed. I assumed it hadn't carried. At the end of the over I walked up to Jim Foat at the other end. 'Funny thing that, Shep. It carried all right and yet no-one appealed.'

I turned to the wicket-keeper: 'Aren't you claiming them this season, Bob?'

He seemed surprised by my remark. Gully had thought I got a touch but Bob didn't. There was no question of a hysterical appeal by a cluster of fielders. What a change from today. Now they're all trying it on. The chorus of appeals makes my head hurt.

Counting up to Six

There's a disturbing belief among many umpires that before long their duties will be confined to counting up to six. In other words they will be employed as mathematicians and not much more; all other responsibilities having been taken from them. They will be cosmetic arbiters in white coats. Or, to interpret it more drastically, for all the decisions they have to make, they may as well stay at home.

During the series with Sri Lanka in 2000/01, especially in the first two Tests, words like 'anarchy' were being bandied about. Frankly, it didn't seem to me that these words were inappropriate. I'm no coward when it comes to taking on the miscreants, but I was grateful that I wasn't involved. I'd have hated the pervasive mood of mutual suspicion and the simmering anger. Things, mercifully, had calmed down when they got to the last Test, at Colombo. The umpires were then South Africa's Dave Orchard and the youthful Asoka de Silva. I must say I worried about the Sri Lankan, fully conscious as he was of what had gone before, but he had an outstanding match. Atherton raised this interesting and valid point in one of his articles. 'He is young and has Test and first-class cricket experience as a player. Does that tell the International Cricket Council anything?'

At the risk of sounding pompous, I feel I must mention something which, within the sporting context, is these days the most demeaned of all qualities – *respect*. I'm talking of respect for the game of cricket. What has happened to it? Has it been crudely discarded as the megabuck takes over? No doubt I'll be accused of having a sentimental and unrealistic view of sport, too influenced by the joys Brother Bill and I shared as village cricketers. I have no guilt on that score. My contention has always been that the players are merely custodians of the game, doing their best to ensure that it survives in the proper spirit for future generations. Am I being too idealistic? It certainly looks like that when I read or experience at first hand what is happening in international matches. The sledging and the cheating have reached wholly unacceptable levels. Players set out to con the umpires. In some top matches the two teams appear almost to despise each other. It shows in their eyes. I heard things said which, if overheard in the street, would be the subject of litigation.

As umpires, we are good and bad. Everyone saw the embarrassing howlers in Sri Lanka. Unfortunately, we are also the convenient scapegoats when controversy rears its unedifying head. Players too easily point in our direction when they know in their hearts they should have walked. *Walked*, did I say? When did we last see a fair-minded batsman do that? He's instructed not to. 'There's too much at stake – leave it to the umpire . . . It's his problem.' And, my God, what a problem it can be!

Steady, Shepherd, steady. There must surely be the exception, shining like a beacon of old-fashioned values. Let me think now. Yes, indeed: Lancashire against Durham early in 2001 in the Benson & Hedges Cup. Lancashire were batting second and had already lost their captain, John Crawley, taken in the slips. Then Mike Atherton nicked one off Neil Killeen. The keeper parried the ball which ended in the hands of Martin Love, the Queenslander. I was at square-leg and couldn't see for sure what had happened. Nor could Roy Palmer, the other umpire. Love held up the ball triumphantly. Atherton, doggedly competitive by nature, didn't really know where the edged shot had gone. He saw Love's gesture of success and walked immediately. There wasn't even an appeal, as far as I recall. It was good to see. Good for the game.

In those Sri Lanka–England Tests there was plenty of good, hard cricket and England did magnificently to come back from 1–0 down to win the series. But I'll also remember the series for the blatant acts of cheating by both sides – by batsmen and fielders. Fielders were accused of 'catching' batsmen on the half-volley and there was so much concentrated appealing. I see no difference between this and a batsman standing his ground when he knows he has hit the ball and been caught fairly. All these acts are cheating of the worst kind and put a fearful amount of pressure on umpires.

The last person I want to sound like is one of those boring oldies who continually make comparisons with what happened in their day, and can find little to applaud about the present game. That is blinkered nonsense. Yet I can't avoid the conclusion that when I started cricket was played competitively, but in good spirit and *honestly*. If a batsman knew he was out, he walked without waiting for a decision – and no fielder would consider claiming a dubious catch. Players only appealed if there was a genuine chance the batsman was out. Word soon went round on the grapevine if anyone cheated, but it was very rare, I assure you. Now, sadly, most players are at it, especially in Tests. Often they don't consider they are cheating, presenting their behaviour as part of the game's ritual. They simply leave all decisions to the umpires. There's no legal onus on the batsman spontaneously to shrug and set off for the pavilion without looking up. That kind of moral duty, it could be argued, went out with the public-school house matches. Yet I'm not so sure it's a complete anachronism. We walked at Instow. Many on village greens around the country still do. Well, perhaps on reflection, not so many. From what I hear – and at times see, as I pull in my car to look over the hedge and watch a few random overs on a day off – even the pattern here of confidence tricks and dissent is being influenced by what happens on the television screens. If Test players can get away with it, why not the village-green sloggers.

As a breed, umpires can feel solitary and vulnerable. Most of us privately resent criticism levelled at us, especially when we consider it is misguided. Several years ago, Dave Houghton, who was then the coach to the Zimbabwean team, was particularly emotive in his language at our expense. Referring to a Test match in Colombo, he said his players felt as if they'd been 'raped' by the umpires. I remember the match, handled by a Pakistani umpire and one from the host country. Alistair Campbell, the Zimbabwe captain, claimed later that he was close to leading his players off the field on the final day. However angered a captain might be, that kind of extreme behaviour could never be justified. What was it we said earlier about anarchy?

England's recent series in Sri Lanka led to more debate about umpiring and the depressing direction the game seemed to be heading than ever before. The ICC sprang into action – or at least serious discussion. High-level meetings were called. There was blanket criticism of some players' conduct and, of course, umpiring standards. Everyone agreed that new guidelines, new warnings and new penalties were urgently required. Society had changed – and so had sport. The cravats and Harlequin caps had long gone. All players were now paid, the top players better than ever before, even if modestly by Premiership soccer standards. Considerable sums of money were being invested in the Tests and one-day internationals. Corporate hospitality had taken over from the boundary deckchairs. Cricket had been revolutionised – but that didn't for a moment excuse some of the things that were going on.

On my long plane journeys around the world I'm apt to thumb through my latest edition of *Wisden*. The laws have often been revised and a new code was introduced in 2000, to supersede that of eight years earlier. As I scanned the relevant pages, I dallied on 'The Preamble'.

Cricket is a game that owes much of its unique appeal to the fact that it should be played not only within its Laws, but also within the Spirit of the Game. Any action which is seen to abuse this spirit causes injury to the game itself. The major responsibility for ensuring the spirit of fair play rests with the captains.

Under the subheading 'Players' Conduct' is the following:

> In the event of a player failing to comply with instructions by an umpire, or criticising by word or action the decisions of an umpire, or showing dissent, or generally behaving in a manner which might bring the game into disrepute, the umpire concerned shall in the first place report the matter to the other umpire and to the player's captain, and instruct the latter to take action.

Mere words, you might say. Such well-intentioned sentiments apparently are not enough. That is why there have been mounting proposals for the banning of those players who blatantly contravene the laws. Yellow and red cards have already been tried out in South Africa. I can imagine that some of our cricket traditionalists will cringe at such a soccer-orientated notion. Nor do I really like the idea. At the same time, I don't rule out the prospect of such a drastic and theatrical penalty.

As a former player, one is well aware of the fearful pressures that bedevil the game nowadays. I think that in passing I should make one point for fairness. We should never lose sight of the need for true balance. Cricket is a game essentially for the *players*. The umpire certainly has his vital role, but he is subordinate to the player.

As I write these words, the game's international administrators, the ICC, are wrestling over the best, most effective way to curb the wrong-doers and bring back some sense of morality. Umpiring as a subject has been consistently high on the agenda. We all accept that in some cases standards have been unsatisfactory. The slow-motion playbacks have emphasised, sometimes brutally, the flaws. So how could matters improve? The setting up of an elite panel of international umpires has found plenty of support. It cuts across the principle of automatic native representation, which has been seen as a block to the progress of some good, young, emerging world-class umpires. There has been, too, the advocacy of two neutral umpires. Selfishly, I see that as a sad end to any Test matches for me in England.

I now return to what I hinted at when I began this chapter of serious reflection. Just how much is a Test umpire to be stripped of his personal judgements and initiative? Is he to become almost incidental to the electronic aids that are now such a factor in the big games? TV technology is here to stay. I accept that and, as I wrote earlier, my initial suspicions have receded. Despite my natural reservations about some aspects of the sophisticated electronic aids, I'm no Luddite and I go along with them. We must strive after all to get everything right. There's an unchallengeable logic to their use and in recent years there has been a less than satisfactory halfway-house attitude in their operation. Some of the TV replays, not used by the umpires, have exposed our occasional frailties and led to rather too much tut-tutting in the commentary boxes. That artificially drawn line down the track has told the broadcaster the ball was going marginally down the leg side when we've given LBWs. What about the bat–pad catch, hardest decision of all, which demands a split-second verdict? Did the ball carry? Was it a bump-ball? So many questions.

I make a few mistakes – not many, I like to contend – but mostly the umpires, with their uncluttered, old-fashioned methods, get things right. This is because, I feel, we are well served by our instincts and intuition. We know the technicalities and the ball's devious tricks. Cricket, for heaven's sake, is a game for people to play – and for people in white coats to administer during the course of the fixture. Mistakes, when they occur, have an uncanny habit of evening themselves out.

It's reasonable enough to retain a measure of healthy cynicism over the visual aids. I would like to quote Mark Nicholas here. He was a county cricketer who went on to become a capable journalist and TV presenter. He knows well enough the advantages that can come from the zooming lens, but this is what he had to say in his *Daily Telegraph* column:

People say why not use television's technology for more decision-making? Because the technology is flawed, that's why. After one claimed catch, low at silly point, Tony Greig and Ian Botham viewed 15 or more replays before Greig went out to the middle during the lunch break and re-enacted the moment. At the end of all that, they still didn't agree. So how will a third umpire make a decision?

Television is an entertainment vehicle, it is not set up as an umpiring aid. Cameras are often in an unsatisfactory position from which to make a decision. They are not guaranteed to be perfectly focused and the cameraman cannot guarantee capturing the moment. The magnifying glass which homes in on most dubiously claimed catches is so blurred as to all but bring a shadow to the picture and therefore confuse the issue further. Most relevantly of all, television is a two-dimensional image of a three-dimensional occurrence. It has no chance of convincing anyone all of the time.

Consequently, on most occasions television is called for, the third umpire will have to say 'not out', as happened with Michael Atherton's catch at slip on the first day of the Kandy Test. And the corollary of that is the players, knowing the loopholes, will claim everything and stand for everything. If television is inconclusive, they will get away with it.

The umpire is still under relentless scrutiny from Big Brother. From my point of view, that giant screen is the real killer. I hate it, recording as it does in that vast, mechanical, impersonal manner every twitch of a player's muscle, every blink of an umpire's eyelids. Then comes the moment of uncertainty. The game stops and all the spectators look in one direction. They simply want to know, in remorseless close-up, what happened. The umpire also looks and on occasion realises that the magnified visual facts are at variance with his instant impression. Just think what this does to his confidence. I don't for a moment blame the spectator for enjoying the drama. He pays a good deal of admission money these days and he reckons he deserves the latest technical aids. Nor do I for a moment blame the TV companies for repeatedly extending their range of visual interpretations. Never before has the cricketing public been better educated in the whims and subtleties of this complex game.

Theoretically, anything that assists the umpires to get everything right must be good for cricket. I've found myself very much involved in this ever-evolving game. Back in 1992–93 I went on the pilot scheme for a neutral umpire – South Africa against India – and before long it was to be adopted. We were moving in the right direction, although, as things turned out, we were still some way from the perfect solution.

'Throwing' has been a recurrent problem within cricket. The history of the game has never been short of rumours that specific bowlers are bending the laws. We've even heard periodic whispers about the great Courtney Walsh, whose achievement of gaining 500 Test wickets in March 2001 ensured his rightful place in the record books. As far as I know, no-one has ever called him. Are we perhaps a little too hasty in casting doubt every time someone comes along who seems to bowl quicker or turn the ball more than anyone else? While Courtney was never called for throwing, there are plenty of sorry cases – tales of bowlers who have been drummed out of the game or forced, with dire results, to change their actions. In the late fifties and early sixties, when I so avidly read every cricket report I could get my hands on (usually when I was delivering them), I remember that a number of Australian quickies were thought to 'throw'. The accusation carried quite a stigma in those days and I usually felt concerned for the players involved. As they used to drag the back foot, some appeared to throw the ball off only eighteen yards or so. Ian Meckiff and Gordon Rourke were two examples.

An English bowler forced to adjust his action was Surrey's Tony Lock. He never seemed the same afterwards: I remember so well when, with his original action, he'd sent the stumps flying out of the ground. Nearer to my West Country home, Somerset had a slow bowler, Eric Bryant, from Weston-super-Mare, who tried to model himself on Lock. He had one horrendous day against my old county at Bath in 1960 and was no-balled for 'chucking' four times in an over by Hugo Yarnold. It was too much for him; he walked out of county cricket for good.

I have definite views about throwing. It has always struck me as terribly difficult to decide with the naked eye whether a bowler throws the ball. Therefore, I argue that it's virtually impossible to call a bowler from square-leg.

A few years ago, at a meeting of the International Umpires' Conference it was suggested that the way to get rid of chuckers at international level was for umpires to call them more often. I don't agree with that. I've never directly reported any player for throwing. I'm convinced that the slow-motion cameras are the best and fairest way to sort things out and come to the right judgement. I don't consider any bowler should attain such a high level in the game if he supposedly has a suspect action. There's TV coverage of all international matches these days and if an umpire is concerned about a bowler's action, then it should be mentioned in his report to the referee. Film of the bowler is forwarded to the International Throwing Committee. It is then up to the committee to adjudicate on the legality of the action.

As things stand at the moment, if an umpire calls a bowler, in effect removing him from international cricket, the umpire can find himself out of the game. This happened to one international-panel umpire, Darrell Hair. He no-balled Sri Lanka's spinning wizard Muttiah Muralitharan and as a result didn't stand in subsequent matches involving that country. Muralitharan poses a problem for any umpire. He is different, but I've never formed the impression that he throws the ball or has an illegal action. I'm well aware that others take a contrary view. In addition, Darrell called Grant Flower, of Zimbabwe, in Bulawayo. The consequence of that was for him to be taken out of matches involving Zimbabwe, too, even though he'd been pencilled in to umpire them in the ICC knockout competition in Nairobi in 2000.

This bothers me. Darrell's opportunities for umpiring on the international circuit have been severely restricted – and his earning capacity reduced. To me, he's a strong, courageous and very good international umpire.

I have tried to convey the monumental problems that at times beset the umpires in a job that must hover uneasily between the electronic and the human. Clearly some countries are better equipped than others in the delicate process of producing first-class umpires. England (and, of course, Wales) has a considerable advantage over some of the others. Its frenetically busy summer programme, incorporating the County Championship and all the one-day matches, offers daily practice at a high level. I hope I won't be accused of letting my patriotism get the better of me when I contend that the standard is reassuringly high. Not all the pitches inspire confidence. There may be uneven bounce for the batsman: there are the greentops and the shirt-fronts, as we call the grassy tracks where the ball seams around and there are those that offer nothing to the bowlers. The sheer variety offers a comprehensive test also for the umpire. In the course of the summer, I stand with a range of partners. It isn't only the reliable, experienced ones who deserve respect. I could nominate three or four outstanding prospects and by the time I have retired, or maybe before, I expect them to be regular members of the international panel on merit.

Clearing the Air

I am blessed with an undeviating optimistic nature. That's why I honestly believe that the acts of villainy that have besmirched the game of cricket increasingly over recent years are being curbed. Going back to what happened in the first two Tests in Sri Lanka – and I could just as easily cite a few other series when the teeth were bared – I think that in an odd way they served a purpose. They caused the international ruling body to take a strong grip on itself. The meetings that followed were positive and devoid of much of the cosmetic good intentions that meant little. In other words the game needed purifying – and I like to think the air is now clearer.

At various stages in this book I have listed aspects of the game that bother me. Let me pluck one at random. You must have seen the way, when a batsman prods the ball gently to mid-off, that the fielder will hurl it back to the wicket-keeper with intimidating venom. Often the keeper will have positioned himself almost directly behind the batsman. The ploy is deliberate and dangerous: it's intended to frighten the man at the crease. I have come across this in county as well as international cricket – and I can find no excuse at all for it.

'I'm only practising my throw, Shep,' a fielder has said to me after noticing my reprimanding glare in his direction.

I disapprove of that tendency towards aggression, just as I did on the occasion when Shane Warne gave two barrels to Andrew Hudson in Johannesburg in 1994. I'm a huge admirer of Warne, the Aussie who has brilliantly repopularised the virtually discarded art of leg-break bowling. I know, too, that he was a much-liked occupant of that minuscule Hampshire dressing room at Southampton in 2000. Yet I can't help wondering how wise it was for the county to invest so much money in his services for one less than successful season. To what extent did Hampshire gain? There's a certain irony that a county which enterprisingly went for Warne and Alan Mullally, neither of whom came cheap, has now been facing worrying financial problems over its new ground.

I have never held passionately strong opinions over the signing of overseas players. On a personal level, I valued the enormous benefits Gloucestershire derived from the signing of Procter, Zaheer and Sadiq. Many others equally brought an added dimension to county cricket: they increased the crowds and gave the ordinary fan the great privilege of seeing famous international stars around the regions. At the same time, I'm aware that some of the overseas players, signed in a hurry as perhaps third or fourth choices, haven't always been worth their place. Worse, they have kept out a promising young local cricketer.

As I was putting these thoughts down on paper, I read that Jimmy Adams, deposed skipper of the West Indies, was likely to be joining Brian Lara for the Maidstone-based team Lashings, which plays in the East Kent League. With a nice turn of phrase, the chairman apparently said that the team was turning itself into the Harlem Globetrotters of cricket. I see this as a harmless one-off exercise in sporting resourcefulness. Not quite so, alas, in the case of a number of clubs around the country who have found local sponsors to finance a summer's cricket for a gifted overseas player. That seems to be a direct snub to some of the bright prospects on the fringes of first-team selection. No wonder too many of them decide it's more rewarding for them to stick to football.

Jimmy Adams is an intelligent West Indian cricketer I rate highly, though his record as the team's captain was painfully undistinguished.

In my mind he never fully recovered from the effects of an injury against Somerset at Taunton in 1995. He ducked into the first ball he received from the towering Dutchman André van Troost. It fractured his cheekbone and put an abrupt end to his tour.

Back to some issues that trouble me. The other day I walked into my local bank in Bideford. I knew the young man behind the counter as a parks footballer.

'How's it going?' I asked.

He shook his head. 'We've had to miss three matches. Not enough refs to go round.'

He was also saying, by implication, that local referees weren't prepared to give up their Saturdays just to be abused and berated. I hear exactly the same from a few of the local cricket clubs The umpires are called everything under the sun. There was one occasion in Barnstaple when a club match had to be abandoned because of the abuse one player was hurling at another. It makes me shudder to think of it. I assure you it's a world away from the cricket scene in which Bill and I grew up. I return to an earlier point: club players see on television the loutish behaviour of some famous cricketers and they feed their egos by copying. No-one suffers more than the umpire. But why should he stand for it? Anarchy on a village green isn't entirely unknown, just ask some of the secretaries of cricket associations. Dissent and even physical threats are reported. Fortunately, such incidents are still rare; the majority of the games being played in town, village and hamlet every weekend retain the eccentric skills and mutual pleasures that represent the best of sportsmanship.

I daresay it's a weakness of mine that I've always seen cricket through idealistic eyes, as a good influence on society. It's something for the spectators as much as the players to enjoy. It's muscle and heart and brain. It's sixes into the cowshed and middle stumps cartwheeling halfway to the boundary. It's cunning rural rivalry and exchanges that never veer far from good humour. And then it's a shared pint. I have seen evidence in our deprived inner-cities of the good effect cricket can bring. Within the confidences of the barside after the close of play, I have heard young players admit that cricket gave them a purpose in life and kept them out of trouble. What a wonderful recommendation for the game.

That is why I remain buoyant and optimistic about the future of this needlessly stained game: the good and the heartwarming continue to surface. When Curtly Ambrose played his last Test match in this country, he put his big arms on my shoulders and said, 'It's been a pleasure having you as umpire, Shep.' David Boon said the same thing when he left Durham and returned home to Tasmania. There have been plenty of kindly, unsolicited compliments. I mention them not to bask publicly in praise from top players but to emphasise the cordial side of cricket.

I've enjoyed being around some of the great characters, listening to them, watching their antics, and occasionally giving them out. Merv Hughes, massive of heart, was Australia's number-one extrovert. Allan Lamb is someone I'd put in the same category. He had a habit of nicking my pen and paper out of my pocket as he walked past me at the end of an over and his South African voice was usually bubbling away. Essex's Ray East was renowned for the sense of comedy he brought to the game. So, in a different way, was Derek Randall; there was invariably something happening when Arkle was at the crease or fielding.

Cricket stories have a timeless appeal. Many have become absorbed into dressing-room folklore. We can't be sure in some cases how much the facts have been embroidered over the years but no-one is too worried ... especially when the tale is as good as the classic about the Essex team travelling to play Glamorgan. The version I heard was that the ruse was dreamed up by those two notorious jokers Ray East (who else?) and David Acfield, a very good off-spinner and an even better fencer, apparently, as his Olympic credentials bear out. They'd got as far as the Severn Bridge when one of them casually asked a few of their team-mates in the car whether they had their passports with them. The conversation was intended for the ears of the popular Barbadian Keith Boyce. He sat up, stirring from his semi-slumbers.

'What do you guys mean? You don't need a passport for Wales, do you?'

'Course you do, Boycey. Don't say you've forgotten it.'

By now he was visibly concerned. The driver pulled on to the hard shoulder. 'Only one thing for it, Keith. We can't go all the way back to Essex. But these officials on the bridge are pretty strict and don't make exceptions. You'll have to be smuggled through – in the boot!'

Boyce squeezed into the boot – and that was how he arrived in Wales for the first time.

An autobiography doesn't have to be exclusively modest, I am told. Some housewives, doing their knitting as they idly watch the cricket on the box, say they find me a bit of a character. That, I assume, is because of my generous waistline, my physical exertions at certain 'mathematical moments' of the day, and rosy cheeks that I hope convey my enjoyment of the match. The cricket writer Mike Carey once came to Bristol to cover a game in which I was playing. I was fielding in the deep when the batsman cracked a high ball in my direction. 'He seemed to be aiming for the distant Post Office Tower, a well-known local landmark,' wrote Carey in his newspaper, and added that it was 'caught by David Shepherd, another local landmark'.

Being a bit of a celebrity, in that I'm always popping up on television in my white coat or finding my picture in the paper, is not something that comes easily to me. I sometimes wish I could relish the publicity in the same way as Dickie Bird always has. Who'd ever imagine me standing with John Major on the pavilion balcony? Dickie could carry that off and treasure the moment. I'd be altogether too shy.

It was at the Oval, after the close of play on one occasion, that I was approached by Canon Derek Carpenter. 'Ah, David, can I have a word? We're holding a special service at my church to commemorate the hundred and fiftieth anniversary of W.G. Grace's birth. Would love it if you'd give one of the readings.'

'Haven't you got the wrong Shep?' I asked weakly. 'Don't you mean the bishop?'

He shook his head. The service was held at St George's Parish Church, Beckenham. Jim Swanton gave the address. The other readings were by Lord MacLaurin and Roger Knight, the secretary of MCC. It was an honour to be asked and I was slightly overawed. I practised my piece and trust it was enhanced by a few warm Devon vowels. Tony Brown, my old captain, once described me as 'pleasantly rustic, a club cricketer who made himself into a county player'. I'll happily settle for that.

Just as Ian Botham settled for the description of him as Gorilla or Beefy. Here was a mighty talent, a match-winner with bat or ball, and a magnificent fielder. Mike Brearley was probably the best captain I came across, and 'Both' responded particularly well to him. A lot of things, not by any means all complimentary, have been said about the great Somerset all-rounder. I played against him for several years at county level and then went on to umpire him. I honestly felt there was mutual respect. He had been too boisterous, too high profile for some of the more staid occupants of the committee room in Taunton. They cringed at the headlines he continually attracted. They resented the unceasing attentions of the tabloids, competing for the latest crumb of scandal about him. There were the pot-smoking allegations and his subsequent confession in the *Mail on Sunday*. Some of us gained the impression that was the result of a bit of journalistic and legal horse-trading.

'Both' broke the rules. He got into a few scrapes off the field. There was the match at Taunton when, seemingly out of form, he was immediately bowled and trudged back towards the pavilion. The crowd was strangely quiet and then someone bellowed a highly un-complimentary comment at the disconsolate England batsman. Botham stopped in his tracks and then marched belligerently towards the offending supporter, who turned out to be a vice-president of the county club. Fielders, spectators and team-mates on the players' balcony held their breaths. Fortunately, only words were exchanged. Somerset CCC acted quickly, taking Botham's part and banning the critical onlooker.

For all his excesses, he was rightly admired by many. He beat the Somerset all-rounder Arthur Wellard's record for the number of sixes in a season. Just like his bosom pal Viv Richards he regularly dispatched the ball out of the ground and into the car park or the River Tone. Then, even when the county pitch was at its most benign to batsmen, he managed to produce remarkable swing bowling. At times he wanted to bowl too fast, or so the coaches said. That fine craftsman Tom Cartwright probably had more influence on his bowling than anyone and said that he found Ian an eager and willing pupil when he first arrived from Lord's, claiming no-one took him seriously as a bowler. 'Let's change that,' Cartwright told him.

When Richards and Garner left Somerset, Botham left too, coming out in sympathy. He was enraged at the county's decision. Those closer to the club than I am assure me there were two sides to the argument and that factions had been created in the dressing room. I know only what I read. That crisis meeting in the cattle sheds of the Bath and West Showground, near Shepton Mallet, appeared to threaten the future of the club itself. The vote went with the establishment, and despite the clumsy manner in which the great West Indians left everyone in Somerset sighed with relief when the county was able to get on with its cricket again. But it took a long time for the lacerations to heal. I am so glad that all three eventually returned to the Taunton ground and that, for Ian, a new stand was named after him. They were all great players and I was privileged to see them at close hand, often at their best.

I certainly didn't know what to expect when it came to my first Test, at Old Trafford. Ian had had his dust-up with Alan Whitehead in the previous Test. What would his relationship be like with me, the novice Test umpire? He came to my end to bowl the opening over of the match and I wondered what, if anything, he was going to say. You never quite knew . . .

He peeled off his sweater and handed it to me. 'Hello, Shep, nice to see you, good luck mate.' He couldn't have been a more calming influence.

Botham and Procter used to compete in single-wicket competitions at Bristol. Often, for these benefit occasions, there were more spectators than for county matches. There'd be the same spinner, to bowl the other end from themselves, the same wicket-keeper and fielders. A stipulated number of runs would be deducted if the batsman was dismissed. As far as I recall, Procter usually won, but they were always keenly contested. Botham was, above all, a competitor.

What monumental power he had in his batting. I was once umpiring a Sunday League game, Somerset against Derbyshire at Taunton. 'Both' was batting with Viv Richards and you couldn't have asked for a more potent duo than that. They were flaying the Derby attack, and Roger Finney, bowling from my end, was being absolutely hammered: they were charging him, smiting fours and sixes. When these two great batsmen were at the wicket together there frequently developed a fearsome rivalry. Fearsome, that was, for the umpire. They are both straight hitters of awesome strength. I can assure you that it was really dangerous that Sunday afternoon alongside the River Tone. I thought of calling for a helmet!

Nowadays we meet from time to time, when Both is working for Sky TV. He has mellowed, like we all have. I think back to all the charity work, especially those arduous walks from one end of the country to the other, he has done. There has been a great deal of hospital visiting by him, much of it unknown to the public. I have considerable admiration for him. As for his playing career, the high point for me was the extraordinary match at Headingley against the Aussies. England were down and virtually out and the fight-back which he engineered along with Bob Willis was, in my opinion, one of the greatest in the history of the game. It still excites me when I see it, yet again, among the nostalgic clips on TV.

On a more modest scale, within the County Championship, I will never forget a specific exceptional performance involving another all-rounder. Phillip DeFreitas had one of those magic matches when everything came off: he could do nothing wrong and I couldn't hide my enthusiasm. That brings me to the question I'm sometimes asked: am I ever sounded out about my opinion of a player by the Test selectors? After all, the umpire is in a good position to make a considered assessment. He sees many matches in the course of a season from close at hand. He's only twenty-two yards away; he can see the flaws or the strengths, can privately make comparisons and form a shrewd judgement about potential. DeFreitas had excelled in a style that made a genuine impact on me. At the end of the season I was surprised to receive a phone call from Mike Gatting, who was then England's captain. 'Seen anyone who looks a bit special, Shep?' I told him how well DeFreitas had played and, encouraged for a second recommendation, I pondered what I'd seen that season and plumped for James Whitaker. The pair were both named in the Test party for Australia that winter. I've no idea whether my words to Gatt had any effect but shall I say I was pleased to see them named in the squad.

David Graveney is, of course, well known to me. Didn't we set up an eighth-wicket record stand in the Gillette Cup once upon a time? Grav, in his elevated days as chairman of the Test selectors, would occasionally ask me: 'Seen anyone lately, Shep?' Craig White was one of those I mentioned to him. When I saw White towards the end of the 1999 season, I teased him by saying, 'Get your bags packed, Craig. You'll be going to South Africa.' He wasn't selected, but he still ended up there, brought in as an injury-replacement from Australia where he'd gone to play some grade cricket.

More recently, after the first Test against the West Indies in 2000 when England were badly beaten, Mike Atherton turned to me in a county match and asked me if I had 'any ideas'. It may just have been a wry reflection on the way the Test had gone; perhaps it was no more than a conversational snippet between overs. But I didn't hesitate in my reply.

'I don't consider Ramps is an opener, Mike. Do you know who I'd like to see there?'

'Go on, tell me.'

'The left-hander they've got at Somerset . . . Marcus Trescothick.'

Based on what happened later, against Pakistan and Sri Lanka, Atherton must have approved of my evaluation of a player who'd run into some technical difficulties with his batting at Taunton and hadn't, during one period not so long ago, even been sure of a place in the county side.

On the Wagon

Some of my mates in the game have noted with alarm over the last season or two that I don't take a drink with the same alacrity at the close of play. 'What's happening to Shep – has he lost his thirst?' they may have asked each other. I'd hate anyone to come to the conclusion that I'm any less convivial or that I'm getting old and staid before my time. So I think that an explanation is in order. I have to put my comparative abstinence down to diabetes.

At the start of the 2000 domestic season I went for my normal medical. I was feeling pretty fit and had lost a little weight, so I was shocked when the medic gave me one of those meaningful looks and said, 'Sugar, I'm afraid.' It was the last thing I'd expected and it worried me. My mother had suffered slightly from diabetes and in her case it had affected her eyes. I argued that my eyes were all-important to me. The doctor put me on pills and told me how necessary it was to watch my diet. He systematically went through the foods and drinks I should avoid. To my horror, beer was high on the list.

'I've always like a pint, Doc. What would you suggest in its place?'

He must have detected the hint of panic in my voice. There followed a bizarre conversation.

'Why not limit yourself to the occasional glass of red wine? There's nothing wrong with that.'

'Does that mean it's good for me?'

'Well, yes.'

'So can I assume the more I drink, the better I'll get?'

Put it down to the dry Devon sense of humour – or a miserable air of resignation that my pint-glass drinking days were over. I thought back to those amusingly misplaced bookings by Gloucestershire in temperance hotels. The prospect now of sitting in a pavilion bar sipping a tulip glass of claret just didn't seem right for me. 'Hey,' I could imagine a few macho players saying to each other, 'what's Shep doing poncing around with some grape-juice? Has he decided suddenly to go up the social scale?'

The doctor's diagnosis did frighten me. Since then, with just the very rare exception, I've followed religiously the dietary and general advice he gave me. When, early in 2001, I was in Bombay for a Test match, the cricket was all over in three days. That resulted in some un-scheduled delays because it was difficult to book an early flight home. One evening, as I had my meal, I surreptitiously ordered a lager. It was strictly the only one and, as far as I know, it did me no harm.

There are other sacrifices, of course, like the day I was walking along a North Devon beach with Jenny and the dog. Suddenly, her eyes on the Front, Jenny told me to wait a moment: 'I've just spotted Hocking's van.' Such an announcement about my favourite ice-cream suppliers has always been music to the ear. My face lit up. Jenny hurried off in the direction of the van; I was again the jolly-faced schoolboy in eager anticipation of a cornet on the Sunday school outing. I was prepared, with Jenny's considerate approval as I saw it, to ignore the doctor's words on this isolated occasion. She returned with one small ice-cream and promptly gave it to Skipper.

I'm coming to terms with the necessary self-discipline. On my next annual medical the news was encouraging: I'd lost a bit of weight but was told not to ease up. Jenny makes sure I don't. When I went to Saffron Walden to umpire an Essex 2nd XI fixture, the county's former scorer Clem Driver came along to watch. 'You know what John Childs says, don't you – you're the only bloke he's aware of who actually *lost* weight after he gave up playing.' I can live with that kind of compliment from a fellow-Devonian.

* * *

However you look at it, cricket has been my life. I inherited my father's sporting genes, though in truth I could never have taken on the Barbarians like he did at rugby. I was lucky enough to grow up in a level-headed, stable, unpretentious family, only a few hundred yards from a lovely club ground. Brother Bill was my great schoolboy mate and, I have to admit, a better cricketer. It was my good fortune to play for my native county in the Minor Counties and then for Gloucestershire. My luck was compounded when, at the second attempt, I got on the first-class umpires' list. Most of my friends have been cricketers. Some play for the top countries of the world, others for isolated Devon villages up twisting country lanes. When I stop for an hour to watch the local lads on one of my rare Saturdays off I like to lean over the scorer's shoulder. Names are familiar to me – in some cases I played with their fathers. That kind of continuity is what I treasure.

I know that the sheep may have had to be driven off the square before the match can start. Then I glance around the improvised boundary and can see the little knots of spectators, offering jocular advice and, more importantly, watching every ball. How I wish all the spectators were just as intent at some of the county fixtures. Instead, too many backs are turned to the play; they are there as business guests, caught up in the aura of corporate hospitality. It all makes sense financially but to my mind devalues a game that is being played supposedly for their benefit.

It isn't only the packed marquees of chattering, sporting indifference that trouble me. I have come to accept that cricket must be a business to survive – and an ominously big business. We depend substantially on sponsorship. In turn our counties depend on their annual handouts, first from the TCCB and then the ECB. But, in 2000 for example, the receipts were down. County clubs, which were beginning to wallow in a new-found affluence, were pulled up with a start. The handouts weren't guaranteed. As for sponsorship, it is proving more difficult to find. I suspect there was real anxiety over the funding of the County

Championship this summer until CricInfo came in at the last minute. Some formerly generous money-bags have withdrawn. It's possible that several of them have been influenced by behaviour on the pitch. And what if, for any reason, televised cricket loses its appeal? There is already some evidence that fewer people watch cricket on TV. The sponsors are aware of this.

I told you earlier how surprised I was by the size of the crowds when I first became a county cricketer. How could the books ever be balanced, I asked myself? Many four-day championship matches are still played in front of miserably sparse crowds. The Test match receipts obscure the reality, but for how much longer? The only mildly consoling thing is that we were saying exactly the same thing in the fifties.

There are amazing, radical changes taking place within the structure of the game. It's hard to keep track of the congested international schedule (and I should know). The players don't have time to unpack their bags; it's one series after another, one new tournament after another. They are geared, with merciless planning, to money. The logistics may be a feat of brilliance, and the hungry TV companies are happy. When I see the players' weary eyes and limbs, I worry about them.

There have been countless gimmicks to accompany the experiments. With the coloured clothing came the astute merchandising which Manchester United and the other till-ringing soccer clubs had put us on to. New competitions and new techniques have encouraged new audiences. Those who come to watch the day–night matches are vastly different from those who stroll the boundaries, delicately to applaud the crafted and restrained singles and twos through mid-wicket. I've umpired big day–night matches abroad, for example India against Australia during the 1995–96 World Cup in Bombay, which have been fantastic spectacles. In India it gets dramatically dark in half an hour or so. In contrast, I have reservations about whether such games will really take off in this country. The floodlights simply don't take effect in the same stunning way.

The innovations go on. We now have tables to show the best and worst Test-playing nations. Domestically, we have seen two divisions in the County Championship. Who ever imagined that would happen? Is it proving a success, stimulating interest and improving standards? The jury, I'm told, is still out. Ask me again in twelve months' time. Three up and three down appears a bit excessive to me, even if there's a valid argument for the need to sustain interest and a competitive edge till the end of the season. At the same time, I sense a danger and it frightens the life out of my Devon bones. Could we be on the way to a soccer-style scenario – think of the top teams in the Premiership – in which just a handful of clubs grow rich and remote at the expense of the others. The ugly name is elitism. If that happens in county cricket, I feel we may as well all pack up. It would serve no useful purpose; it would marginalise the smaller, struggling counties; and I am sure it would damage our national game.

Already we detect far greater movement of players at the end of each season. If the rich get richer, they will be in an unchallengeable position to filch the best of the talent from the smaller counties. In turn, the latter will need to sell to survive. Only the affluent will be able to afford top players' salaries. The mere thought of such a trend gives me nightmares. Whatever happens, I'm convinced the interchanging of personnel between seasons will increase. With it will disappear, I fear, a feeling of regional identity. When I played in the Minor Counties, long ago, I relished the sound of those melodic Devon vowels all around me. Then, in Gloucestershire, my next adopted home, the feeling of belonging was strengthened for me by Bobby Etheridge's Gloucester accent, Ron Nicholls's from Berkeley country, Graham Wiltshire's from Chipping Sodbury and Smudge Smith's from Fishponds. In the winter months I tend to switch on the television to watch a top football match. There's barely a home-based player on view. It's just the same in senior club rugby. I'd hate that to occur in county cricket, even though I accept that some movement is inevitable and, in some cases, beneficial to the club.

As part of the game's evolution, I can't overlook the fact that a few counties could go under and I can't see this as an altogether bad thing. Perhaps some will be able to continue in some form, using part-timers and taking part in various limited-overs competitions. The argument that at the moment we have too many first-class counties and too many competitions, leaving players exhausted by the demanding schedules and treks across the country at the close of play, can't be rejected idly.

Australia remain pre-eminent among the cricketing nations. They keep discovering new talent; at home, they nurture and develop, all of it underpinned by an envied competitiveness and psychology that others do their best to copy. By comparison, what has been happening to the West Indies? Their cricket strategy has let them down; they have neglected young players. I'm told they suffer from to many sporting distractions. Ambrose has disappeared from the Test scene, and now Walsh is due to follow him. Where are the fast bowlers, the fearsome talented breed that once annually came off the conveyer belt, to take the place of those two towering stars? West Indian cricket has been disturbingly in the doldrums and some of their Test performances have been embarrassingly poor.

I read of several of their more promising young players, like Ramnaresh Sarwan, being sent to Australia's outstanding Cricket Academy. This was a surprising development, it seemed to me, when the Windies were just about to tour Australia. It told us something about the state of their domestic game. The schools, I'm told, have been failing; the youngsters, whose fathers were once caught up in what was then a passion for the game, look instead to basketball and football. Cricket is becoming a poor relation. Where, one has to ask, are the personalities emerging to take over from Brian Lara and fire youthful imaginations?

Lara's own partial eclipse, after that historic 501 at Edgbaston and some magnificent innings for his country, was a matter of concern and no doubt mystery, not least to his doting admirers in Trinidad. I've seen the little left-hander at his sublime best, as well as in the doldrums, sparring and agonising. At the time of his decline, I had sympathy for him. All his senior players had gone, virtually at the same time, and he was left with a mammoth responsibility as the principal batsman and captain. Much was being heaped on those slender shoulders. His period as a county cricketer here wasn't entirely happy, of course. The dressing room at Birmingham was said to throb with undercurrents. Lara, as the overseas player, was not only generously recompensed; he (or perhaps his agent) was asking for privileges that niggled some of the jobbing pros at Warwickshire. The West Indian's relationship with that outspoken county coach Dermot Reeve added to the weeks of unease.

The Caribbean inter-island rivalries, emanating from different cultures and backgrounds, is a constant problem for anyone leading the Test team. Clive Lloyd coped with that as successfully as anyone. He had both the authority and the respect for a job that called for positive action and tact. He had the considerable bonus, however, of great players around him, as had Viv Richards later. Captaincy is that much easier when you're winning.

By far the most encouraging news from that part of the world was the emergence in 2001 of the Shell Cricket Academy of St George's University in Grenada. The small island may seem an unlikely location, but the enthusiasm is real enough, not least from the founder, Dr Rudi Webster, a Barbados-born fast bowler who played for Scotland and then sixty times for Warwickshire in the sixties. The project, which has the backing of the West Indies Board, bubbles with overdue idealism and pragmatic hopes. Some famous names have been recruited as coaches and advisers.

I take great heart at England's signs of resurgence, despite the recent setbacks against the Australians. There were misgivings in some quarters when Nasser Hussain was appointed captain. So there were, of course, when Duncan Fletcher took charge of the coaching side. The two hardly knew each other, yet they have forged a positive and at times imaginative partnership. Team spirit soared in the series against Pakistan and Sri Lanka. Central contracts and with them a comprehensive team plan have clearly helped. At the same time, many of us feel a natural sympathy for the county clubs who are losing their best players for the majority of the season. It's bound to have some effect on membership. 'What chance do we have of winning the championship when our finest batsman and bowler are away all the time on their England calls?' I hear that all the time from Somerset and Yorkshire supporters – and yes, I have to feel sorry for them. But the logic of a central pool of England players, properly paid and excused some of the grind of a typical domestic season, can't possibly be contested. It's the only way for international progress to be made. Nothing was more unsatisfactory than the manner in which our top players were left fatigued, physically and mentally, by the onerous commitments, four-day and one-day, of a county side's summer.

As for international tours, the intention is to make them shorter. This is a move that had to come. With so many Test-playing nations now and the innovation of a ICC Test Championship, it's going to be a fearful challenge to squeeze in all the additional matches. Australia already looks on cricket as something to be played twelve months of the year, backed by indoor arenas and the latest scientific aids in multi-purpose stadia. Shorter tours could bring one welcome revision in the traditional pattern for our English players – more Christmas Days at home with their families. From my experience, I'm well aware that many of our cricketers are sentimental family men who don't enjoy being away from the domestic Christmas turkey and their young children's company. Those pictures, annually wired back, of the fancy-dress parties on tour always strike me as a thin disguise over how the boys are really feeling.

Cricket has brought me much, including the MBE, which I received from the Queen in December 1997 'for services to the game'. I hired the obligatory grey topper and was honoured to have more than a perfunctory chat with Her Majesty. I can appreciate the sheer diversity of subject-matter that she must address as she meets so many people, from so many walks of life, on the day of the investitures. Maybe Prince Philip, the cricket buff, suggested a question or two. She asked when and where I was standing next. Both of us had recently returned from Pakistan and that stimulated words of genuine interest on her part. Jenny and I spent a few days in London, relaxing, going to West End shows and mostly keeping the subject of cricket off the agenda. Fond as we are of Skipper, we decided not to take him to London for the special break. I couldn't be sure how well he'd get on with the corgis!

I began this book by extolling the virtues of Devon and I'll never live anywhere else. It isn't exactly a cricketing backwater, as most recently Peter Roebuck demonstrated in his days as a county skipper. The stylish left-hander Nick Folland could assuredly have established himself as a first-class cricketer – and he did play briefly for Somerset – if he hadn't chosen to return to teaching. Mark Lathwell, that mighty little enigma, lives just down the road from me at Fremington. He offered so much as a fluent stroke-maker for Somerset but Test recognition came prematurely; he hated the fuss that was being made about him. There were also attempts to change his technique at the crease. That's invariably fatal. He was comfortable with the way he batted and with foot movements that didn't come straight from the manual. Then there were his injuries. Lathwell and Trescothick were chums, hungry for runs and rich in promise. While the left-hander sorted out his technical problems and went on to open for his country, Lathwell, with an amiable temperament which is said to favour a game of darts in his village local, bravely works at his relaunched career.

Let no-one say that Devon lacks cricketers. The Tolchard brothers, Roger and Jeff, came from Torquay, and so did their nephew, Roger Twose. There's John 'Charlie' Childs and farmer's son Tony Allin, who played thirteen times for Glamorgan in 1976. He was a fine slow left-arm bowler who headed Glamorgan's averages that summer. They offered him a two-year contract but Tony preferred to play his cricket for Devon between the haymaking and harvesting.

Brian Roe, an insurance worker from Barnstaple, made 131 appearances for Somerset before having several seasons with Devon. 'Chico', as he was known, was small in stature and possessed envied powers of application. As a club cricketer in North Devon he was a prolific scorer. At the last count he'd chalked up more than 200 centuries. It used to be said that because of his lack of inches elderly ladies on the Taunton boundary always wanted to mother him.

Mike Garnham was born in South Africa but settled near Barnstaple and played for North Devon CC. As a teenager he began to impress as a wicket-keeper–batsman. I'd heard about him and asked my brother what he thought. 'He's a bit useful' was the reply. By then I was coming to the end of my playing career for Gloucestershire. Twice I went along to the Instow ground to watch young Mike, and I had no hesitation in recommending him to my county club. The coach, Graham Wiltshire, invited him to Bristol for a trial and he joined the staff. Mike was an ambitious as well as a talented young player. He didn't like kicking his heels. At Gloucestershire he was number-two keeper to Andy Stovold most of the time so, in the main, he played for the 2nd XI, and I captained him in a few matches. It seemed to confirm my opinion that he had a future in county cricket if he remained patient for a little longer.

I hoped in vain. By late July he'd made only three senior appearances in the championship. He came with me to Blaby for a 2nd XI game with Leicestershire and, apart from his tidy wicket-keeping, he composed a nice-looking half-century. What was more significant to me was the sight of him walking around the boundary with Jack Birkenshaw, who'd at that time played something like 400 matches for Leicestershire and knew a promising cricketer when he saw one. I murmured to myself, 'He's on the way.' The following season Garnham was a Leicestershire player and he stayed with them for six years.

He had come to Bristol on my recommendation and I was sorry to see him go after so brief and barely recognised a stay. His keeping was of a high standard and, as a bonus, his batting had markedly improved, with some particularly useful strokes, I remember, off the back foot. Unfortunately, Mike had an infuriating habit of upsetting people. He showed good form for his new county before appearing to become disillusioned with the game. Then, perhaps surprisingly, in a burst of renewed enthusiasm he played ninety-five times for Essex.

There was no reason at all why Mike Garnham had to show loyalty to Gloucestershire. If, as he saw it, he was destined to stay in the 2nd XI he might as well go to pastures new. All the same, I retain an old-fashioned regard for loyalty in all walks of life. In my fledgling seasons as a county cricketer I would sometimes play for a pub team known as F Troop, run by landlord Gerry Collis, later the Gloucestershire president. Gerry must have had some influence – we used to play on the Close at Clifton College. For one fixture he idly asked Arthur Milton if he'd like a game. Arthur, Gloucestershire and England, Arsenal and England, showed some casual interest and made a mental note of the date.

At the time, Arthur was the Oxford coach. It so happened that F Troop's game coincided with the Varsity match. Gerry discreetly forgot about the invitation. To everyone's surprise, however, Arthur turned up with his kit at the Close. 'But shouldn't you be at Lord's?'

'No, never like to turn down a game, you know,' said Milton, eyes twinkling. He was a shy man and didn't much like the fuss and ritual of Lord's. 'Cambridge were about to be beaten. And I felt my work was done by then.'

Arthur had life in perspective. So, I like to think, have I. I've become older and wiser, better known as an umpire than I was as a player. Yet my life hasn't really changed too much. My age-old expressions continue to bring tolerant sighs from Jenny. When I pass the baker's in Bideford, I continue to ask if they have any stale crusts left. When I go out for a meal in a restaurant, maybe miles from the West County, I question the range of puddings and enquire whether they have any Hocking's ice-cream. I know they haven't, but I can't help myself.

The warm, bygone images of Instow will live with me forever – the hissing locos and the dozens of wide-eyed tourists spilling on to the pre-Beeching platforms, the weather-beaten ferrymen on their daily route to Appledore, the cascading Christmas mail at our little post office on the Front, the endless good fellowship at the close of play under the thatch at North Devon CC. They will always be more important to me than the brash transitory cricket headlines of belligerent exchanges among players who should know better. The big screens and bated breaths, 'Hawkeye', the latest device for determining LBWs, the surfeit of TV pundits, the white balls and the black moods, the open-ended debate about where the game is going, the misplaced notion that consumerism is of more relevance than the cover drive . . . All are part of my living.

Cricket remains full of surprises. As I write this I haven't yet seen Colin Miller, who I know has the habit of changing the colour of his hair as startlingly as he can turn the ball from the off. I look forward to the 2001 Ashes series because the Australians are the ultimate challenge. To me, Brett Lee is the quickest bowler of all. The first time I saw him was in a Boxing Day match against India in 1999. Umpires are allowed to express no emotions but his sheer speed – and he isn't a tall man – made me want to catch my breath. I was rather grateful I was safely stationed out of range, and not one of the lower-order batsmen. At the end of the match, I turned to him and said, 'Young man, if you keep your head on your shoulders, you'll go a long way.'

It has been a privilege to see the world's great players at close range, noting their personalities and whims, as well as their rich sporting gifts. I admire so much that marvellous trio of spinners: Warne, Muralitharan and Saqlain Mushtaq. All different; all exponents of such finger and wrist wizardry that they take their place in cricket's timeless roll of honour. What fascinates me most of all is their facility to turn the ball both ways. I'd never seen an off-spinner do that until I watched Saqlain in beguiling action.

England's own revolution and discernible improvement has been a systematic and gratifying exercise. It pleases me to detect how the selectors are taking more notice of the A tours. I think of players like Ian Ward and Ryan Sidebottom. Ward, need I mention, was born in Plymouth; his father and grandfather played for Devon. There, that is positively the last blatant regional plug you will find in this book! What is the point of an A tour if the party is not made up of potential Test players? All of us can think, sadly, of dozens who over the winters should not have gone on A tours in the first place or who, in some cases, were to drift before long into relative obscurity.

This is certainly not about to turn into a bout of crystal-gazing. I do, however, share the general enthusiasm about players like James Ormond of Leicestershire, Usman Afzaal of Nottinghamshire and Jon Lewis of Gloucestershire. No-one can seem to make up their mind about emerging wicket-keepers. I go no further than Surrey's Jon Batty, someone whose name is not too often mentioned.

While I'm in this reflective mood, I should like to nominate Graham Gooch's undefeated 154 in the first Test against the West Indies at Leeds in 1991 as the best I've ever seen at that level. He stayed with tremendous resolve for seven and a half hours when, in England's second innings, the next highest score was 27. And my best batsman overall? I am tempted, despite all the wondrous competition, to go for Sachin Tendulkar. Many of his runs, I accept, have been scored on the sub-continent, but he has never allowed the slow bowlers to dominate. He plays the great ones, like Warne, perfectly. I can find little fault with either his technique on the field or his disposition off it.

I've cited in these pages some of the surprises that can confront an umpire. We go on to the field never knowing what is going to crop up. I'm thinking of unscheduled incidents that cause us mentally to consult the complicated laws of the game. Leicestershire's championship match with Lancashire at Grace Road in May 2001 is a good example. Everything was bubbling up to a tense and exciting finish on the third day. The game was see-sawing, the crowd were rapt for probably the first time in a fixture which had been full of bad early season batting. I wasn't umpiring, though the reports soon got back to me. Lancashire appeared to be edging to victory. Leicestershire were short of bowlers because of injury and Darren Maddy was brought on. Then came a hint of real sensation from Mike Smethurst, someone with no especial claims as a batsman. He straight-drove Maddy, who fielded briskly and hurled the ball back towards his keeper. Smethurst, for a reason only he will know, played the ball into the covers. Maddy immediately appealed loud and earnestly. Others gave him throaty support. They all peered at umpire Barry Dudleston. He went off to consult Mervyn Kitchen, and the batsman survived. If Smethurst had been out of his ground, he would have gone for obstructing the field. It became a talking point as *Wisdens* were pulled from travel bags all around the boundary, I'm told. It was the right decision – and one on which I haven't yet had to adjudicate. Not something we like to occur in the closing overs of a tight game.

The umpires in that match told me there were some wonderful catches, including the last two, by Daniel Marsh, Leicestershire's overseas player. Maybe the pedigree says it all. He's the son of Rodney, who has been director of the Australian Cricket Academy since 1991. Daniel, shortish and sturdy, is a talented batsman, a slow left-arm bowler and a spectacular fielder. And no, he hasn't played for Australia. I offer this intriguing list: Darren Lehmann, Jimmy Maher, Jamie Cox, Andrew Bichel, Michael Hussey, Michael DiVenuto, Greg Blewett and Martin Love. They all played county cricket in England in 2001 and so far there hasn't been too much Test-match recognition (none in most cases) for them. Some may never play for Australia. Yet all, in their different ways, have class and much talent. What a staggeringly rich seam of outstanding cricketers Australia produces. I marvel at this almost inexhaustible supply and I'm sure my list is far from complete.

Here is another surprise for the umpires, a poignant one this time, and one in which I was involved. The match was at Grace Road and I was in nearby digs with Vanburn Holder. We always stayed there, at the home of Dorothy Hopkins, who was an infallible early riser. There was no sign of her when we got up. The back door was open but she wasn't in the garden. Vanburn went to buy the papers and I continued the search. I looked in various rooms and then found her … dead in an armchair. We were both fond of her and you can imagine how unsettling it was. I was grateful that it rained all day and there was no play.

In the course of this book I may have hinted once or twice that I possess a sensitive side and that a few things I overhear, or read, upset me. I'm lucky enough to have had a friendly relationship with the press and I should be grateful for that. There have still been stray newspaper reports which cause me to ask myself: 'Is he having a go at me?' I've known dozens of journalists, going back to my North Devon and then Bristol days. Perhaps I've warmed to some a little more than to others. I suppose it comes down to trust – and there are some cricket writers I'd trust with my life. Then again …

Early in my umpiring career I was standing with Sam Cook at Hove, where Sussex were playing Somerset. My next appointment was at Eastbourne, so I stayed down in Sussex and idly read the local paper. Sam and I had both been slated for our handling of the match. Sadly the cricket writer got some of his facts wrong. He attributed decisions to me which were Sam's and vice versa. It made my blood boil. Some years later met I the reporter concerned and wasted no time in telling him of the inaccuracies in his piece. Nor did I approve of the comments that he had claimed were made by the then Sussex coach, Stewart Storey, at our expense. I'm afraid a Devon man doesn't always forgive easily if he feels he has been maligned. And, even if he has to wait a few years, he won't let it rest.

Some umpires have an easier relationship with the press than others. I prefer to keep my head down. It doesn't give me a buzz to see my name in print. If a Test has produced a glaring controversy, the journalists will inevitably be moving on to it. They will want a 'nanny' (goat – quote) from the umpire involved and I may be a biggish bloke but I can be pretty adept at being elusive. The authorities are anxious, in any case, to keep us well away from those notebooks and cassette recorders.

I would be untruthful if I attempted to give the impression that cricket is morally in a healthy state. Grimly, we all know differently. Not long ago there was even talk of murder, threats and kidnapping when Sir Paul Condon's anti-corruption report was made public. The findings sounded melodramatic and sensational. Many famous names have already been mentioned for varying degrees of misdemeanour. The innuendoes seemed at one stage to be multiplying by the day; the difficulty was in substantiating the evidence. Several South African and Asian players have been banned for life. No doubt there have been many conflicting statements, smokescreens, nudge-nudge compromises and too much pussyfooting. How much hard evidence will ever emerge? How many players will be named and indicted? None of us know.

The claim that some of the murky dealings could be traced back to England in the seventies shocked most of us. Meanwhile, the rumours won't go away. It's possible that some well-known players are being unfairly tormented by the allegations. The game has been tainted irreversibly and the crucial factual information at hand is exasperatingly elusive and hard to nail. There will be more disclosures, I've no doubt, and more denials, as well as perhaps criminal proceedings. 'Bent' cricketers are beyond my comprehension and, as I wrote earlier, the tawdry allegations may at last have stopped the match-fixers in their tracks and given the game some clean air to breathe again.

My God, that Condon document, which was published at the end of May 2001, made for disturbing reading. It shook cricket's establishment to the core. The ICC came in for a fearful hammering, accused of being too loose and fragile. There were disquieting revelations and the kind of intrepid condemnation you would expect from an ex-Met copper on nearly every page of the report, but I'm even more worried about what wasn't said. The anti-corruption unit didn't receive the amount of co-operation to which they were entitled. Some interviewees were too timid – they feared for themselves and their families, it appears.

I turned on my TV the day the report came out and heard Lord MacLaurin talking about 'a dreadful cancer' in the game. Was I so naïve, so blissfully in love with cricket as I'd always known and cherished it, that I hadn't a clue about dirty deals being done and the public consequently being short-changed? I've talked ceaselessly over the issue with my fellow-umpires. If I was unaware of irregularities, we all were.

The whole rotten business is, I've gradually come to realise, so much more than the transgressions of Hansie Cronje, Salim Malik and Mohammad Azharuddin. I'm not at all sure the once utterly whole-some old game will ever fully recover. There has been too much betrayal.

At the moment I don't know my long-term future. There are positive moves to recruit younger international umpires, who supposedly have added energy and stamina. It only seemed like yesterday – in fact it was early 2000 – when I officiated in my fiftieth Test in Mumbai, India. I was presented with a specially commissioned silver award before the start of the match between India and South Africa. David Richards, as chief executive of the ICC, said flatteringly: 'Shep has been at the top of his profession for a number of years and this award is due recognition of his ability and durability. He has become without question one of the best and most respected umpires in international cricket and he is one of the sport's most popular figures.'

It has been a career of rich experience and boundless pleasure, joyfully untouched by the evil and greed which has more recently been creeping in. As I know Dickie Bird and a few other contemporaries of mine accept, we are left with a vast emotional void when it's time to give up.

Yet, in my case, does there have to be? I'm off down the road now to sniff the salty sea air again – and stroll on the beach with Jenny and Skipper. That, for me, is real living. With not a white coat or a set of red barrel counters in sight.

Index